CARIBBEAN BY CRUISE SHIP

DOCUMENTATION		
Passenger Name_____		
Ship Name _____		
Date of Voyage_____		
Stateroom_____		

Trunk Bay, St. John, U.S. Virgin Islands

CARIBBEAN
By Cruise Ship

THE COMPLETE GUIDE TO CRUISING THE CARIBBEAN

FIFTH EDITION

ANNE VIPOND

YOUR PORTHOLE
COMPANION

OCEAN
CRUISE
GUIDES
Vancouver, Canada   Pt. Roberts, USA

Published by: Ocean Cruise Guides Ltd.

Canada:
325 English Bluff Road.
Delta, B.C. V4M 2M9

USA:
PO Box 2041
Pt. Roberts, WA 98281-2041

Fifth Edition

Editors: Mel-Lynda Andersen, Richard Rogers
Contributing Editors: William Kelly, Michael DeFreitas
Additional Photography: Michael DeFreitas, Gordon Persson, Martin Gerretsen
Artwork by Alan H. Nakano
Cartography: Reid Jopson, Doug Quiring, Cartesia, OCG
Design: Ocean Cruise Guides
Publisher: William Kelly

Visit our web site: www.oceancruiseguides.com

We welcome comments or suggestions from readers. Contact us at our email address: info@oceancruiseguides.com

Printed in China

Library and Archives Canada Cataloguing in Publication

Vipond, Anne, 1957-
    Caribbean by cruise ship : the complete guide to cruising the Caribbean / Anne Vipond. -- 5th ed.

Includes index.
ISBN 978-0-9688389-8-3

    1. Cruise ships--Caribbean Area--Guidebooks. 2. Caribbean Area--Guidebooks. I. Title.

F2165.V56 2007   917.2904'53   C2007-903221-4

Great Bay, St. Maarten

CONTENTS

PART TWO

THE VOYAGE & THE PORTS

The island-dotted Caribbean Sea is perfectly suited to a cruise vacation. Ever since the concept of cruising was pioneered in the 1960s, when jet planes became the main mode of transatlantic travel and shipping companies sought new roles for their ocean liners, the Caribbean has been the most popular cruising area in the world. The beauty of its beaches is legendary, and its turquoise waters remain warm year round – ideal conditions for swimming, snorkeling and other water sports.

The region is also rich in culture. The West Indies were once the most important colonial region in the world, their sugarcane plantations a lucrative source of wealth for Britain, France and other European powers. As a result, each island nation has its own history and local flavor – an exotic mix of Indian, African, European and Asian influences. The African influence is reflected in the rhythmic music and the bold use of color in everything from folk art to batik clothing to colonial architecture. West Indian homes boast crayon-colored shutters, and the local fishermen paint their skiffs a combination of rainbow reds, yellows and blues, inspired no doubt by an aquamarine sea shimmering across the colorful corals and tropical fish.

Sailing vessels have long plied the Caribbean's warm waters, riding the constant trade winds that temper the region's heat and humidity. North Americans yearning to escape the gray grip of winter soon find their senses reawakened by the Caribbean's warm breezes, fragrant flowers and the carefree mode of travel that a cruise vacation provides. The ships usually pull into port as dawn is breaking, treating their passengers to the magic of a seaborne arrival as the golden pink sun rises above a rippled sea and the verdant shores of a volcanic island draw ever nearer. The departure is equally special, the ship easing away from shore and heading out to sea as the setting sun casts its Caribbean colors across the sky. For a vacation of relaxation and romance, nothing surpasses a cruise among these islands of endless summer.

Anne Vipond

PART I

GENERAL INFORMATION

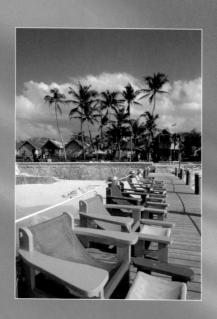

CARIBBEAN CRUISE AREAS

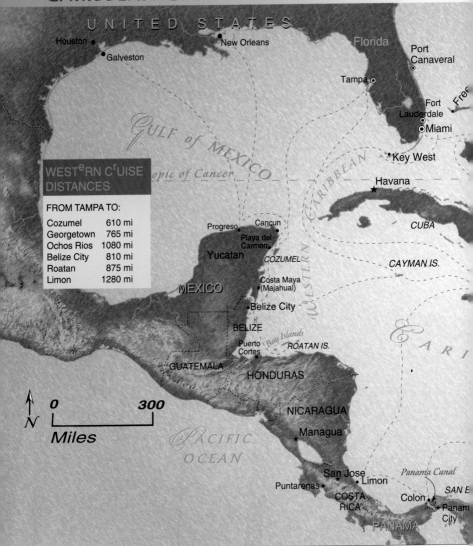

WESTᵉRN CʳUISE DISTANCES

FROM TAMPA TO:

Cozumel	610 mi
Georgetown	765 mi
Ochos Rios	1080 mi
Belize City	810 mi
Roatan	875 mi
Limon	1280 mi

Choosing Your Cruise

The West Indies extend in a wide, 2,500-mile arc from Florida to Venezuela, separating the Atlantic Ocean from the Caribbean Sea. They are comprised of the Bahama Islands, the Greater Antilles (which are the larger islands of Cuba, Haiti and Dominican Republic, Jamaica and Puerto Rico) and the Lesser Antilles, which are the smaller islands to the east and south. The Lesser Antilles are further divided into the Leeward and Windward groups, terms from the days of sail in reference to the prevailing trade winds.

The many cruise ships plying the Caribbean can spread out and

offer a variety of routes and combinations of ports. They use several base ports, the major ones being Miami, Fort Lauderdale, and San Juan, Puerto Rico. Other base ports include Port Canaveral, Jacksonsville, Tampa, New Orleans, Houston, Galveston, and Mobile, as well as New York, Baltimore, Norfolk and Charleston.

The cruise lines arrange their itineraries to give passengers a good diversity of ports. Various European nations colonized the region and to this day a number of islands remain colonies of Britain, regions of France or members of the Kingdom of the Netherlands. The colonial architecture, customs, language and cuisine of each island reflect its

Spanish, Danish, British, French or Dutch past. But the differences between islands are not only cultural. Some are flat and arid, others are lush and mountainous. Some are noted for their beautiful beaches, others for their excellent snorkeling and diving. One island might be included specifically for duty-free shopping, yet another for its natural beauty of volcanic mountains and tropical rain-forests.

A Western Caribbean cruise includes such destinations as Key West, Jamaica, Grand Cayman, Cozumel, the Yucatan Peninsula and several countries of Central America. An Eastern Caribbean cruise often takes in the Bahamas, the U.S. Virgin Islands (specifically St. Thomas with its famous duty-free port) and the half-Dutch/half-French island of St. Maarten/St. Martin. Southern Caribbean cruises, many of which depart from San Juan, stop at a few Eastern ports but also proceed southward along the Lesser Antilles, often right to the Venezuelan coast, venturing into less-travelled waters and visiting quieter islands where tourism is not as highly developed and the authentic West Indian lifestyle is still predominant.

Caribbean cruises vary in length, from weekend getaways to extensive 16-day voyages. Seven-day itineraries – with three or four ports of call – remain as the standard cruise, with some lines offering the option of booking back-to-back cruises on alternate routes. Ten-day cruises are also popular, with a few more ports of call added and usually departing from Florida to the Southern Caribbean. The ideal itinerary for many is a 14-day

A Caribbean cruise – having fun and relaxing in the tropical warmth. (Left) Celebrity Cruises' private beach stop at Catalina Island, Dominican Republic.

(Above) A large ship with all the amenities approaches St. Thomas. (Below) A small, luxury ship docks in Castries, St. Lucia.

cruise deep into southern waters, stopping at a variety of islands. Simply put, the Caribbean is such a diverse destination, it warrants several visits.

Which Ship?

The selection of ships cruising the Caribbean is exhaustive. Since this is the world's most popular cruise destination, every kind of ship – megaships, small luxury ships and sailing vessels – is available here. In recent years, the major cruise lines have been launching increasingly larger ships, and the array of onboard facilities has transformed them into impressive floating resorts, providing myriad activities for passengers. In addition to several swimming pools, a sports deck, health spa and fitness center, standard features also include a show lounge, movie theater, shopping arcade, library, internet cafe and youth center. And the traditional selection of lounges has been joined by alternative restaurants for passengers who would rather not dine in the main dining room each evening. The passenger capacity on these large ships is generally about 2,000, with a few ships accommodating more than 3,000. Five-star ships are generally more spacious than the mainstream ships and have a more refined atmosphere.

In contrast to the large ships are the small luxury ships carrying 100 to 300 passengers. Being aboard one of these upscale vessels is similar to being on board a billionaire's private yacht. The service is attentive and personalized and, although the onboard facilities are not as extensive as

The smaller ships anchor off secluded islands and pull into the less-visited Caribbean ports.

on the large ships, all appointments are of the highest quality and some of the features are unique, such as a stern that folds out into a swimming platform, from which passengers can partake in various water sports while the ship is at anchor.

The romance of sail is a strong allure on the many sailing cruise ships, which range from small windjammers to large clipper-style ships carrying a few hundred passengers. While these ships use engines to help propel the vessel, the sails are often raised in the trade winds of the Caribbean. Passengers can usually participate in sail handling through informal classes on board. Life on these vessels is unstructured, the cabins are compact and the meals less elaborate than on large ships, although some sailing vessels – such as the Windstar fleet – offer premium accommodations and service.

The large ships pull into the popular ports while the small lux-ury ships and sailing vessels tend to visit quieter, less developed islands. Major cruise lines often include a private island stop in their itineraries, anchoring off a small undeveloped island (usually in the Bahamas) where passengers can spend a day on shore enjoying the cruise company's private beach, water sports equipment and snack bar facilities.

The Glossary of Cruise Lines at the back of this book provides a brief description of the various lines and ships servicing the Caribbean. To obtain more information on picking a cruise line, peruse the Internet or book stores, and visit a travel agent. In North America, look for an agency displaying the CLIA logo, indicating its agents have received training from the Cruise Lines International Association. Cruise agents are an excellent source of information, with personal knowledge of many ships. An experienced agent can provide important detail, including specific itineraries and cabin choices, and obtain the best deals available – both early-bird specials and last-minute promotions.

When to Go

The weather varies little throughout the year in the Caribbean, due to the moderating effect of the surrounding water and steady breezes. The average temperature – about 80 degrees Fahrenheit (26 degrees Celsius) – fluctuates less than 10 degrees between the warmest and coldest months. The hottest, wettest months are in summer, marking the start of the hurricane season, which begins in July and continues through to November, the peak hurricane season being late August to early October. Cruise ships receive weather information from the National Hurricane Center and stay well away from the track of any approaching hurricane.

The topography of each island determines its local climate, with the low-lying islands receiving about half the rainfall of the mountainous ones, their leeward sides being dryer than their windward sides. On mountainous islands with many rivers, run-off during spells of heavy rain will send sediment into the water and reduce visibility for divers.

The most popular months for Caribbean cruising are mid-October to mid-April, with the peak season starting at Christmastime and lasting to the end of March, at which time the majority of ships leaves the area to spend the summer in either Alaska or Europe. Some, however, remain in the Caribbean year-round.

Although air connections to and from your cruise can usually be arranged by the cruise line, there may be a premium for this convenience and the routing could be convoluted, with stopovers and plane changes. Paying the deviation fee ($50 and up) offered by most lines gives you some latitude in choosing the airline, routing and schedule. Most cruise lines offer transfers and pre- or post-cruise hotel packages.

If your cruise departs from a U.S. mainland port, the cruise line may offer a coach shuttle service to the pier (check with your travel agent). Long-term parking is available at the drive-to cruise ports.

Key West is an easy drive from Miami for passengers embarking on a pre- or post-cruise land tour of Florida.

A pre-cruise stay in Florida is a chance to enjoy the state's fine beaches. (Below) Racing a 12-meter yacht off St. Maarten.

Land Tours

A cruise is a good opportunity to combine a vacation at sea with a land-based holiday. If time allows, fly to your port of embarkation at least a day before the cruise begins and avoid the stress of making same-day travel connections. Better yet, stay two or three nights at the base port and take the time to enjoy the local sights. Cities such as Fort Lauderdale, Miami, Tampa, New Orleans and San Juan, Puerto Rico are all tourist destinations in themselves and warrant a brief stay, either at the beginning or end of a Caribbean cruise. Most cruise lines offer hotel packages at these turn-around (home) ports, and several offer extensive land tours.

The walled city of Old San Juan is especially fun to explore on foot, with its romantic setting of colonial buildings, excellent restaurants, fine beaches and some of the best shopping in the Caribbean. Florida also has numerous tour options and there is lots to explore in the Sunshine State, including the John F. Kennedy Space Center near Port Canaveral and the scenic drive south to the Everglades and Key West. Your travel agent should be able to sort through the hotel and tour options at any of these ports and arrange a complete cruise-tour package that suits your schedule and budget.

Shore Excursions

See each chapter in Part II for more details.

In the Caribbean, many 'shore' activities actually take place in the water – swimming off soft sand beaches, snorkeling among

(Above) Kayaking is a popular shore activity at the ports of call. (Below) Island drives often include panoramic lookouts, such as this one at Estate St. Peter Greathouse on St. Thomas.

coral gardens, scuba diving to shipwrecks, and skimming across the water on a windsurfer, catamaran or 12-meter racing yacht. For those who prefer to stay dry, submarine rides, semi-submersibles and glass-bottomed boats afford effortless views of the underwater world. There are also boat trips to secluded beaches, river rafting through mangrove forests, kayaking across tropical lagoons and hiking in tropical rainforests, where waterfalls, crater lakes and freshwater pools create a paradisal setting for the birds and animals living there.

In addition to the Caribbean's natural beauty, its colonial history can be explored on island drives to such points of interest as Nelson's Dockyard on Antigua and Brimstone Hill Fortress on St. Kitts. Some of the islands' former sugar plantation estates are open to the public, their grand mansions now museums and the grounds now parkland containing picnic tables and botanical gardens. The ports themselves often have numerous historical sites, with colonial forts, churches and government buildings lining narrow cobblestone streets, where restored warehouses now contain

shops and restaurants. A number of ports have local botanical gardens for easy viewing of the many indigenous and exotic plants that grow in the region.

Most cruise lines offer organized shore excursions for the convenience of their passengers. These are described in a booklet enclosed with your cruise tickets. Onboard presentations are also given by the ship's shore excursion manager. There is a charge for these excursions, but they are usually fairly priced, and the tour operators are reliable, monitored by the cruise company to ensure they maintain the level of service promised to passengers, with the added advantage that the ship will wait for any of its overdue excursions, so there's no concern about missing the ship.

Ship-organized shore excursions cover a whole range of activities and are attractive for their convenience. You are transported to and from the ship, any needed equipment is provided and you know ahead of time how long the tour will last and how much it will cost. And while ship-organized shore excursions are not the only option, they are recommended for certain activities such as scuba diving. Several cruise lines, such as Princess and Royal Caribbean, offer scuba certification programs sanctioned by PADI (Professional Association of Diving Instructors), which include academic study, pool practice and open-water dives with professional guides.

Also recommended are ship-organized golf tours (some island courses limit play to residents and cruise passengers who purchase advance tee times). Tennis, on the other hand, is best arranged independently. Many Caribbean resorts let non-guests use their tennis courts for a fee, and the

(Left) Atlantis submarine rides are offered at several Caribbean islands. (Below) Mullet Bay Resort, St. Maarten, is one of many golf courses open to cruise passengers.

ship's shore excursion office can usually provide current information for each port of call.

For independent sightseeing, renting a car is an option on most islands. However, driving is often on the left, the roads can be narrow and winding, and a temporary driver's license is usually required in addition to the rental fee, bringing the total cost above that of hiring a taxi for a few hours. However, it's fun to strike out on your own, and the roads are often quiet once you get away from the port area. Just be sure to give yourself plenty of time to get back to the ship – distances can take longer to cover than anticipated on some of the islands' narrow and winding roads. Good islands to explore with a rented car include Barbados (with well-maintained roads, a scenic east coast and numerous countryside attractions), St. Kitts (with a new highway to the Southeast Peninsula) and the U.S. Virgin Islands. To save time and ensure the availability of a rental car, it's best to reserve ahead. Major car rental companies operate on most islands.

Hiring a taxi is another option. If you decide to take a taxi tour, chat with a few drivers and choose one who is friendly and shows promise as a tour guide. Most drivers are a wealth of information and represent an opportunity to learn more about the local people while seeing the island's natural and historical

Professional taxi drivers operate well-maintained vehicles and are usually excellent tour guides.

sights. Always agree beforehand on the price of the tour and exactly which stops are included. If you enjoyed the tour, a tip is appropriate. Fares to popular destinations are usually set by the local taxi association and posted near the cruise ship pier. At some ports a taxi director is stationed at the cruise pier to quote fares and direct passengers to qualified drivers. Other ports may provide pierside information booths.

Beaches are often within walking distance or a short taxi ride away, and most are open to tourists, although it's not unusual for there to be a small admission charge. The beaches on volcanic islands can vary in color, while those on flat coral islands have white sand. Beaches on the Caribbean side of an island are sheltered; those on the Atlantic side will have a surf. Beachfront hotels often rent lounge chairs, beach umbrellas and the use of lockers and change facilities to the public, as well as watersports equipment. Bring your own beach towel, which your room steward can supply.

Documentation

A valid passport is the best proof of citizenship a traveler can carry, and may soon be required for all travelers entering the United States through sea border crossings. Canadian citizens arriving by air into the United States must have a valid passport, and American citizens returning to their country by air must have a passport. Thus, the cruise lines strongly recommend that all passengers booking a Caribbean cruise have an up-to-date passport.

Before your departure, leave a detailed itinerary with a family member, friend or neighbor. Be sure to include the name of your ship, its phone number and the applicable ocean code, as well as your cabin number – all of which will be included in your cruise documentation. With this information, a person can place a satellite call to your ship in an emergency. Another precaution is to photocopy on a single sheet of paper the identification page of your passport, your driver's license and any credit cards you will be carrying in your wallet. Keep one copy of this sheet with you, separate from your passport and wallet, and leave another one at home.

Taking out a travel insurance policy at the time of booking is recommended. A comprehensive policy will cover travel cancellation, delayed departure, medical expenses, personal accident and liability, lost baggage and money, and legal expenses. You may already have supplementary health insurance through a credit card, automobile club policy or employment health plan, but you should check these carefully. Whatever policy you choose for your trip, carry details of it with you and documents showing that you are covered by a plan. If you plan on doing any scuba diving, bring your diving certification.

Currency

Each island has its own legal tender, but American currency is accepted everywhere in the Caribbean, as are major credit cards and traveler's checks. Cab fares are usually paid in cash. It's a good idea to carry some small U.S. bills for minor purchases rather than receive large amounts of local currency in change. Traveler's checks should be cashed on board the ship unless you are planning a large purchase. Prices quoted in this book are in U.S. dollars, unless otherwise noted.

Health Precautions

No vaccinations are necessary for a Caribbean cruise, but if you are at risk of complications from the flu or other respiratory illnesses, you may want to get a flu shot. To avoid traveler's diarrhea, it's best to drink bottled water when

ashore and never eat a piece of unfamiliar fruit you see hanging from a tree. The poisonous manchineel tree, which grows near beaches, bears fruit resembling small green apples. Contact with these or the tree's leaves, sap or bark will cause a chemical burning. Signs usually identify these trees but the best approach is to stay on designated paths to avoid potentially harmful vegetation. Insects are not a problem, although some Central American ports and Mayan jungle sites can have mosquitos, so take along some insect repellent. Visit your family doctor or local travel clinic several weeks prior to your cruise to determine if you are travelling to any malaria-risk areas requiring preventative measures.

Modern cruise ships use stabilizers to reduce rolling motion when underway, so seasickness is not a widespread or prolonged problem with most passengers. However, there are several remedies for people susceptible to this affliction. One is to wear special wrist bands, the balls of which rest on an acupressure point. Another option is to chew Meclizine tablets (often available at the ship's front office) or take Dramamine pills. It's best to take these pills ahead of time, before you feel nauseous, and they may make you feel drowsy. Check with your doctor when deciding on medication. Fresh air is one of the best antidotes to motion sickness, so stepping out on deck is often all that's needed to counter any queasiness. Other simple remedies include sipping on ginger ale and nibbling on dry crackers and an apple. Lying down also helps. Should you become concerned about your condition, simply visit the medical center on board for professional attention.

The overall standards of cleanliness on board cruise ships are extremely high. However, contagious viruses (such as the Norwalk stomach virus – a brief but severe gastrointestinal illness) are spread by person-to-person contact. To avoid contracting such a virus, practise frequent and thorough handwashing with warm soapy water.

All large ships have a fully equipped medical center with a doctor and nurses. Passengers needing medical attention are billed at private rates, which are added to their shipboard account. This invoice can be submitted to your insurance company upon your return home.

What to Pack?

Pack casual attire for daytime wear – both on board the ship and in port. Cool, loose cottons are best. Include sunglasses, a wide-brimmed straw or cotton hat, and comfortable rubber-soled shoes or sandals. Sunscreen is also important, one with a protection factor of 15 or higher, to shield your skin from the sun's burning rays. Apply generously before going outside and reapply frequently if you are spending time at the beach, even when the sky is overcast. A light sweater will come in handy, as the air conditioning in dining rooms, stores and museums is much cooler than the temperature outside. Your evening wear should include something suitable for the two or three formal nights held on board most ships. Women wear gowns or cocktail dresses and men favor suits. For informal evenings, women wear dresses, skirts or slacks, and men wear sports jackets with either a shirt and tie or an open-necked sports shirt. Shops on board often sell formal and casual wear, and colorful tops and shorts can be purchased at good prices at ports along the way.

Many ships have coin-operated launderettes with an iron and ironing board, or you can pay to have your laundry done, as well as steam pressing and dry cleaning. Basic toiletries, such as soap, shampoo and hand lotion, are usually provided, and other toiletries can be purchased in the onboard shops. A hair dryer may be installed in the stateroom. (Details about a particular ship's

amenities can be confirmed with your travel agent.) Beach towels are supplied for use on shore, and it's not necessary to pack snorkeling or diving gear, or golf clubs, because this equipment is usually included in ship-organized shore excursions or can be rented. For boat excursions, deck shoes or light-colored rubber-soled sneakers are needed.

Keep prescribed medication in original, labeled containers and carry a doctor's prescription for any controlled drug. If you wear prescription eyeglasses or contact lenses, consider packing a spare pair. And keep all valuables (traveler's checks, camera, expensive jewelry) in your carry-on luggage, as well as all prescription medicines and documentation (passport, tickets, insurance policy). It's also prudent to pack in your carry-on

Good walking shoes are imperative for exploring the brick-and-stone walks common in many Caribbean ports of call.

bag any other essentials you would need in the event that your luggage is late arriving. Last but not least, be sure to leave room in one of your suitcases for souvenirs.

Security

While security is not a major concern when on the ship, you should take some precautions when venturing ashore. Property crime can occur anywhere, but tourists are especially vulnerable. Keep all credit cards and most of your cash securely stowed in an inside pocket of your clothes or shoulder bag, and keep a few small bills in a readily accessible pocket so you're not pulling out your wallet to pay for small impromptu purchases from street vendors. Don't wear expensive jewelry ashore, and leave your passport and other valuables in your cabin safe when going ashore. Do not leave valuables unattended on a beach, and never leave anything of value in a rented car.

Connecting With Home

The internet and email are replacing the telephone for most long distance communication and large ships have computer centers where you can send and receive email. Internet time is quite reasonable and ships will charge either a flat rate for 10 to 15 minutes (about $8) or by the minute. Passengers can call home from the ship, either through the ship's radio office or by placing a direct satellite telephone call. This is

(Below) A Caribbean phone card and a ship's internet cafe.

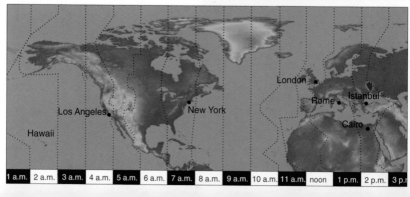

expensive, however, and unless the call is urgent, you may want to place it from a land-based phone. Pre-paid Caribbean calling cards are sold at most ports and allow the user to make international calls from any touchtone phone. Cell phone coverage is also widespread in the Caribbean. Three time zones encompass the Caribbean. Islands east of Dominican Republic are on Atlantic time; those west to the Cayman Islands are in the Eastern time zone. Cozumel and the Yucatan peninsula fall within the Central time zone.

Vacation Photos

Photographs are often the most cherished souvenirs we have of our vacation, and even casual

photographers will enjoy capturing the vibrant colors of the Caribbean on film. If you are taking a brand new camera on your trip, shoot and develop a roll of film at home beforehand to make sure the camera works properly and that you understand all of its features. For automatic cameras, 200-ASA print film is your best choice for all-around lighting conditions and is unlikely to be damaged by the powerful X-ray machines now used at airports. Exposed but undeveloped film should not be put in checked luggage but placed in a carry-on bag where it can withstand about five X-rays at walk-through security checkpoints before becoming damaged. Another option is to ask for a hand inspection, or have your film developed on board the ship.

If you're using a digital camera, take an extra battery pack and be sure to have a total of at least 128 mb of flash card memory storage. Most ships' photo departments can now develop digital images into prints.

When shooting underwater photos, be aware that water absorbs light, with red and orange colors reaching only a short distance below the surface, which is why the color blue dominates underwater photos (see example at left) unless special lighting is used. When shooting aboard an Atlantis submarine use high-speed film (up to 800 ASA).

(Above, left) An underwater photo. (Left) Photography gear.

Shopping

The Caribbean is famous for its 'free ports' where the selection and savings on luxury goods are among the world's best. With few local manufacturing industries to protect, most Caribbean countries charge no duty on imports, nor is there sales tax, resulting in savings of up to 50%. These savings are passed on to visitors who, in turn, are allowed a duty-free allowance on goods they take home. Special permits are required to bring home restricted animal products made from certain species, including sea turtles and corals.

Before you embark on your cruise, you may want to visit your local customs office and register any valuables you plan to take with you (i.e. cameras, jewelry) so that you have no problem reimporting them duty- and tax-free. Separate from goods bought at duty-free prices are those that are duty-exempt. Any item purchased in its country of manufacture is duty-exempt such as locally made handicrafts. Loose gems – emeralds, diamonds, rubies and sapphires – are also duty-exempt.

Your ship's port lecturer will offer valuable advice on what to look for and where to shop at each port of call. Although recommended merchants often pay a promotional fee to the cruise line, they must guarantee the integrity of goods they are selling to the line's passengers. If you are considering an expensive purchase, it's prudent to shop at stores known or recommended by the cruise line.

(Above) Shopping in Philipsburg, St. Maarten. (Below) A store window in Pointe-a-Pitre, Guadeloupe.

(Above) Clothings stalls at Needhams Point, Barbados. (Below) Jewellers line the streets of Charlotte Amalie.

When buying a piece of jewelry, its quality grades, carat weight, gold content and purchase price should all be noted on the receipt, an important document for insuring the item when you return home. Gold content is measured in karats, with one karat equalling 1/24 part gold. Pure gold is 24 karats while an alloy containing, for example, 75% gold is 18 karats. Precious stones are weighed in carats, one carat equalling 200 milligrams.

Diamonds are graded for clarity and color. Only trained gemologists can accurately determine a diamond's grade, but there are a few features you can look for. If, for instance, you are buying a cluster ring or tennis bracelet, look to see if all stones are fairly well matched without any one being a different color than the rest. To test for brilliance, stand back from the bright lights of the showcase and see if the gems maintain their sparkle. Good buys in the Caribbean include large single diamonds and tennis bracelets.

The world's finest emeralds are mined in Colombia and many of these stones are brought directly to the Caribbean, where jewellers sell them at impressively low prices. Emeralds, like diamonds, are sold by weight but the cut of the stone is less important than its color. The darker the emerald, the higher its value, yet shoppers should buy the color they personally prefer. All emeralds are flawed so be suspicious of someone offering you a dark green stone with no visible flaws at a low price, for it might be a fake. Also, a green oil is sometimes

rubbed on an emerald to hide its flaws and deepen its color – until the oil wears off – so it's important to buy an emerald from a reputable dealer.

While the selection of brand-name luxury goods, including leather, linen, perfumes, cameras and electronics is truly tantalizing, not to be overlooked are locally made goods. Look for Caribbean clothing made of high-quality, sea island cotton. Batik and tie-dye processes are often used to color the clothing with bright floral patterns. Colorful Caribbean artwork, widely influenced by Haitian primitive art, ranges from folk art to fine art. Wood crafts, basket weaving, pottery and doll-making are practiced throughout the islands and these unique souvenirs can be bought at local markets and craft shops. Crafts tables are often set up near the cruise pier and some terminals contain shopping malls with a selection of duty-free goods and locally made arts, crafts and clothing.

(Above) In St. John's, Antigua, the cruise ships dock adjacent to Redcliffe Quay, where upscale shops are housed in heritage buildings. (Below) A resident of Dominica sells flowers near Trafalgar Falls.

Cruising the Caribbean provides many opportunities to ponder the complex workings of a modern cruise ship. Where once a voyage took months from South America to Florida, it now takes only days. Even a modern yacht, equipped with highly efficient sails, an auxiliary engine and satellite navigation equipment, can transit the Caribbean with a fraction of the effort required in Columbus's time.

Navigational Challenges

The Caribbean poses a number of navigational challenges, not the least of which are hurricanes from June to November. However, weather information has become very accurate and ship's officers are aware of approaching storms well in advance. If necessary they take evasive action and alter course for other ports. Ships are usually safer at sea than near land, where wind strengths can increase dramatically, and there is the danger of a ship being blown onto a reef or suffering damage while moored to a dock.

Pinpoint navigation is lesson number one for all junior officers on a cruise ship, who must always be aware of local hazards, such as reefs or strong ocean currents. Specifically, currents are strong in the Straits of Florida (between Florida and Cuba) where the Gulf Stream flows north at speeds up to five miles per hour. Old Bahama Channel and the Windward Passage (between Haiti and Cuba) also have north-flowing currents, as does Cozumel Channel, where currents can reach four m.p.h. If undetected, a strong current can slowly push a ship off course and lead to danger. During the days of the Spanish Main in the Caribbean, a number of galleons came to ruin when pushed by currents onto sandbars or reefs.

The Caribbean is now well charted and the numerous reefs and submerged hazards are indicated on nautical charts. Ships also use sophisticated depth

The upper decks of modern cruise ships provide excellent viewing for passengers.

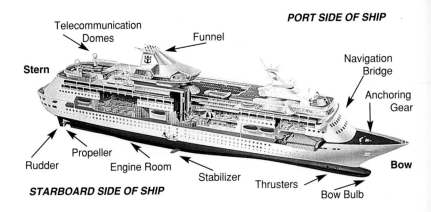

PORT SIDE OF SHIP

Telecommunication Domes

Funnel

Navigation Bridge

Stern

Anchoring Gear

Rudder

Propeller

Engine Room

Stabilizer

Thrusters

Bow Bulb

Bow

STARBOARD SIDE OF SHIP

sounders, which give the officers an accurate picture of the seabed to ensure there is ample water below the keel. A pilot is usually aboard to guide a ship into and out of each port, drawing on his local knowledge to advise the captain .

A few Caribbean ports present special challenges during docking. The most difficult ports are: Cozumel for strong currents and afternoon wind, Ocho Rios for strong winds that start early in the evening, and Barbados for the port's twisting, narrow entrance and strong afternoon winds. Grand Cayman also gets a mention by various captains for the swell that rolls into the bay where cruise ships anchor. Curacao can also present difficulties with its narrow entrance and cross winds that develop in the evening. Tampa is a beautiful harbor to exit or enter, with a long entrance to Hillsboro Bay and narrow channels leading to Garrison Seaport, but it can be a navigational challenge during bouts of fog, which occur from January to April.

How Ships Move

Ships are pushed through the water by the turning of propellers, two of which are mounted at the stern. A propeller is like a screw threading its way through the sea, pushing water away from its pitched blades. Props are 15 to 20 feet in diameter on large cruise ships and normally turn at 100 to 150 revolutions per minute. It takes a lot of horsepower – about 60,000 on a large ship – to make these propellers push a ship along at 20 knots. The bridge crew can tap into any amount of engine power by moving small levers that adjust the propeller blades to determine the speed of the ship. Most modern ships use diesel engines to deliver large amounts of electricity to motors that smoothly turn the propeller shafts. The use of electric motors to turn prop shafts greatly reduces ship vibration and passengers rarely detect the workings of the ship. Some ships use electric motors mounted on pods hung from the stern of the ship, like huge outboard engines. These pods can swivel 360 degrees.

Ships normally cruise between 15 and 20 knots in the Med, although in the Greek islands – where distances are not great – ships go slower. Distances at sea are measured in nautical miles (1 nautical mile = 1.15 statute miles = 1.85 kilometers).

Most of the cruise ships currently sailing the Mediterranean were built in the last decade or two – a testament to the booming cruise industry. These new ships have been dubbed 'floating resorts' for their extensive onboard facilities, from swimming pools and health spas to show lounges and movie theaters. Cabins, formerly equipped with portholes, now are fitted with picture windows or sliding glass doors that open onto private verandas. Modern cruise ships are quite different from those of the Golden Age of ocean liners, which were designed for the rigors of winter storms in the North Atlantic. Ships built today are generally taller, shallower, lighter and powered by smaller, more compact engines. Although their steel hulls are thinner and welded together in numerous sections, modern ships are as strong as the older ocean liners because of advances in construction technology and metallurgy.

A ship's size is determined by measurements that result in a figure called tonnage. There are approximately 100 cubic feet to a measured ton. Cruise ships used to be considered large if they exceeded 30,000 tons. Most new ships being built today are over 80,000 tons and carry about 2,000 passengers.

At the stern of every ship, below its name, is the ship's country of registry, which is not necessarily where the cruise company's head office is located. Certain countries grant registry to ships for a flat fee, with few restrictions or onerous charges, and ships often fly these 'flags of convenience' for tax reasons.

A ship's bow bulb reduces the vessel's fuel consumption.

The Engine Room

Located many decks below the passenger cabins is the engine room, a labyrinth of tunnels, catwalks and bulkheads connecting and supporting the machinery that generates the vast amount of power needed to operate a ship. A large, proficient crew keeps everything running smoothly, but this is a far cry from the hundreds of workers once needed to operate coal-burning steam engines before the advent of diesel fuel.

Technical advancements in the last 40 to 50 years have helped to reduce fuel consumption and to improve control of the ship. These advancements include the bow bulb, stabilizers and thrusters. The bow bulb, just below the waterline, displaces the same amount of water that would be pushed out of the way by the ship's bow. This virtually eliminates a bow wave, resulting in fuel savings as less energy is needed to push the ship forward. Stabilizers are small, wing-like appendages that protrude amidships below the waterline and act to dampen the ship's roll in beam seas. Thrusters are port-like openings with small propellers that are located at the bow (and sometimes at the stern) which push the bow (or stern) of the ship as it is approaches or leaves a dock. Thrusters have greatly reduced the need for tugs when docking.

The Bridge

The bridge (located at the bow of the ship) is an elevated, enclosed platform that bridges (or crosses) the width of the ship, providing an unobstructed view ahead and to either side. It is from the ship's bridge that the highest-ranking officer – the Captain – oversees the operation of the ship. The bridge is manned 24 hours a day by two officers working four hours on, eight hours off, in a three-watch system. They all report to the captain, and their

The bridge on a modern cruise ship has space-age features.

various duties include recording all course changes, keeping lookout and making sure the junior officer keeps a fresh pot of coffee going. The captain does not usually have a set watch but will be on the bridge when the ship is entering or leaving port, and transiting a channel. Other conditions that would bring the captain to the bridge would be poor weather or when there are numerous vessels in the area, such as commercial fishboats.

An array of instrumentation provides the ship's officers with

pertinent information. Radar is used most intensely in foggy conditions or at night. Radar's electronic signals can survey the ocean for many miles, and anything solid – such as land or other boats – appears on its screen. Radar is also used for plotting the course of other ships and for alerting the crew of a potential collision situation. Depth sounders track the bottom of the seabed to ensure the ship's course agrees with the depth of water shown on the official chart.

The helm on modern ships is a surprisingly small wheel. An automatic telemotor transmission connects the wheel to the steering mechanism at the stern of the ship. Ships also use an 'autopilot' which works through an electronic compass to steer a set course. The autopilot is used when the ship is in open water.

Other instruments monitor engine speed, power, angle of list, speed through water, speed over ground and time arrival estimations. When entering a harbor, large ships must have a pilot on board to provide navigational advice to the ship's officers. When a ship is in open waters, a pilot is not required.

Tendering

At some ports, the ship will anchor off a distance from the town and passengers are tendered ashore with the ship's launches. People on organized shore excur-

Ships at anchor transport their passengers ashore in tenders.

sions will be taken ashore first, so if you have booked an excursion you will assemble with your group in one of the ship's public areas. Otherwise, wait an hour or so to board a tender, when the line-ups will be shorter.

Ship Safety

Cruise ships are one of the safest modes of travel, and the cruise lines treat passenger safety as a top priority. The International Maritime Organization maintains high standards for safety at sea, including regular fire and lifeboat drills, as well as frequent ship inspections for cleanliness and seaworthiness.

Cruise ships must adhere to a law requiring that a lifeboat drill take place within 24 hours of embarkation, and many ships schedule this drill just before leaving port. You will be asked to don one of the life jackets kept in your cabin and proceed to your lifeboat station. Directions are displayed in your cabin, and staff are on hand to guide passengers through the safety drill.

Hotel Staff

The Front Desk (or Purser's Office) is the pleasure center of the ship. And, in view of the fact that a cruise is meant to be an extremely enjoyable experience, it is fitting that the Hotel Manager's rank is second only to that of the Captain. In terms of staff, the Hotel Manager (or Passenger Services Director) has by far the largest. It is his responsibility to make sure beds are made, meals are served, wines are poured, entertainment is provided and tour buses arrive on time – all while keeping a smile on his face. Hotel managers typically have many years' experience on ships, working in various departments before rising to this position. Most have graduated from a university or college program in management, and have trained in the hotel or food industries, where they learn the logistics of feeding hundreds of people.

The front desk handles all passenger queries and accounts.

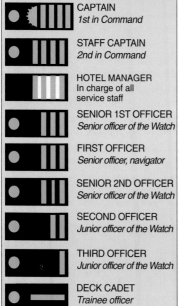

	CAPTAIN	1st in Command
	STAFF CAPTAIN	2nd in Command
	HOTEL MANAGER	In charge of all service staff
	SENIOR 1ST OFFICER	Senior officer of the Watch
	FIRST OFFICER	Senior officer, navigator
	SENIOR 2ND OFFICER	Senior officer of the Watch
	SECOND OFFICER	Junior officer of the Watch
	THIRD OFFICER	Junior officer of the Watch
	DECK CADET	Trainee officer

A Hotel Manager's management staff includes a Purser, Food Service Manager, Beverage Manager, Chief Housekeeper, Cruise Director and Shore Excursion Manager. All ship's staff wear a uniform and even if a

The ship's hotel manager oversees all of the service staff.

hotel officer doesn't recognize a staff member, he will know at a glance that person's duties by their uniform's color and the distinguishing bars on its sleeves. The hotel staff on cruise ships come from countries around the world.

Checking In

Upon arrival at your cruise ship pier, you will be directed to a check-in counter and asked to offer up a credit card to be swiped for any onboard expenses. In exchange, you will receive a personalized plastic card with a magnetic strip. This card acts both as your onboard credit card and the door key to your stateroom. It is also your security pass for getting off and on the

A standard outside stateroom with balcony.

ship at each port of call. Carry this card with you at all times.

Life Aboard

Cruise ship cabins – also called staterooms – vary in size, from standard inside cabins to outside suites complete with a verandah. Whatever the size of your accommodation, it will be clean and comfortable. A telephone and television are standard features, and storage space includes closets and drawers ample enough to hold clothes and miscellaneous items. Valuables can be left in your stateroom safe or in a safety deposit box at the front office, also called the purser's office.

If your budget permits, an outside cabin – especially one with a verandah – is preferable for enjoying the coastal scenery and orienting yourself at a new port. When selecting a cabin, keep in mind its location in relation to the decks above and below. Being above or below the disco is fine if that is where you plan to be in the wee hours, but if you are below the dining room, you'll likely hear the scraping of chairs as a wake-up call. For those prone to seasickness, cabins located on lower decks near the middle of the ship will have less motion than a top outside cabin near the bow or stern. If you have preferences for cabin location, be sure to discuss these with your cruise agent when booking. Cruise lines often reward passengers who book early with free upgrades to a more expensive stateroom.

Both casual and formal dining are offered on the large ships, with breakfast and lunch served in the buffet-style lido restaurant or at an open seating in the main dining room. Dinner is served at two sittings in the main dining room and, when booking your cruise, you will be asked to indicate your preference for first or second sitting at dinner. Luxury

Specialty restaurants (above) are an alternative to the main dining room (left and bottom).

cruise lines usually have one open seating for dinner, while several of the premium lines - such as **Princess Cruises** and **Norwegian Cruise Line** – have introduced options to the traditional two-sittings format.

Most ships also offer alternative dining – small specialty restaurants that require a reservation and for which there is usually a surcharge (about US$20 per person). Room service is also available, free of charge, for all meals and in-between snacks.

Things to Do

There are so many things to do on a modern cruise ship, you would have to spend a few months onboard to participate in every activity and enjoy all of the ship's facilities. A daily newsletter, delivered to your stateroom, will keep you informed of all the ship's happenings. If **exercise** is a priority, you can swim in the pool, work out in the gym, jog around the promenade deck, join the aerobics and dance classes or join in the table tennis and volleyball tournaments. Perhaps you just want to soak in the jacuzzi, relax in the sauna or treat yourself to a massage and facial at the spa.

Stop by the **library** if you're looking for a good book, a board game or an informal hand of bridge with your fellow passengers. Check your newsletter to see which **films** are scheduled for the movie theater or just settle into a deck chair, breathing the fresh sea air. Your days on the ship can be as busy or as relaxed as you want. You can stay up late every night, enjoying the varied entertainment in the ship's lounges, or you can retire early and rise at dawn to watch the ship pull into port. When the ship is in port, you can remain onboard if you wish or you can head ashore, returning to the ship as many times as you like before it leaves for the next port. Ships are punctual about departing, so be sure to get back to the ship at least a half hour before it is scheduled to leave.

Although **bridge tours** (of the navigation area of the ship) have been largely discontinued due to security concerns, tours of the kitchen and of backstage entertainment areas are available on most ships. If you have an interest in these areas, check with the front desk for tour opportunities.

Children and teenagers are welcome on most cruise ships, which offer an ideal environment for a family vacation. Youth facilities on the large ships usual-

(Top) A large ship's central atrium. (Above) The games room. (Below) Celebrating a birthday at sea.

(Top to bottom) Pool decks on modern ships are expansive and often include dedicated areas for children. Outside teak decks are excellent venues for excercising.

ly include a playroom for children and a disco-type club for teenagers. Supervised activities are offered on a daily basis, and security measures include parents checking their children in and out of the playroom. Kids have a great time participating in activities ranging from ball games to arts and crafts, all overseen by staff with degrees in education, recreation or a related field. Each cruise line has a minimum age for participation (usually three years old), and some also offer private babysitting. Youth facilities and programs vary from line to line, and from ship to ship.

Extra Expenses

There are few additional expenses once you board a cruise ship. Your stateroom and all meals (including 24-hour room service) are paid for, as are any stage shows, lectures, movies, lounge acts, exercise classes and other activities held in the ship's public areas. If you make use of the personal services offered on board – such as dry cleaning or a spa treatment – these are not covered in the basic price of a cruise. Neither are any drinks you might order in a lounge. You will also be charged for any wine or alcoholic beverages you order with your meals. Some cruise lines offer beverage programs for teens and children, in which their parents pre-pay for a booklet of soft-drink tickets or for unlimited soda fountain fill-ups.

Tipping is extra, with each cruise line providing its own guidelines on how much each crewmember should be tipped – provided you are happy with the service. On some cruise lines tipping is a personal choice while on others it is expected. A general amount for gratuities is US$3.50 per day per passenger for both your cabin steward and dining room steward, US$2.00 per day for your assistant waiter, US$.75 per day for the assistant maitre d', and 10 to 15 percent for the wine steward (unless this is automatically added to your receipt). Tips are usually given the last night at sea, preferably in American cash. Some cruise lines offer a service that automatically bills a daily amount for gratuities to your shipboard account. Most ships are cashless societies in which passengers sign for incidental expenses, which are itemized on a final statement that is slipped under your cabin door during the last night of your cruise and settled at the front office by credit card or cash.

(Above) A poolside bar is an ideal spot for relaxing. (Below) A couple enjoys a romantic moment at the ship's rail.

Tectonic Beginnings

Volcanism, massive uplifting, fluctuating sea levels and large-scale erosion have all played a part in forming the West Indies. The earth's surface is divided into crustal plates, and most of the Caribbean islands lie close to the boundaries of the Caribbean Plate. Some 70 million years ago, the Caribbean Plate began pushing against the much larger American Plate, which encompasses the western half of the Atlantic Ocean. Tectonic pressures produced three volcanic mountain ranges, which now comprise the Greater Antilles and some of the Lesser Antilles, including the Virgin Islands, St. Maarten and Antigua. Meanwhile, volcanic forces were also forming the Andes Mountains of South America, branches of which extend to the north coast of South America where their partially submerged peaks are now islands, including the Dutch islands of Aruba, Bonaire and Curacao, and, to the east, the islands of Trinidad and Tobago.

All of this volcanic activity was followed by an era in which the sea temporarily covered the newly formed islands. Sediments of sandstone and limestone built up as the bodies of marine animals decayed, and some of the islands were flattened. Uplifting returned these islands to the sea's surface, and the Caribbean Plate began to move slowly eastward, creating a deep-sea subduction zone between it and the American

DISASTER AT YUCATAN

Scientists have long agreed that the dinosaur, after roaming the Earth for 140 million years, suddenly faced worldwide extinction. Many theories have been proffered to explain the dinosaur's demise, one being that the formation of mountain ranges brought colder climates. A more recent theory, however, now points to a massive meteor or asteroid as the instigator.

Some 65 million years ago this huge asteroid – estimated at six miles in diameter – apparently crashed into the Yucatan region of Mexico, its impact triggering the atmospheric and climactic effects that forever changed our planet's life forms. For instance, a winter lasting several years killed the vegetation upon which dinosaurs depended for food.

Artist's impression of a meteor hitting the Yucatan some 65 million years ago.

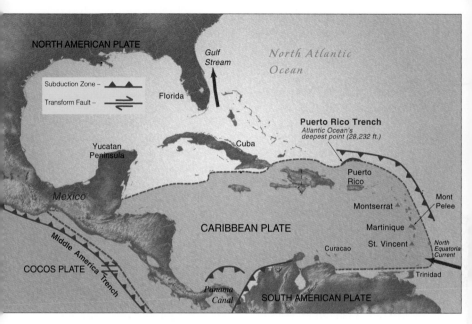

North Atlantic Ocean

NORTH AMERICAN PLATE

Gulf Stream

Subduction Zone –

Transform Fault –

Florida

Puerto Rico Trench
Atlantic Ocean's deepest point (28,232 ft.)

Yucatan Peninsula

Cuba

Puerto Rico

Mont Pelee

Montserrat

Mexico

Martinique

CARIBBEAN PLATE

St. Vincent

North Equatorial Current

Curacao

Middle America Trench

COCOS PLATE

Panama Canal

Trinidad

SOUTH AMERICAN PLATE

Plate. As the spreading Atlantic floor was driven downward beneath the Caribbean plate, a new chain of volcanoes erupted along this boundary, their conical peaks now comprising an arc of mountainous islands that extends from Saba, at the top, to Grenada, at the bottom. Sea mounts (under-water volcanoes) also lie along this boundary.

Not all of the islands are volcanic in origin. Barbados began to form about 700,000 years ago, when tectonic forces slowly pushed a section of seabed to the surface. The eastern half of Guadeloupe also formed in a similar manner, whereas its western half is volcanic in origin. The Bahamas, some of which stand only a few feet above sea level, are elevated areas of the Bahamas Bank and were likely part of a large land mass before rising sea levels submerged all but the highest points.

Volcanic Eruptions

Volcanoes form around an aperture in the earth's crust, through which gases, lava (molten rock) and solid fragments are ejected. A volcano's crater, its floor often covered with steam vents, is formed when the cone collapses during an eruption. A dormant volcano quickly loses its conical shape to erosion, so any mountain that is cone-shaped can be considered a potentially active volcano.

Numerous volcanoes in the Lesser Antilles are active, including St. Vincent's La Soufriere, which erupted in 1979, and Montserrat's Soufriere Hills volcano, which, after standing dormant for nearly 400 years, roared back to life in 1995, its most devastating eruption spewing forth an avalanche of scalding rock, ash and gas in June 1997. By then, two-thirds of Montserrat's 11,000 residents had already evacuated the island. Most of those who had chosen to remain were crowded into the north end of the island, but 19 people died when seven villages in an off-limits zone were engulfed by the pyroclastic flow which travels at speeds approaching 100 miles per hour. The island's abandoned capital of Plymouth was destroyed, and the southern two-thirds of this once verdant island lay in ash-covered ruins. In late 1999, vulcanologists reported a new lava dome growing in a crater left by a July 1998 eruption, and this dome collapsed in the summer of 2001, sending boiling rivers of ash and rock into the sea. By early 2002, the volcano's increase in rockfalls and levels of sulphur dioxide were warning of yet another eruption.

The 1902 eruption of Mount Pelee on Martinique killed all but one of St. Pierre's residents.

The Caribbean's most violent eruption in recent times was that of Martinique's Mount Pelee on May 8, 1902. Gases within the volcano reached such a critical pressure that masses of solid and liquid rock erupted into the air and a superheated cloud of burning gas and fine ash swept down the mountainside, blanketing the nearby town of St. Pierre and destroying all life in its path. Torrential rain, caused by the condensation of steam, often accompanies such an explosion. There had been warnings that Mount Pelee would erupt, but the 30,000 residents of St. Pierre chose to ignore the earth tremors, the rumbling sounds within the volcano, and its emissions of steam and light ash. The local wildlife, however, followed their instincts and evacuated the area. When the volcano finally erupted, all but one of St. Pierre's residents – a prisoner protected by the walls of his jail cell – died in the massive explosion.

Earthquakes

Earthquakes are generated by blocks of rock passing one another along fault lines (fractures in the earth's crust). Their relative movements can be vertical, horizontal or oblique, and are usually measured in inches per year, except when a sudden release of stress along a fault triggers an earthquake. An earthquake begins with tremors, followed by more violent shocks that gradually diminish. The origin (focus of a quake) is underground or underwater, and the epicenter is a point

on the surface directly above the focus. The magnitude and intensity of an earthquake is determined by the Richter scale, which measures ground motion to determine the amount of energy released at the quake's origin. A reading of 4.5 on the Richter scale indicates an earthquake causing light damage; a reading of 8.5 indicates an earthquake of devastating force.

The Caribbean Plate is no longer moving north, so volcanic activity has ceased in the Greater Antilles, but there is faulting and fracturing due to the plate's moving eastward. In 1692, Port Royal on the south coast of Jamaica was completely destroyed by an earthquake. The Lesser Antilles have also experienced earthquakes in historic times, with a number of ports suffering damage over the centuries, including Basseterre on St. Kitts, where a quake occurred in 1974.

Hurricanes

Of the natural phenomena affecting the Caribbean, hurricanes are the most widely feared, causing widespread loss of life and billions of dollars in property damage. Leaves are stripped from trees, palms are toppled, roofs are peeled off buildings and flying debris is scattered. For the people huddled inside boarded-up homes, the noise is deafening. A storm surge – a wall of water pushed by the hurricane – may form and crash onto shore, and reefs lying offshore are often

Devastating hurricanes can strike anytime between June and early November.

damaged by the pounding wave action. Even if an island or coastal region is spared the winds, the torrential rains from the tail of a hurricane often cause floods that wash out roads and swell rivers to dangerous levels. In a hurricane's wake, tens of thousands of residents can be without electricity, running water or telephones. Some might be missing a roof, or even an entire house if poorly built.

The first human records of Atlantic tropical cyclones appear in Mayan hieroglyphics. By building their major settlements away from the hurricane-prone coastline, the Mayans practiced a method of disaster mitigation, which greatly reduced their losses. The word hurricane originated from the Arawak language and meant 'evil spirits and big winds.' In other parts of the world, terms such as typhoon and cyclone apply to the same sort of intense storm. Meteorologists in North America describe an intense trop-

ical storm with winds exceeding 74 miles per hour as a hurricane.

Past storms have left their mark in history. One hurricane was immortalized in 1609 when a fleet of ships carrying settlers from England to Virginia was struck by a hurricane. Several of the ships were damaged and part of the fleet grounded at Bermuda, their passengers becoming Bermuda's first inhabitants, their stories an inspiration for Shakespeare's The Tempest. The deadliest known hurricane occurred in October 1780 when over 22,000 lives were lost in the Lesser Antilles. A 1900 hurricane severely damaged Galveston and that city's preeminence as the financial capital of southern Texas.

The hurricane season for the Caribbean and the eastern seaboard of the United States starts in June and lasts through November. The northward shift of the sun increases the temperature of the Atlantic Ocean and of the air mass lying between Africa and North America. In an average year, more than 100 disturbances (low-pressure systems) with hurricane potential are observed in the Atlantic Ocean, Gulf of Mexico and Caribbean Sea; on average only 10 of these reach the tropical-storm stage and about six mature into hurricanes. The 1950s and 1960s were active years for hurricanes in the Caribbean, when rainfall over Africa's western Sahel (where hurricane seedlings originate) was above normal.

All storms in the northern hemisphere spin in a counter-clockwise direction at sea level and hurricanes are no exception. The wind speed is caused by heavy, cool air rushing to fill a low-pressure area where the warmer, lighter air is rising. If the low-pressure area is large and the pressure gradient (the rate of pressure change over distance) between it and adjacent pools of air is steep, it will attract larger amounts of cooler air. As the cooler air spins around the eye of the low-pressure system, it can begin to tighten the eye, making it smaller in diameter. This begins a cycle of intensifying winds and of increased air flowing upward. The warm, rising air loses heat and, as a result, water is condensed to form massive nimbo-stratus clouds. Heavy torrential rain is always a precursor of an approaching hurricane.

Although a hurricane's greatest wind strength (usually between 100 and 200 m.p.h.) is along the wall or edge of its eye, where the winds create a churning sea and dense spray, the eye itself is very calm with little wind and a warmer air temperature. A hurricane can have a diameter of 500 miles or more, but the strength or intensity of a hurricane is unrelated to its overall size. Very strong hurricanes usually have relatively small eyes – less than 10 miles in diameter. Other factors come into play, such as the proximity of large, high-pressure systems and whether the storm track is over warm, shallow water.

Hurricanes often create large tidal surges, which are perhaps the biggest concern for coastal communities. These surges are sometimes referred to as domes and are caused by the low pressure of the hurricane lifting the ocean's water into a mound one to three feet higher than the surrounding surface. This mound can result in coastal surges, with the sea level rising 20 feet or more. Swells from a storm can pulse out along the water's surface for thousands of miles. Pacific surfers often ride the oceanic memory of distant typhoons.

Hurricanes are assigned different categories, depending on their storm surge, wind speed and other factors that provide a measure of the storm's destructive power. The United States National Oceanic and Atmospheric Administration (NOAA) uses five categories, beginning with category one. A hurricane of this strength will produce winds of 75 to 95 mph that can damage unanchored mobile homes and vegetation. A category-five hurricane is potentially catastrophic, packing winds in excess of 155 mph. Such winds can rip roofs off buildings and residential areas within 10 miles of the shoreline are evacuated.

The deadliest hurricane in the Caribbean occurred in the Lesser Antilles in mid-October 1780, and has become known as The Great Hurricane. The storm caused an estimated 22,000 deaths, with about 9,000 lives lost in Martinique, 4,000-5,000 in St. Eustatius, and 4,300 in Barbados. The number of fatalities from this hurricane exceeds the cumulative loss in any year and, in fact, in all other decades.

In 1992, Hurricane Andrew annihilated homes and businesses along a 30-mile swath through Dade County in Florida. When it was over, more than 60,000 homes were destroyed and 200,000 people were left homeless. Insurance pay-outs and government recovery expenditures topped $29 billion – one of the costliest hurricanes on record. But it could have been even worse. The National Hurricane Center in Miami estimates that if

This spectacular view of the eye of Hurricane Mitch (1998) was shot by NOAA and shows the intense center of the storm – the deadliest one to hit the Caribbean in 200 years.

Andrew had tracked only 20 miles further north when it hit Florida, losses would have topped $75 billion. One of the deadliest hurricanes to hit Central America was **Hurricane Mitch** in late October 1998, its five-day rampage through Central America claiming over 11,000 lives and dumping several feet of rain that triggered huge floods and mudslides in Honduras and nearby countries. And of course New Orleans is still recovering from the disastrous aftermath of widescale flooding following Hurricane Katrina in 2005.

The last decade has been one of increased hurricane activity in the Atlantic. In 2004, an unprecedented four hurricanes hit Florida in a single season. The 2005 season was worse, with so many hurricanes making landfall the World Meteorological Organization nearly ran out of names. An official list of alphabetical names (excluding Q, U, X, Y and Z) is drawn up annually for the naming of each tropical storm that forms in the Atlantic, even if it doesn't reach hurricane force.

The prediction and surveillance of hurricanes has improved dramatically in the last 40 years. The National Hurricane Center in Miami provides accurate hurricane forecasts, and warning stations have been established throughout the West Indies. Weather systems in the Atlantic are monitored 24 hours a day, with highly advanced radar and satellites to give hurricane forecasters the ability to detect and track storms long before they hit land, while reconnaissance planes measure the approaching storm's strength. Residents of the region are warned of an approaching hurricane up to three days in advance – time enough to nail plywood over windows and retreat to public shelters, built of solid concrete, to wait out the storm.

Cruise ships receive hurricane information from the National Hurricane Center and NOAA, and stay well away from the track of the hurricane.

Hurricane Katrina heads for
New Orleans in August 2005.

The history of the West Indies is one of the richest stories ever to unfold. In less than a century, the islands ringing the Caribbean Sea went from tropical paradises to prizes of European imperialism, their fates determined by battles and revolutions staged on both sides of the Atlantic. Yet, the Caribbean was once an unimaginable place to Europeans, including Christopher Columbus who, to his dying day, believed he had found the Far East.

The Early Natives

The Caribbean Islands were initially inhabited by three major Amerindian native groups – the Ciboney (the oldest and most primitive tribe), the Arawak and the Carib. All came from around the Amazon basin and migrated to the north coast of South America before travelling by canoe to the Caribbean. The Ciboney were first to ride winds and currents north along the island chain, followed by the Arawaks who settled first on the Lesser Antilles and then, pushed from these small islands by the warlike Caribs, moved to the Greater Antilles and the Bahamas.

By the time Columbus arrived in 1492, the aggressive and proud Caribs had settled most areas of the Caribbean, their largest populations located on the Lesser Antilles. The Ciboneys had been reduced to settlements on the northwest coasts of Cuba and Hispaniola, where they lived in small shelters and caves, surviving on shellfish, wild fruits, herbs and small game. They wore little clothing, painted their bodies and their only implements were stone tools.

More is known about the Arawaks, who lived in simple houses of brush and practiced *conuco*, a unique agricultural method of growing root plants by placing their cuttings in large mounds of ash and earth. Columbus described Arawak homes as "simple and clean, very high with good chimneys." Arawaks rested on woven nets strung between trees and called these hammocks.

A surplus of leisure time allowed them to develop skills for making pottery, baskets, woven cotton clothing, stone tools and jewelry including rings, necklaces and masks shaped from gold found in local riverbeds. They also enjoyed games, including a form of soccer, and they built rectangular playing courts similar to those of the Maya, whose influence was widespread.

The peaceful Arawaks, content with their simple housing needs and easily obtainable food, enjoyed a tropical paradise. Politically, they were organized as loose federations of provinces within an island, with the local village headman holding the greatest sway over

A pre-Columbian Arawak carving.

his people. Women were equal to men in most areas.

Equality of the sexes was not the case with the Caribs. Tasks between genders were strictly defined and men treated their wives as servants. The Carib men excelled at boat building and navigation – useful skills for fishing and raiding other islands. The Caribs, who had little difficulty pushing the Arawaks from desirable islands, were fearless in battle. They were one of the few native groups in the Caribbean region to defeat Europeans in battle and, unlike the Arawaks who welcomed the first Spaniards with open arms, the Caribs consistently resisted attempts to conquer or enslave them.

They also developed a reputation for cannibalism, a word derived from the Spanish word *caribal*, but human flesh was not part of their regular diet. They did occasionally eat parts of warriors taken in battle, and Columbus, who witnessed this ritualistic act, used it as a pretext for enslavement.

Columbus Discovers the Caribbean

Europe's discovery of the New World came as a result of the ambition and persistence of one man – Christopher Columbus. Born in Genoa, Italy in 1451, Columbus's first sea adventure took place in 1476 when he was sailing with a small fleet of cargo ships that was attacked by pirates. Over 500 men were killed, but Columbus managed to escape by swimming six miles to the Portuguese shore. He married a Portuguese woman of high birth whose father was governor of the Madeira Islands. While living there, Columbus formulated his audacious plan of reaching the Far East by sailing due west.

Finding no support in Portugal, Columbus turned to Spain. In 1486, he presented his plan to King Ferdinand and Queen Isabella, who were interested but preoccupied with driving the Moors from their country. For five years Columbus stayed near the court and campaigned the Queen for financial support. Finally, in January 1492, upon Spain's defeat of the Moors, an agreement in principle was reached.

With three ships – the *Nina*, the *Pinta* and the flagship *Santa Maria* – Columbus set out from Spain on August 3, 1492. This first voyage across the Atlantic was completed in 33 days, when he arrived at an island at the south

A replica of Columbus's favorite ship, the Nina.

end of the Bahamas island group, which he named San Salvador (also known as Watling Island). Here Columbus met some friendly Arawaks (also known as Tainos) who viewed these newcomers as protection against the Caribs. Columbus convinced a few of them to guide him further west, and they sailed on to discover Cuba, and then Hispaniola, where he left the crew from the wrecked *Santa Maria*. After finding a small amount of gold, Columbus returned home to a hero's welcome.

Columbus completed three more voyages to the Caribbean, each less successful than the last. On his second voyage, Columbus had a skirmish with some Caribs at Salt River on St. Croix (the first fatal confrontation between Europeans and New World natives) which claimed the lives of two Caribs and one Spaniard. On his third voyage, Columbus and his brother were sent home in chains by the Governor of Hispaniola on charges of misrule.

By this point, relations with the natives had deteriorated dramatically and Columbus now saw Indians simply as a labor force for mining gold and gathering food. He introduced the dreaded system of *encomiendas*, which allotted to Spanish settlers the lands and lives of natives. On his last voyage (1502-04), Columbus sailed his four ships along the coast of Central America in search of a strait leading to the Indian Ocean. He found no strait, no gold and lost all four ships. He returned to Spain near collapse and died in 1506 in obscurity.

The Columbus monument in Barcelona, Spain.

Extermination of the Arawaks

The impact of Spanish colonialism on the indigenous population was rapid and devastating. Many natives perished from overwork and murder, but even more died from various European diseases, such as influenza and small pox. Isolated for thousands of years, the Arawak simply did not have the natural immunities needed to fight off even a common cold. By the end of 16th century, the friendly Arawaks, of whom Columbus said, "There is no better nor gentler people in the world," were extinct.

Population estimates at the time of Columbus's arrival range from half a million to as high as six million, but whatever the number, this was soon reduced to zero for the Arawaks. This genocide was denounced by outspoken religious leaders living in the Caribbean. One of the most influential was a Dominican priest named Bartolome de Las Casas, who wrote a scathing critique of the Spanish conquerors in his book called *A Short Account of the Destruction of the Indies*. Las Casas's disturbing firsthand account of Spanish atrocities had a profound and lasting impact on European politics. Printed in 1552, it became a bestseller (and is still in print) throughout Europe and was translated into every major language. For 300 years it upheld an image of the cruel Spanish conquest of America. Protestant countries regarded the book as proof of the unholy greed of Catholic Spain and used it in support of an ongoing campaign to attack and plunder treasure ships returning to Seville.

Colonizing the Caribbean

Fifty years of empire building followed Columbus's discovery of the New World, and from the mid-1500s to the mid-1700s, two armed convoys were sent annually from Spain to collect precious gems, gold and silver. The New Spain flotilla, bound for Mexico, would sail in April to Veracruz to load silver from Central Mexico. The Tierra Firme fleet would sail in August to Cartagena and wait for the gold and silver to arrive from Portobelo. Both fleets would rendezvous in Havana to reprovision for the long trip home through the Florida Straits and past the Bahamas. Although many vessels fell prey to pirates, storms and reefs, most ships made the journey safely back to Seville.

Following Columbus's last voyage, thousands of Spanish settlers arrived in the Greater Antilles eager to find gold. The Spanish conquest of Mexico and Peru prompted many to leave the exhausted island mines to seek fortunes on the mainland. Almost all of the Lesser Antilles were abandoned once it was deter-

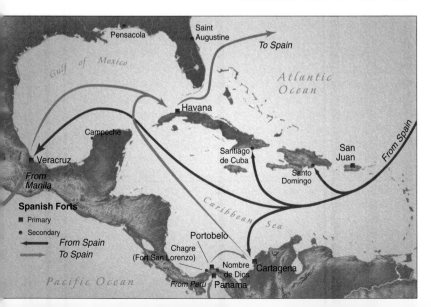

mined they were 'useless' for lack of gold. The natives were carted off as slaves and by 1570 the islands were empty and forgotten. All that remained was wild Spanish livestock which, ironically, sustained Dutch, English and French privateers while they preyed on Spanish fleets.

By the late 16th century, English, French and Dutch interlopers had spent more than 50 years harassing Spanish treasure fleets. Exploits of various captains, most notably Sir Francis Drake, made pirating a romantic career option for young Englishmen. It was the Dutch, however, who first turned the West Indies into a viable trading zone, when a Spanish embargo in 1598 forced them to look elsewhere for salt and tobacco. At that time the Netherlands owned half of the world's merchant fleet, and Amsterdam was the center of international trade. For a brief period the Dutch monopolized the slave and sugar trade in the Caribbean, their greatest victory against the Spanish occurring in 1628 when Piet Heyn captured the entire Mexican treasure fleet near Cuba. By 1630, the Dutch West India Company, operating as a commercial venture based in Amsterdam, had settled on St. Maarten, Curacao and Bonaire.

Dutch attempts to usurp Spanish control in the Caribbean and South America eventually failed, but the net gainers were adventurers from France and England who, encouraged by high tobacco prices, looked around the Lesser Antilles for suitable land. On January 28th, 1624, Thomas Warner, with 20 fellow adventurers from Guyana, landed on the beautiful island of St. Christopher (St. Kitts) and founded the first British settlement in the Caribbean. Some French sailors arrived about the same time and the two groups divided the island, with local Caribs their mutual enemy. St. Kitts became the Caribbean mother colony for further settlements by the British and French. Warner's tobacco plantation was a huge success and news of the fortunes being made in tobacco prompted rapid settlement of other islands – Barbados, Montserrat, Nevis, Antigua and the British Virgin Islands by English farmers; Martinique, Guadeloupe and the western half of Hispaniola (Haiti) by French farmers. The Carib natives, after being pushed off St. Kitts, retained strongholds on Dominica, Grenada and St. Vincent.

Sir Francis Drake (1540-1595)

The second largest fortress in the Caribbean, the British citadel of Brimstone Hill on St. Kitts was known as the 'Gibraltar of the West Indies'.

Tobacco was still the crop of choice for settlers arriving at new islands, but it was soon observed tobacco, like most weeds, will grow almost anywhere. Supply soon outstripped demand, prices fell and the tobacco boom burst. Then settlers on Barbados began planting sugarcane after visiting Brazil to learn of Dutch innovations in planting and harvesting. The first successful crop on Barbados set off a frenzied boom and by 1647 most planters had switched to sugar, a luxury commodity with far greater staying power than tobacco. Demand for labor soared and the population grew from 10,000 in 1640 to 43,000 by 1655. Sugar became the new 'white gold' of the Caribbean and thousands of English peasants signed themselves into years of indentured work.

The French colonies grew at a slower pace until the early 18th century, when sugar production lifted their prospects. Like the British, the French crown tried to enact trade restrictions that kept its colonies under exclusive control. The effort was unpopular and Caribbean planters – both British and French – soon got their own way in commercial matters as well as winning control of their local governments.

The Struggle for Caribbean Control

Spain's influence in the West Indies declined significantly in the 17th century. The Dutch, with the greatest number of ships and least amount of regulatory baggage, succeeded in controlling trade, their merchants providing the best service and highest profits for Caribbean farmers. However, during a determined effort in the latter half of the 17th century, England and France finally wrenched control from the Dutch who were left with six small islands – Sint Maarten, Sint Eustatius, Saba and the ABC's –

Aruba, Bonaire and Curacao.

By this time, both English and French merchants had increased their Caribbean possessions. In 1655, a fleet under Cromwell's government took Jamaica, while the French solidified their hold on Martinique, Guadeloupe and Saint-Domingue (later renamed Haiti), and took possession of St. Barts, St. Croix and Grenada. The Caribs continued to suffer at the hands of Europeans. A massacre of natives was organized by the French on Grenada in 1653, where 40 desperate Caribs jumped to their deaths from a cliff that became known as Morne des Sauteurs (Leapers' Bluff).

In 1654 the French failed to eliminate the Caribs on St. Lucia and St. Vincent but did slaughter those remaining on Martinique. Finally, in 1660, a treaty was signed reserving Dominica and St. Vincent for the Caribs.

One other European country got into the act of taking and settling Caribbean islands. The Danish West India Company was the first to permanently settle St. Thomas when its sponsors, encouraged by the Dutch,

The Danes built Fort Christiansvaern on St. Croix.

believed they could make large profits by carrying slaves from Africa to St. Thomas for resale in the West Indies. The company went on to acquire St. John and St. Croix, but went out of business in 1754 when the Danish crown purchased the islands.

Throughout the 18th century, France and England engaged in a series of wars of which the Caribbean was a major theatre, with islands changing hands several times. Both sides erected forts to protect their islands from enemy attack, but the battles were fought mainly by their navies. Britain permanently stationed squadrons of warships in the West Indies while France sent over fleets in response to specific issues or conflicts. The first of these conflicts was the War of Jenkins Ear from 1739 to 1748, which ended inconclusively. Next was the Seven Years War, from 1756 to 1763, which resulted in Britain receiving Canada in exchange for Guadeloupe, valued by France for its sugar plantations.

America's War of Independence

Caribbean sugar helped push the American colonies to revolution in 1776. For decades Britain had been charging high duties to American merchants buying sugar products from non-British islands in the Caribbean. But when Britain prohibited the importation of any foreign rum or molasses, such restrictions infuriated the Americans and became a major grievance leading to revolution in 1776.

The American Revolution received support throughout the Caribbean, where the same conflict of interest between home countries and colonies existed. Troops from Saint-Domingue

Sail loft pillars remain intact at Nelson's Dockyard in Antigua.

fought for George Washington under Lafayette. The Jamaica Assembly demanded equality with England and the Bahamas openly supported the mainland colonies. It seemed, without the British Navy to stop them, the islands of the British West Indies would have joined the Revolution. The Dutch island of St. Eustatius became the first territory in the New World to recognize the independence of the United States.

The Caribbean's sugar industry also gave the United States the very symbol of its independence – the Capitol. It was designed by a planter from Jost Van Dyke in the British Virgin Islands, Dr. William Thornton, a Quaker interested in architecture. After seeing an advertisement for a competition to design the Capitol, he presented his winning design to President Washington.

The after-effects of American independence were devastating for the Caribbean islands. Britain blockaded the mainland American ports from West Indies trade and, with exports and imports suddenly cut off, food became a scarce commodity and thousands died of famine. Eventually Britain reopened trade and relaxed the embargo. In the meantime, however, the French West Indies enjoyed boom times as the main supplier of rum and sugar to America. But the sweet life was not to last, for the upheaval of the French Revolution eventually spread to the Caribbean. Saint-Domingue (Haiti) convulsed in a terrible civil war led by slaves yearning for freedom. Guadeloupe and Martinique were also caught in the struggle, enduring battles and a reign of terror after Jacobin republicans arrived to take control. In 1793, the local white planters on these islands sought protection from Britain, which quickly took advantage of the chaos to capture almost all French possessions in the Caribbean. This was reversed in the fall of 1794, when Victor Hugues, leading a squadron of troops, retook Guadeloupe and sent more than 1,200 white planters to the guillotine. Hugues went on to stir up rebellion on other islands and successfully expelled the British from St. Lucia. On Grenada, the British just managed to hang on to their main fort while fighting an insurrection led by the Creole planter Julien Fedon. In Saint-Domingue, Britain endured its most serious losses, both in money and men, during a conflict that dragged on until 1798 when a Creole slave named Toussaint L'Ouverture successfully repelled the British.

SLAVERY

In the early years of sugar planting, white indentured laborers, serving terms of three to five years, were far more common in the islands than black slaves. An important boost for planters came when Cromwell sent thousands of Scottish and Irish people to Barbados in the 1650s. However, Barbados was a death sentence for white laborers and as many as three out of four white workers perished soon after arrival, many dying from tropical diseases. Black workers generally fared better at adjusting to the climate, but survival meant a constant routine of hard work between cutting the cane or working in the sugar mill, where temperatures reached 120 degrees.

By 1650 it was clear that a massive labor force was needed to grow sugar. Africa was already supplying slaves to Asia, the Middle East and Europe, and

Slaves push hogsheads of sugar to a tender for loading onto ships.

slave traders were quick to satisfy the labor needs of Caribbean planters. Trade in human cargo was underway and about to take place on a scale never before seen. Europe's acceptance of slave labor in the Americas for over 300 years is, today, difficult to understand. Although slavery was practised worldwide, it had virtually disappeared in Europe by the Middle Ages and had been replaced with the notion of semi-freedom under which most serfs labored. The Portuguese had been the first to enter the lucrative trade of transporting black labor from the west coast of Africa back in the 15th century, and by the middle of the 17th century, French, English and Dutch slavers were actively buying and selling from African warlords. From Senegal to Angola, forts were built to protect slave companies, and cities such as Luanda, Accra and Lagos existed for centuries as human warehouses.

West African tribes, some living hundreds of miles inland, were under continual onslaught by slave traders, who would march whole villages to a slave depot.

The Atlantic triangle brought manufactured goods from Europe to Africa, slaves from Africa to the Caribbean, and sugar, cotton and tobacco back to Europe. It was a system that suited accepted economic dogma of the time and was so profitable it seemed providential. The triangle made the West Indies among the most valuable colonies the world has ever known, and England's Liverpool was transformed from a fishing village into a center of international commerce, becoming one of the largest ports in Europe devoted to the slave trade.

Over four million Africans, between 1601 and 1870, were shipped to the Caribbean. (The United States, by comparison, imported about half a million slaves.) The appalling rate of mortality, both on the plantations and on the slave ships, kept the death rate far in excess of the birth rate, and new slaves for the islands were always in demand. For every 100 slaves put on a ship bound for the Caribbean, only 56 would be alive after three years.

Planters had complete control over their slaves, who had little

recourse against injustices, although some – called Free Coloreds – earned their freedom through faithful service or bought it with money raised by selling handicrafts or garden produce. Desperate slaves simply ran away, and on most islands were quickly captured and severely punished. Runaway slaves stood a better chance on the Greater Antilles where they hid in the dense rainforests and rugged mountain areas. Jamaica was home to the best known and most successful group of runaways who became known as the Maroons. They successfully raided frontier plantations, established towns and beat off numerous attacks by British troops, finally gaining two homelands of more than 2,500 acres.

Abolition and the Road to Freedom

In the latter part of the 18th century, the Age of Enlightenment resulted in new ideas about freedom and equality. Confidence in human reason and progress lent credibility to radical beliefs, and people were open to change. During this time, anti-slavery movements throughout Britain gained momentum and, led by a number of powerful parliamentarians, they won the support of the prime minister, William Pitt. The chief spokesman for abolitionists, William Wilberforce, initiated a series of parliamentary inquiries publicizing the horrors of the Middle Passage – from Africa to the colonies.

Armed with information to reveal the slave trade as a vast graveyard for African slaves and British sailors who died from various tropical diseases, the abolitionists spread their campaign across the country and found a receptive public willing to sign petitions. The result was a success and the British Parliament scheduled an abolition bill for 1796. However, revolutionary France's Reign of Terror discredited radical ideas, and not until May 1806 did the British government pass the Foreign Slave Bill prohibiting the shipping of slaves

Huts for slaves working the nearby salt pans still stand at Lacre Punt on Bonaire.

to foreign colonies. Two years later, it abolished the importing of slaves into British colonies.

Convincing planters to accept abolition was a different matter, but resistance from planters only stiffened the resolve of abolitionists. The slaves themselves began revolting with increasing frequency. In 1816 a revolt ravaged Barbados, which had not known a slave conspiracy since 1701. Ironically, the very measures enacted to end slavery made the situation worse. The labor force dwindled at the cessation of the slave trade in 1808 and masters forced their existing slaves to work harder, moving women, children and older domestic servants out to the fields to work.

By 1830, Caribbean slaves and British abolitionists were losing patience with the slow progress towards freedom. A large slave rebellion in Jamaica led by a Baptist lay preacher named Sam

Cutting sugarcane from dawn to dusk during harvest (January to June) was backbreaking work.

Sharpe brought events to a head when more than 60,000 slaves revolted by burning 200 sugar estates in the northwestern parishes. News of the revolt and its repression galvanized British abolitionist groups to organize a final drive to end slavery. More than one and a half million people signed petitions which were presented to Parliament early in 1833. The Abolition Act was passed in August, ordering the end of slavery by the following year, making Britain the first European power to abolish slavery. Parliament voted to pay planters about £25 per slave, which went a long way toward encouraging passage of the Emancipation Bill in colonial assemblies.

France passed an emancipation decree in 1848, and the Netherlands ended slavery in the Caribbean in 1863. The Spanish colonies, which were enjoying a boom in sugar production in the 19th century, took longer, eventually abolishing slavery in Puerto Rico in 1873 and in Cuba in 1886. The Danish Virgin Islands

introduced slavery reforms in 1839 and issued an emancipation decree in 1848.

Following emancipation, the freed slaves either moved off the plantations to form 'free villages' and grow their own food on small plots of land, or they continued working on the estates as wage earners. As labor costs climbed, sugar prices fell, due to the large quantities of beet sugar being successfully grown in Europe as well as cane sugar exports from countries, such as Brazil, that were still using slave labor. The slave trade continued in Africa and other parts of the world long after the nations of Europe had abolished slavery.

Abolitionist leader William Wilberforce at the age of 29.

Caribbean Politics in the 19th and 20th centuries

After emancipation, the Caribbean islands all beat to a different drum. The British islands became Crown colonies and remained thus until powerful labor movements in the late 1930s prompted several to seek full autonomy from Britain. Jamaica, Barbados and Trinidad and Tobago were led by forceful, populist leaders with socialist leanings, who borrowed ideals and slogans from Britain's Labour party. The 1940 Moyne Report recommended self government for the islands and, although the British government agreed, it wanted to hand over the reigns of power to moderate political leaders who enjoyed popular support. Jamaica and Trinidad and Tobago were the first colonies to gain independence in 1962, followed

Cover of abolitionist pamphlet in late 18th century. Millions of similar tracts were circulated in England before emancipation.

by Barbados in 1966 and the Bahamas Islands in 1973. Next was Grenada (1974), then Dominica (1978), St. Lucia (1979), St. Vincent and the Grenadines (1979), Antigua and Barbuda (1981), and St. Kitts and Nevis (1983). Most of these sovereign states are members of the British Commonwealth of Nations and, as recently as 1997, were allowing legal appeals to the judicial committee of Britain's Privy Council in London. A number of the smaller islands have chosen to remain British Crown colonies, these being Anguilla, the British Virgin Islands, the Cayman Islands and Montserrat.

Following a plebiscite in 1945, the French Antilles chose assimilation and political union with France. Both Martinique and Guadeloupe are overseas departments and administrative regions of France, the latter including the

After emancipation, many former slaves tended small plots of land to grow food for themselves and the local market. (Below) A street scene in Christiansted, St. Croix, circa 1910.

dependencies of St. Barthelemy and St. Martin.

The Dutch islands of Aruba, Curacao, Bonaire, St. Eustatius, Saba and St. Maarten have also retained links with their home country, remaining part of the Kingdom of the Netherlands. In 1986 Aruba separated from the Netherlands Antilles, but remains part of the Kingdom. Curacao, the capital of the Netherlands Antilles, prospered during the oil boom of the 1960s and 1970s, but refining capacity has been cut since the 1980s and the state has taken over ownership.

Finally unburdened of trade restrictions in the late 18th century, the economies of Spain's colonies improved. Cuba became a huge sugar producer but resentment against Spanish rule and taxes continued, leading to civil wars in the latter part of the century. A separatist movement, with strong support in the United States, resulted in an open conflict between Spain and America, which lasted for 10 weeks in 1898. After two naval losses to the American fleet, Madrid surrendered. Cuba was granted independence and Puerto Rico and

other possessions were ceded to the United States which became the main economic and political force in the Caribbean. American capital provided the means to rebuild sugar, banana and coffee industries in the Greater Antilles and, by the 1920s, American-owned companies were producing most of the world's cane sugar.

To protect American shipping, the United States purchased the Danish West Indies during the First World War in 1917. Renamed the Virgin Islands of the United States, they are strategically positioned along the approach to the Panama Canal. America's presence in the Caribbean has brought stability to the region and such benefits as building roads, establishing institutions and improving communications.

The Caribbean Today

Any island, with its limited resources, is challenged to meet the economic needs of its citizens and this is especially true in the Caribbean. Tourism has been a bright spot for many islands and the cruise ship industry, with a total economic impact estimated at $4 billion annually, has created over 80,000 full-time jobs in the Caribbean region .

Notwithstanding Cuba, the Caribbean region's political determination is adherence to democracy. The acid test of this occurred in 1983 when countries of the Caribbean refused to tolerate the murder of Grenada's prime minister, Maurice Bishop, by an unelected military regime and backed intervention by the

Under Governor Peter von Scholten, slavery was abolished in the Danish West Indies (now U.S. Virgin Islands) in 1848.

United States to restore civil order. Grenada has enjoyed democratic elections ever since.

The West Indies, physically isolated from one another by the Caribbean Sea, remain fragmented politically. A case in point is the secessionist movement in Nevis, the smaller member of the twin-island federation of St. Kitts-Nevis. The two islands, separated by a narrow channel, have a shared history, common language and much inter-island travel, yet the residents of Nevis – many of whom feel their union with St. Kitts was imposed upon them in 1871 by a British colonial government – voted 62 per cent in favor of secession in a 1998 referendum. However, the St. Kitts-Nevis constitution states that 66.6 percent of Nevisians must vote for secession before it can take place. With democracy a valued institution, peace and stability prevails.

The immense wealth brought back to Spain from Mexico and Peru was a constant source of envy for other European countries, and resentment grew when Spanish claims were confirmed by papal decree. Without the resources to attack the Spanish empire directly, northern European nations relied on piracy to tap into the New World's gold supply.

Piracy was called privateering when it received tacit approval from British, French and Dutch crowns in the form of licensing or commissions. This subtle distinction gave captains latitude to pursue innocuous activities, such as collecting livestock on Caribbean islands, when the real purpose was to pillage Spanish towns and ships. The captains would return home to divide their spoils with the crown while receiving the royal pardon.

San Juan's 'new' El Morro fortress was Drake's undoing. The Spanish, unlike in earlier days, were ready for the much-feared privateer.

France, almost continuously at war with Spain until 1559, was the first to attack Spain's source of wealth. When news that French privateer Jean d'Ango seized four Spanish ships laden with treasure near the Azores in 1523, men throughout France boarded ships bound for the Caribbean to prey on Spanish vessels. As many as 30 French ships raided the West Indies annually, the climax of these efforts coming in 1555, when corsair Jacques de Sores took Havana and burned it to the ground.

The exploits of Sir Francis Drake fired the imagination of all Europe when he captured an entire year's production of Peruvian silver in 1572. With only two ships and 73 men he took the city of Nombre de Dios (near today's location of the Panama Canal) and captured three mule trains transporting 30 tons of silver. This voyage brought Drake wealth and fame, and inspired generations of adventurers to seek their fortune in the West Indies.

Drake made a number of sorties to the Caribbean and is also credited with being instrumental in the defeat of the Spanish Armada in 1588. Drake met his end in 1595 during a siege of the newly built El Morro fortress in San Juan, Puerto Rico. After failing to penetrate the settlement, he sailed to other ports looking, without success, for treasure. Returning to his old haunt of Nombre de Dios, he met his fate when he died of dysentery and was buried at sea near Portobelo.

The struggling Spanish colonies, limited by crown decree to trade only with Spanish ships, were themselves participants in piracy. When ships from Seville were captured by pirates, the motley crew would sell the prized cargo to Spanish merchants in the Caribbean at prices well below the official tariffs.

The term 'buccaneer' derives from French colonists who, hiding out on Hispaniola, sold the meat and hides of cattle left by the Spanish. These buccaneers began setting up camps on various islands to repair their vessels and rest before venturing back onto the high seas. One of the first such camps was on Isla Tortuga off the north coast of Haiti. Established in the late 16th century, this multinational settlement was perhaps the earliest independent European community in the New World, owing alle-

Howard Pyle's illustrated 'Book of Pirates' depicted pirates as a colorful and ruthless bunch taking big risks in small boats.

giance to no crown and trading with every nation. The Bahamas, Turks and Virgin Islands were also excellent pirate hideouts, for they were windward of Spanish bases in the Greater Antilles and difficult for the lumbering galleons to approach.

One of the best harbors was Charlotte Amalie on St. Thomas, which became a haven for pirates who brought booty to sell to local merchants. Collusion with pirates became so blatant that an international incident unfolded at Charlotte Amalie in 1683, when the island's governor refused to hand over a pirate ship to a British man-of-war.

However it was Jamaica that had the most infamous reputation as a pirate enclave in the 17th century and for 30 years, from 1643, it offered hospitality to thousands of pirates from Europe and the Caribbean. The most celebrated of all pirates at Port Royal was Henry Morgan. A bold captain who knew the coasts of the Spanish Main well, Morgan's first great success was taking the rich city of Portobelo in 1666. This astounding achievement garnered Morgan a pardon from the Jamaican governor and earned him a reputation throughout the Caribbean as a shrewd and fearless leader.

More exploits followed, climaxed by the spectacular capture of Panama in 1671. When the pirates marched back across the isthmus, they took a string of 200 pack mules laden with gold, silver and other valuables, plus a large number of captives. While the crew quarreled over their share of the loot, Morgan slipped away in his ship with the greater part of the booty, leaving his followers without food or ships.

Although Morgan was sent to England to stand trial (England and Spain had recently signed a treaty) he was exonerated as a hero, knighted by the king, and sent back to Jamaica not as a prisoner, but as Deputy Governor of the island. Sir Henry finished his days on his sugar plantation and, unlike others of his kind, died in his bed in 1688.

Pirates were often an unpredictable and contradictory bunch. Many a notorious captain would, upon sinking a ship and killing the survivors, call his crew together for prayer service. Some skippers forbade swearing, drinking and gambling, and some even displayed empathy for their hapless victims.

Two female pirates, Anne Bonny and Mary Read, made the annals of pirate history in the early 18th century for their exploits and method of escaping the hangman's noose. Convicted of piracy in Jamaica, Bonny and Read successfully pleaded for their lives, claiming they were

S.ʳ HEN. MORGAN
Part. 2. Chap 7.

Sir Henry Morgan's life (1635-1688) as a pirate, living in luxury to his dying day, was the exception rather than the rule. After being knighted by Charles II, he was sent back to Jamaica as Deputy Governor to rid Port Royal of pirates. Morgan's Lookout, his famous retreat, is located near Ochos Rios on Noel Coward's Firefly estate.

pregnant. On the day that Bonny's lover 'Calico' Jack Rackam was hanged, he obtained permission to see Anne for a farewell interview in which she apparently told him that she was sorry to see him there, but if he had fought like a man, he need not have been hanged like a dog.

One of the most interesting pirates was Major Thomas Bonnet. He was not raised for a seafaring life and, before taking to piracy, he was apparently enjoying a quiet retirement on his large estate in Barbados. A married man, he lived in a fine house and was much respected by his neighbors and other gentry of the island.

But one day, something snapped. Bonnet decided to fit out a ship armed with ten guns and a crew of 70 men. To satisfy the curious, he said he intended to trade between the islands. Without so much as a word of good-bye to his wife, Bonnet slipped out of Bridgetown harbor at night and began looking for victims off the coast of Virginia, capturing half a dozen small ships.

His undoing was meeting the infamous Edward Teach (better known as Blackbeard) who had terrorized the Bahamas and American mainland for years. Teach attracted warships like flies to molasses and both he and Bonnet were finally captured by armed sloops. Bonnet was found guilty and hanged in November 1718. When news of Bonnet's exploits and demise reached Barbados, his neighbors were shocked and found it difficult to

(Above) Piratess Anne Bonny was a tough pirate who fought bravely against being captured. (Below) Captain Thomas Bonnet is the only pirate actually known to make his victims walk the plank.

imagine what had caused this sudden change in one of their own. It was suggested his mind had become unbalanced from the unbridled nagging of Mrs. Bonnet, whose husband was one of few known pirates, other than those in fiction, who actually made his prisoners walk the plank.

The archetypal pirate was Blackbeard. Notorious for his cruelty, he tortured victims and crew with equal enthusiasm. Once, after blowing out the candle in his cabin, he fired at his guests in the darkness, severely wounding one. He said afterwards that if he didn't shoot one or two, they would forget who he was. A great practitioner of psychological warfare, he would stick lighted candles in his bushy black beard to enhance his fear-

some image. Blackbeard was successful for many years in the Caribbean and the U.S. eastern seaboard before being trapped by British warships off the North Carolina coast in 1718. A physical giant who wore 12 pistols and several cutlasses when heading into battle, he killed several Marines before falling to the pistol shots and sword wounds that finally killed him.

These were the dying days of piracy as Britain began stationing naval ships in the Caribbean and installing governors determined to clean up their islands. Some, like Henry Morgan of Jamaica and Nassau's Captain Woodes Rogers, were former pirates who knew where in the 'faggot heap to search for the ferret.' Woodes Rogers, who was an extraordinary navigator (he found Alexander Selkirk, a.k.a. Robinson Crusoe, on a small island in the Pacific) and a natural leader, rounded up 2,000 pirates in the Bahamas and convinced most to give up piracy.

Pirates were always in the market for stone watchtowers, such as this one overlooking the harbor in Charlotte Amalie on St. Thomas. Built by Danes in 1678, Skytsborg is said to have been used as a hideout by the infamous pirate Blackbeard.

SHIPWRECKS

Over the centuries, storms, reefs, sea battles and pirates have claimed many a ship plying the waters of the Caribbean. Those that foundered on shallow reefs kept wreckers employed in salvaging their contents, while those that settled in deeper water have, in many instances, become prime diving sites. It's estimated that some 700 ships lie wrecked on the bottom of the Caribbean Sea, and many are still being discovered. High-tech private salvagers, also known as treasure hunters, are often employed by the governments of developing countries to extract artifacts and treasures from sunken ships. This practice is opposed by archeologists, who believe historic shipwrecks should be protected from what they consider to be modern-day piracy. When the wreck of *Queen Anne's Revenge*, Blackbeard's flagship which sank off the North Carolina coast in 1718, was discovered by treasure hunters in 1996, the state claimed the wreck and its artifacts, imposing an exclusion zone around the site. The salvage company that discovered the wreck after years of research into historical documents, plans to recoup its costs by selling film and book rights.

Cartanser Sr., an encrusted World War II cargo ship, sits in 35 feet of water off St. Thomas.

SUGAR AND RUM

Sugar, initially a luxury good, had a tremendous impact on the world economy in the 17th and 18th centuries, when it became a staple of the masses. British consumption in particular soared, and the Caribbean's highly prized 'sugar islands' were often used as bargaining chips at peace conferences between warring powers. Sugarcane grew so well in the Caribbean, and such huge profits were being made, that almost all the Lesser Antilles turned themselves completely over to its cultivation.

Cane cultivation usually took place from June to December, during the rainy season, when slaves planted cane cuttings and nurtured the growing plants. After 18 months, the cane was eight to 10 feet tall and ready for harvesting during the dry season

Wind-powered mills for crushing cane were more common on low-lying islands such as Barbados and St. Croix.

from January to June. Early methods of extracting juice required an enormous amount of cane; about 20 pounds were needed to produce a pound of sugar. Heavy bales of cane stalks were brought from the fields to the mills where the cane was crushed and juice was extracted. The cane was run through the mill's rollers at least twice to squeeze as much juice out of the stalk as possible. The juice would run by trough to the boiling house where it was boiled and clarified in a series of copper vats to remove excess water and impurities. Workers would skim off gross matter and strain the juice before finally allowing it to flow into cooling troughs. The resulting raw sugar, called *muscovado* (unfinished sugar), was put in huge barrels called hogsheads which weighed 1,600 pounds. The hogsheads were placed on racks and left to stand for 12 to 16 hours when a plug at the bottom was removed and the molasses drained off. The barrels were then topped up with sugar and ready for export.

The refining of this raw sugar product was normally completed in Europe or North America but the production of rum, at least for domestic consumption, was usually carried out on the individual islands. Early rum was made by fermenting a mixture of water and molasses (five parts to one) in a vat with a measure of skimmings, oranges and herbs to taste. After fermentation, the mix was heated in a still through condensing coils, emerging as rum of 120 proof or stronger. It was sometimes rough, usually uneven, but it was rum.

RUM

Known as *ron* in Spanish and *rhum* in French, rum is a versatile spirit with a range of taste and characteristics unique to each producing island. The history of rum runs parallel with that of the Caribbean. Sir Henry Morgan glowingly described rum as, "A friend and brother to one alone in the dark, a warm blanket on a chilly night, an excitement in the cheek and an inspirer of bold and brave deeds." Many islands have a long history of producing rum. In the tropics, rum has long been the preferred drink, and not just for its taste. Alcohol dilates the peripheral blood vessels and actually has a cooling effect on the body, which makes rum more refreshing than ice water.

Rum, which is produced from either molasses or cane juice, is unique in that it retains more natural taste factors from its product of origin than any other spirit. Starch-derived spirits, such as vodka (made from potatoes) or whisky (from grain), must be cooked or malted to produce a sugar for fermentation. Since rum is derived from sugar, it doesn't have to go through a cooking process, nor does it have to be distilled at very high proofs, so it receives the minimum of chemical treatment.

A St. Croix distillery with pot stills shown on the left while workers roll a hogshead barrel filled with raw sugar along the loading dock.

Production begins with the fermentation of either cane juice or molasses to make the originating product for the start of distillation. The method of distillation and aging, along with the strain of yeast used, and the type and amount of caramel used in coloring, are what differentiate the various rums. The traditional pot still (also known as batch production) and the more modern continuous column stills are both used in the distillation process, with some rums being a blend of each method.

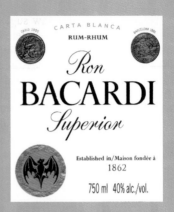

Like whiskey and brandy, rum needs to mature, and full bodied rum is normally aged three years or more while drier, lighter rums are generally aged only one year. Rum is naturally colorless but it will pick up some color if it is aged in charred casks (which also adds aroma) or, more usually, if sugar caramel is added. These darker rums are often used in hot drinks in cold damp climates while the drier light rum is popular as a chilled summer cocktail.

Different Types of Rum

Popular rum distilleries hold regular tours for visitors and are well worth the visit for rum aficionados. Most Caribbean rum is produced from local sugar cane products, although imports from Mexico and Central America are sometimes used. Here is a quick overview of various island rums.

Puerto Rico: The rums produced here are dry and light bodied. The molasses is fermented in gigantic vats using mash from a previous fermentation. If the rum is matured for only a year in uncharred oak casks, it is light-bodied, neutral in flavor and white in color. Two years in charred barrels and the addition of caramel produces a somewhat darker rum with more body and a stronger aroma.

Puerto Rico's best-known rum is Bacardi – the top selling rum in the world. Bacardi, using continuous stills which impart a remarkable consistency in taste, has a range of rums aged one to six years, including an excellent reserve rum (six years old) best savored neat. The bat on the logo is from the company's beginnings in 1862, when Don Facundo bought the distillery which was then home to a colony of fruit bats. The bat symbol was, at that time, an easily recognized trademark for illiterate customers.

Jamaica: The traditional Jamaican rum, full bodied with a pungent aroma, has in recent decades been blended lighter with the taste and aroma toned down. However, most Jamaican rum is still made using pot or batch stills and aged a lengthy three to five years. The molasses is allowed to ferment naturally, which can take up to three weeks but allows for greater saturation of cane flavor. A number of fine rums are produced on Jamaica and the major producer is Appleton, which makes an excellent range of rums from its own sugar cane, blending pot-still and continuous-still rums to make its popular brands. Appleton produces a 12-year-old rum, one of the oldest and finest available. Appleton Estates is often included in most cruise line's shore excursions to Jamaica and, for rum fans, is well worth the visit.

Barbados: Rums from this island are semi-light in body and color, with an almost smoky flavor. Distillation methods include pot and continuous stills, and most Bajan rums are a blend of the two. Cockspur, Mount Gay and Doorly's are popular brands. The world's oldest rum is claimed by Mount Gay, its production traced prior to 1703. Mount Gay rums are distilled from molasses using natural spring water from the island. Different aged rums are blended to make its final smooth-tasting Eclipse product.

French West Indies: A considerable amount of full-bodied rum is made on Martinique and Guadeloupe. On Martinique alone there are nearly a hundred cane growers and over a dozen large distillers. French West Indies rum is different from other islands in that the product is distilled from the concentrated juice of sugar cane rather than from molasses. It is produced by pot still and takes on a dark color.

Other Islands: The U.S. Virgin Islands produce a light-bodied rum, with Cruzan on St. Croix enjoying a very good reputation, while the British Virgin Islands are producers of Pusser's famous Royal Navy Rum, a dark rum which can be bought in a traditional clay jug. Antigua produces a decent and inexpensive rum called Cavilier, and Westerhall distillers on Grenada produce a limited pot-still rum from sugar cane juice aged in oak. Each bottle is numbered, which somehow makes the sipping of this light rum all the more delightful.

The Caribbean is a sea of cultures, its people as diverse as the world itself. Their official languages include English, French, Spanish and Dutch, yet it's a Creole dialect, based on a French vocabulary and African grammar, which is used on many of the islands and is incomprehensible to most outsiders. Local customs and cuisine also vary from island to island, but what does prevail throughout the Caribbean is exuberance, especially during each island's Carnival.

Carnival is a celebration of life and no where is it displayed with more fervor than in Trinidad, where the music of Carnival – calypso and steel band – was born. Pulsating Afro-Caribbean rhythms provide the beat and the brilliant costumes worn by dancing paraders provide the color. A year of preparation produces elaborate, three-dimensional costumes, some up to 10 feet tall and weighing 300 pounds. Competition for prizes is fierce – not for the money, but for the honor.

Mocko jumbie stilt walkers – the traditional symbol of Carnival – originate from the traditions of West Africa. They parade atop 10-to-20-foot stilts, dressed in bright colors and covered in mirrors because these 'elevated spirits' are said to be invisible and onlookers see only themselves. Carnival celebrations vary from island to island, and not all are held in the days prior to Lent. In the Bahamas, a festival called Junkanoo is held right after Christmas, with people flocking to Nassau to participate in the parades. In Puerto Rico, fiestas honoring patron saints are held in central plazas and include religious and costumed processions. In the U.S. Virgin Islands, Carnival is celebrated on St. Thomas in April, on St. John over

(Left) Some school-girls on Grenada. (Opposite page) A Dominican woman walks with easy grace and swaying hips while balancing a basket on her head.

July 4th, and on St. Croix in December. Crop Over Festival in Barbados – a revival of the traditional celebration of the end of the sugar harvest – is held each summer, as is Antigua's annual festival celebrating the abolition of slavery.

Whether it's called a 'jump-up' or a 'mas' (masquerade), the celebration is uninhibited and the mood joyful, with spontaneous street parties, reggae concerts, calypso competitions, food fairs and the crowning of a Carnival king and queen.

Each port has a bustling marketplace, located in a central square, where fresh produce is sold along with other wares. Traditionally a social gathering place as well as the town's commercial hub, with island farmers, fishermen and traders bringing their goods here to sell, the market reflects traditions long rooted in Africa. Matriarchs called 'market women' often control, through mutual understanding, a specific spot in the square and acquire goods to sell either by purchase or on consignment.

The fresh fruits, vegetables and spices on colorful display at the market are the mainstays of creole cooking. Root vegetables, including yams and sweet potatoes, are commonly used, as are breadfruits, tomatoes, peppers and ackee which, when removed from its ripened pod and cooked, resembles scrambled eggs. Rice, peas, beans and fried plantains (a type of banana) are served alongside a main dish of saltfish (salted cod), curried goat or conch fritters. Stews are also popular, such as kalaloo which consists of okra, spinach, goat, crab, fish and West Indian spices.

The flavorful dishes created in West Indian kitchens incorporate a number of local spices. Allspice, chives, curry, ginger, nutmeg, turmeric (the 'poor man's saffron') and thyme are all favored. Jerk, a popular Jamaican cooking technique introduced by African slaves, involves marinating pork, chicken, sausage or fish in a mixture containing Scotch Bonnet (a very hot chile pepper), thyme, allspice, scallions, garlic and nutmeg, then cooking the meat in an outdoor pit over a pimento wood fire. This traditional dish was likely introduced by African slaves, but the Arawak natives before them were already grilling meats and fish. The Arawaks introduced many tropi-

(Above) Colorful batik clothing is made through-out the West Indies. Here, a worker applies wax to cloth at the Caribelle Batik factory on St. Kitts.
(Left) Bahamian wood carvings.
(Below) A fisherman mends his nets at the coastal village of Anse-la-Ray, St. Lucia.

(Above) Business is brisk at the public market in Pointe-a-Pitre, Guadeloupe. (Right) Race day at a school in Basseterre, St. Kitts. (Below) Cricket is a popular sport on the British-colonized islands of the Caribbean.

cal fruits to the West Indies, as well as vegetables such as corn, callaloo (similar to spinach) and cassava (resembling sweet potatoes and the source of tapioca).

Rum is another important ingredient in Caribbean cooking, used widely in deserts featuring bananas and coconut. A typical Caribbean fruit punch, with or without rum, consists of orange and pineapple juice, with grenadine syrup and nutmeg added. Limes, mangos, pineapples and papayas are just some of the delicious fruits grown locally and served up Caribbean style.

In a region where self expression and creativity are evident in the dancing, singing and easygoing nature of the people, it's easy to forget there's a more serious side to Caribbean culture, one that has produced a number of critically acclaimed writers and poets. Nobel-winning writer Derek Walcott, born of mixed-race ancestry on St. Lucia in

1930, was educated in Jamaica where he immersed himself in classical literature. His poems draw both on the folklore of a West Indian childhood and the teachings of a higher education, a dichotomy that once caused him to complain that he felt more at ease describing an English cherry tree than the breadfruit tree under which he sat while writing.

Another famous West Indian writer is V. S. Naipaul, considered a master of English narrative, who was born in poverty to Indian parents in Trinidad in 1932. Apparently hating both his mother and his tiny country's provincialism, Naipaul moved to England at the age of 18 to study at Oxford. Knighted in 1990, Sir Vidiadhar Surajprasad Naipaul has written a sweeping selection of novels, travel books and documentary works, and in 2001 he was awarded the Nobel Prize in literature for his vivid portrayal of post-colonial society and his critical assessments of Muslim fundamentalism. A highly educated street fighter, Naipaul is unflinching in his opinions and his legendary brusqueness is described in Paul Theroux's unflattering book *Sir Vidia's Shadow: A Friendship Across Five Continents.*

Also making her mark on the world is Antigua-born Jamaica Kincaid, who ran away to New York City at age 17 to escape an unhappy childhood which, along with the bitter realities of her

A Jamaican girl in her school uniform smiles for the camera.

homeland, are frequent subjects of her writing.

Caribbean visual artists have been widely influenced by Haiti's primitive art, which developed in isolation among the peasantry until discovered by the outside world in the 1940s. Colorful and vivid, Haitian art often depicts voodoo images based on African tribal practices. African motifs – animal patterns and geometric designs – are often incorporated in Caribbean works, both fine art and folk art, and the works of local painters and artisans are widely displayed in island shops and galleries.

Prominent singers and song-writers who hail from the Caribbean include Cuban-born songstress Gloria Estefan, Puerto Rican pop star Ricky Martin, and the late reggae superstar Bob Marley of Jamaica, whose music was introduced to an international audience by record producer Chris Blackwell, the founder of Island Records (which he sold to Polygram in 1989). The actor Sidney Poitier was raised on Cat Island in the Bahamas, and fashion designer Oscar de la Renta was born in the Dominican Republic, his namesake perfume inspired by his mother's garden in Santo Domingo.

West Indian men and women are leaders in many fields. St. Lucian-born Sir Arthur Lewis won a Nobel prize for economics in 1979, and Dominican prime minister Eugenia Charles, dubbed the 'Iron Lady of the Caribbean' for her outspoken personality and political strength, led her country in the 1980s and 90s. Famous Caribbean athletes include Puerto Rico's baseball legend Roberto Clemente, and two of the world's fastest 100-metre sprinters – Donovan Bailey (winning Olympic gold for Canada in 1996) and Linford Christie (Britain's gold medalist in 1992) – are from Jamaica.

Empty pews await Sunday worshipers at the 18th-century Santa Anna Church in the community of Noord, Aruba.

Caribbean music, drum laden and danceable, has direct connections with the music of West Africa. The Gankogui (or double African bell), which provides a steady repeating pattern and is the rhythmic basis to West African music, evolved from a 12-count rhythm into the eight-count 'clave' rhythm that is the foundation for most Caribbean music. Wooden concussion sticks, called claves, produce a beat that guides all other instruments in their rhythmic variations. The clave sticks may or may not be used in a particular piece of music, but their underlying rhythm is always present.

Many Caribbean songs are lyrically linked to the experience of slavery, both in style and subject matter, for although slaves were not allowed to speak to one another in the fields, they could sing. After emancipation, former slaves maintained their musical

Calypso is heard everywhere during Trinidad's Carnival.

heritage at social events and church services, passing on rhythms, techniques and lyrical motifs to successive generations.

The main rhythm of reggae – in which the accent is put on the second and fourth beat of a four/four time signature – has been traced back to the Yela rhythm created by women in southern Senegal by alternating hand claps with the pounding of grain. The African wellspring from which Caribbean music evolved is also the source of jazz, which developed in New Orleans in the latter part of the 19th century and was based, in part, on black work songs and field shouts.

In an evolving tapestry of musical sounds, Caribbean music has been influenced by American jazz, along with other, less closely related musical forms, including European waltzes, quadrilles and mazurkas, as well as Latin styles such as the Cuban rumba. American Gospel, rock and roll and rhythm and blues also have played a big part. The following

is a compilation of the different styles you will hear when visiting ports of the Caribbean.

Calypso

Originally from Trinidad, calypso is popular throughout the Caribbean. The beauty of calypso is twofold: sophisticated lyrics with clever word play and driving rhythms for a festive unwinding. The music is thought to have progressed from the field songs of slaves employing allegory to pass along information and gossip. This interest in subtle lyrics, to hide meaning from slave masters, was turned into a source of entertainment and art. The game evolved with work crews fighting mock battles in song and the number of bon mot lyrical strikes determining the winner. Instruments were added to the sound in the 19th century, when calypso was first recorded. Today, driven by syncopated bass rhythm, calypso is filled in with drums, guitars and occasionally tenor and alto steel drums.

Steel bands play calypso arrangements on drums called steel pans.

Calypso, like its offspring soca, is a favorite at Carnival in Trinidad, where there are competitions for lyrical quality and party-pleasing rhythms. Popular artists include Chalk Dust, Mighty Sparrow, David Rudder, Roaring Lion (who at 89 years of age released a hit album) and Eddy Grant. Another recent offshoot of calypso is "ringbang" developed by Eddy Grant which marries a modern sound utilizing synthesizers and recording techniques with classical calypso lyrics and melody. A major record label for calypso (and soca) is Ice Records, which has a dazzling array of artists and releases a selection of Carnival competitors each year. Hot and Sweet, recorded by calypso king Mighty Sparrow in the 1970s, is a classic.

Steel Band

The steel pan, the only contemporary instrument created in the

Caribbean, is made from a 55-gallon oil drum. The base of the drum is heated and stretched into a concave shape, and the surface is then pounded out in graduating rectangles to create different notes. Steel bands normally arrange popular calypso songs for their drums. The Rising Stars of St. Thomas are a popular steel pan band. Cruise lines often arrange for steel bands to play their music during arrival or departure of their ships

Soca

A blend of soul and calypso, soca is jumped-up calypso with bawdier lyrics. The music of choice on Trinidad, soca is popular throughout the Caribbean and played non-stop at Carnival time when famous calypso and soca artists perform at competitions. Well-known artists include the versatile Mighty Sparrow (who has the longest straight number of wins at the Road March King competition in Trinidad) as well as Superblue, Fab 5 and ring bang artist Viking Tundah. Cuban per-cussionist Changuito, often referred to as the father of modern soca, developed the soca rhythm while playing with the group Los Van Van. One of the best known soca songs is Hot Hot Hot, recorded by Hot Hot Hot Arrow, a native of Montserrat.

Goombay

Unique Bahamian music with a fast-paced tempo driven by a range of skin drums, goombay is directly linked with West African dances and drums. Nassau holds an annual Goombay Summer Festival featuring this and other Afro-Caribbean music.

Reggae

Perhaps the biggest revolution in Caribbean music, reggae literally lifted Jamaica from a post-colonial funk in the late 1960s to an era of new confidence and hope. Born in the slums of Kingston, reggae quickly became popular around the world as mainstream artists such as Eric Clapton, Paul Simon and the Rolling Stones produced hits using the reggae beat. Evolved from ska (Jamaican dance-hall music) and a slow rock-steady beat, reggae was slower still with a greater emphasis on bass and, traditionally performed outdoors, was played loudly. Reggae's early lyrics were social, political and spiritual, exerting a real impact on Jamaican politics in the early 1970s. Its main artist was the late

Bob Marley performing at one of his last concerts.

Bob Marley, whose songs of redemption, salvation and prophecy made him a leader for poor Jamaicans (see profile in Jamaica chapter). Bob Marley and the Wailers produced a string of reggae hits with bestselling albums such as Catch a Fire and Natty Dread and became the leading reggae group of the 1970s. *Get Up, Stand Up, I Shot The Sheriff* and *One Love* are some of Marley's well-known songs.

Although local DJs gave reggae its big push in the mid-to-late 60s, it was record producer Chris Blackwell's early support that gave reggae an audience in the markets of Europe and the United States. One of the first albums to become an international hit, now a classic, was Jimmy Cliff's *The Harder They Come* which was actually a soundtrack to a movie about the hardships of attaining success as a musician in Jamaica. Other reggae artists from this era include the Maytals, Desmond Dekker and Burning Spear. Marley's son Ziggy and wife Rita continue to record, and other popular artists include Beres Hammond, Buju Banton, Shabba Ranks and Maxi Priest.

Salsa

Hot, sensuous dance music with a distinct call-and-response singing style, salsa is popular in Puerto Rico. Its strong emphasis on brass and percussion is derived from the Cuban salsa which uses timbales, bongos and congas to carry the rhythm. Popular artists include Eddie Palmieri and Bobby Valentin.

Other Musical Styles

Merengue, created during the 19th century in the rural townships of the Dominican Republic, utilizes the cylindrical, double-headed tambora drums and brass instruments. Merengue is experiencing a comeback in its country of origin, and both it and Cuban salsa are currently the hip music rage in Madrid night clubs.

Cadence is popular in Martinique, Guadeloupe and Dominica. It began as a sort of Caribbean jazz fusion (featuring clarinet and trombone), which synthesized various musical forms, including soca and reggae, with exuberant driving drum rhythms.

Zouk is popular French Caribbean music that grew from cadence and is very fast with lots of Latin influences. Vocal harmonies are featured in zouk music, which was originally used to describe parties on Martinique and Guadeloupe.

Jazz has become increasingly popular in the Caribbean on several islands, including St. Lucia, Jamaica, Grenada and Puerto Rico, which host annual festivals which feature local and international performers.

Gospel is American religious music that developed in the southern slave-holding states and can be heard in many a Caribbean church. A fusion of jazz, blues, reggae and calypso, gospel evolved from a combination of plantation work songs and Protestant hymns. When a West Indian congregation raises its unified voice in a jubilant gospel song, the spiritual inspiration of the music is a salve for tired ears.

(Above) The customs house in San Juan reflects the Plateresque style of contrasting bare walls and ornamental doorways.

(Below) Spanish and French colonial buildings featured overhanging grilled balconies, built over the sidewalk to provide shade, such as those lining a Marigot street in St. Martin.

The sturdy West Indian house is both functional and visually pleasing. Its steep, gabled roof withstands strong winds, sheds rain quickly and, vented at both ends, allows hot air to escape. Hoods and louvered wooden blinds keep out the hot sun and driving rain while admitting light and fresh air. Solid wood shutters are another feature on islands where hurricanes are an annual threat. Gingerbread fretwork, in a variety of patterns, is often added as decoration.

Dutch colonial buildings are often baroque in style, their gabled roofs embellished with ornamental trim. (Above) The Penha building in Willemstad, Curacao.

British plantation owners lived in 'great houses', their outer walls often built of large limestone blocks up to 20" thick to absorb the sun's heat. (Middle left) St. Nicholas Abbey in Barbados is one of the oldest great houses in the West Indies. It was built by a British colonel around 1650 in the Jacobean style, with gables and corner fireplaces – an unlikely feature for the tropics.

(Below, left) Barbadian chattel houses – moveable wooden homes built by freed slaves – were a miniature version of the Georgian-style manor house.

Features of West Indian neo-classical architecture include rows of arches running the length of arcaded sidewalks and upper-floor galleries designed to catch the breezes and provide shade from the tropical sun. (Above) Government House in Christiansted, St. Croix,

(Above, right) The Sacred Heart Basilica in Balata, outside Fort-de-France, Martinique, is a smaller version of the famous Montmartre landmark in Paris, its design a revival of the Byzantine-Romanesque style.

European technological advances in the 19th century included the widespread use of metal, as evidenced in the Schoelcher Library (shipped in pieces from France; see photo on page 281) and the Saint-Louis Cathedral (shown at right). Both buildings are located in Fort-de-France and were designed by French architect Henri Pick (a contemporary of Gustav Eiffel, builder of the Eiffel Tower).

Bird of Paradise

Amazon Parrot

The Caribbean's plant and animal life is rich in diversity and beauty. Flowers, both indigenous and exotic, flourish here amid the lush, tropical greenery, as do nearly 300 species of butterflies and hundreds of species of birds.

Heliconius Ismenius butterfly

Hibiscus

Torch Lily

PLANT LIFE

The vegetation on a single island can vary considerably, with a jungle-like growth of dense foliage proliferating on its windward side, and stunted plants that tolerate arid soil growing on its leeward side. The vegetation zones occurring on mountainous islands are well defined. At the summits of the higher peaks is an elfin woodland of matted mosses, lichens and ferns, which can survive in wet and windy conditions. A montane (mist) forest grows on the mountains' upper slopes and

The massive trunk of this tropical tree is supported by buttress roots.

ridges, and consists of small trees and ground vegetation of grasses and ferns.

At lower elevations is the rain forest, its tall trees and interlaced foliage forming a dense canopy, through which little sunlight can penetrate. **Bromeliads** (air plants) sprout from massive tree trunks and ferns grow at their bases. A secondary forest will grow in areas previously cleared through natural disaster or cultivation for crops, its open canopy allowing the growth of shrubs and small plants at ground level. Often intermingled with secondary forests are seasonal formations, which contain many of the flowering trees that blossom during the dry season.

In addition to being sources of food and material for handicrafts and construction, a number of island plants and trees are also used for bush medicines and herbal remedies, their leaves boiled to make therapeutic teas and soothing baths for treating such ailments as rheumatism and the common cold. Children use young green fruits for playing marble games and a broad leaf on a stick can serve as a parasol.

Many of the tropical hardwoods, such as mahogany, are deciduous but are considered evergreen because, rather than shed all their leaves at once, they do so sporadically throughout the year. In addition to supplying oxygen, tropical trees support vines and air plants, an example being the banyan tree, which sprouts roots that hang between the tallest branches and the ground. Tree roots supply nutrients to the soil and prevent soil erosion during heavy rains.

Forests are important watersheds, with almost all fresh water originating in forest rivers and lakes. The widespread cutting of tropical rain forests has become a controversial practice due to its destruction of freshwater sources as well as its destabilization of the earth's temperature, humidity and carbon dioxide levels. Island rainforests, being self-contained ecosystems, are much more susceptible to extinction than those on a continental land mass. On some Caribbean islands, the removal of vegetation around watersheds has caused rivers to dry up, and fresh water must be imported or produced by desalinization plants.

The importance of forest preservation is recognized by a growing number of Caribbean nations that are countering development with the establishment of national parks, nature reserves and wildlife sanctuaries. Guided tours are offered throughout the islands, which allow visitors to see first hand such species of tree as the soapberry, fig and maho, its bark used for making rope. Limes, bananas, papayas and other fruits can be seen hanging from tree branches, as can cocoa tree pods containing cocoa beans. These and other species, such as the nutmeg tree, were introduced to the West Indies for cultivation. Banana plants are widely grown,

Rainforest conservation is critical to the survival of an island's watershed.

their leafy, palm-like aspect a familiar sight. The overlapping bases of the banana plant form a false trunk, from which emerges the true stem of a mature plant, bearing the male and female flowers. The latter develop into clusters of upturned bananas, called 'hands', with each banana a 'finger'. The plant is cut down for harvesting, since it bears fruit only the once.

Exotic flowers blossom everywhere. Introduced to the islands during the colonial era, they provide brilliant splashes of color amid the green tropical foliage. Some of the popular flowers are bougainvillea, hibiscus, orchid, frangipani, flamboyant (royal poinciana) and the trumpet-

shaped yellow cedar. Indigenous plant species include bamboo, guava trees, wild pineapple, dodder vines, century plant, soursop, tamarind and coconut palms.

Palm trees grow throughout the Caribbean, their flowing crowns of frond leaves swaying in the breeze and providing welcome shade. Palms grow to heights of 100 feet or more, their smooth cylindrical stems marked by ring-like scars left by former leaves. The towering royal palms, often seen lining avenues, reach heights of up to 120 feet and were traditionally used as boundary markers for sugar plantations.

The coco palm, from 60 to 100 feet tall, readily establishes itself on shorelines and small islands because its seeds, enclosed in a large buoyant pod, can float. Its fruit is the coconut, a hard woody shell encased in a brown fibrous husk, and a single coco palm can bear more than 200 nuts annually. A coconut has three round scars at one end, its embryo lying

Three Palms Beach, Puerto Rico

against the largest, which is easily punctured to drain the nutritious juice inside. Copra, from which oil is extracted to make soaps, cooking oil and suntan lotion, is produced when a ripened coconut is broken open and dried.

Every part of a coco palm has value, its leaves used for making fans, baskets and thatch, its coarse coconut husks turned into cordage, mats and stuffing, its nutshells polished and carved to make attractive cups and bowls. Even the fibrous center of old trunks can be used for rope. In addition to its fruit being a staple food, the young head of its tender leaves – called palm cabbage – is cooked as a vegetable.

Called 'trees of life' for the many functions they serve, coco palms are susceptible to lethal yellowing disease, caused when minute insects called planthoppers infect the palm leaflets with a mycoplasma-like organism. The yellowed leaves soon die, as does the tree's trunk. This disease devastated Key West's coco palms in 1955, before spreading north to

Miami where, by the mid-70s, the disease had eradicated 90% of the city's coco palms. In the early 80s Mexico's Yucatan Peninsula was hit by the disease. Although a palm infected with lethal yellowing can be treated with regular applications of tetracycline funneled through a hole that is bored into the trunk, the most workable solution is to replace the stricken palm with a resistant variety.

ANIMAL LIFE

Over the centuries various animal species have been introduced to the West Indies, such as the mongoose, a ferret-sized mammal imported from Asia to hunt rats and snakes but which also destroys much of the native fauna. Others are indigenous to the region, such as the **iguana**, a herbivorous lizard common to Mexico's Yucatan peninsula and a number of Caribbean islands. Being cold blooded, it derives body heat from the sun and basks on rocks and tree tops for much of the day to maintain a body temperature high enough to digest the leaves and fruits it consumes. Peaceful and harmless, iguanas grow to three feet in length and can weigh over 400 pounds. The larger males are gray with a tall crest on the back, while the females retain the bright green body of a young iguana. The female burrows a nest in sandy soil, laying her eggs at the end of a tunnel, which she then refills for concealment. When the young iguanas hatch, they dig their way to the surface where they are vulnerable to predators.

Found in the Caribbean, iguanas can weigh up to 400 pounds.

The American **crocodile**, found in South Florida, the West Indies and Central America, lives in both fresh and salt water and does not attack humans without provocation. Crocodiles are large, carnivorous reptiles that live in swamps or on river banks, slipping into the water to hunt for prey with their powerful jaws. Its eyes, ears and nostrils are on top of its head, with valves closing on the ears and nostrils when the crocodile submerges. The average length of a crocodile's flat body and tail is about 10 feet but the saltwater variety is often 14 feet long, sometimes growing to 20 feet.

Alligators, which are found in the southern United States, are generally less aggressive than crocodiles, have wider snouts and, unlike the crocodile, the lower fourth tooth does not protrude when the mouth is closed. Caimans are similar to alligators, growing to lengths of 15 feet, and are found in Central America.

Jaguars have a unique coat with rings surrounding spots, and it is this pattern of rosettes that distinguishes jaguars from leopards. Jaguars are good swimmers and can live in trees for months when the jungle floor is flooded. Belize has a world famous jaguar reserve.

Birds

The Caribbean's abundant bird life ranges from tiny hummingbirds to the high-flying frigate bird. Because the West Indies are close to both South and North America, there is some crossover of range between tropical birds and those commonly seen in the United States.

The magnificent **frigate bird**, also called man-o'-war bird, is the most aerial of the water birds with a wingspread of 7-1/2 feet – the largest in proportion to its body of any bird. Highly skilled fliers, frigate birds can be seen riding thermal updrafts along

Frigate Bird

Brown Pelican

coastlines for extended periods of time. They feed mainly on fish they spot while in flight and they will harass other birds, such as pelicans, until they drop their catch, which is then snatched in midair or retrieved from the water or beach. Its long tail, deeply forked and scissor-like, is opened only while maneuvering in flight. Although classed as a sea bird, it is awkward in the water.

The **brown pelican**, in contrast to the frigate bird, is heavy bodied with a long neck and large, flat bill. It too is a graceful flier, as well as a skilled swimmer, and it will glide in circles in the air before suddenly diving straight into the water to scoop a fish into the large, expandable pouch hanging from its lower jaw. Brown pelicans nest on shore and the young feed from their parents' pouch.

The **flamingo** is a tall, tropical wading bird related to the stork and heron. Now an infrequent visitor to southern Florida, the American flamingo nests chiefly in the West Indies, with sizeable breeding colonies located on Bonaire and on the southernmost Bahamian island of Inagua. Flamingos build conical mud nests, one to two feet high, with mates taking turns incubating one or two eggs.The flamingo feeds in the shallow water of marshes and lagoons, where it scoops water into its large bill, the serrated edges of which strain algae and shellfish from the water. The bird's pink color comes from its diet of shrimp and other crustaceans containing the pigment carotene.

The **Great Egret** (also called Common Egret) is a type of heron that feeds in shallow water on small aquatic life. Threatened in the early 20th century when its white, silky plumage was used to adorn ladies hats, the egret is now a protected species.

Parrots, with their brilliant plumage, longevity (up to 80 years in captivity) and ability to mimic human voices, have for centuries been popular cage birds. Their natural habitat is the tropical rainforest and the smaller species tend to be mostly green, a camouflage defense against predators. The best mimics are the Amazons, which are found in the West Indies.

Flamingo

Coral Reefs

Some of the most unusual animal life in the Caribbean is found beneath the water's surface, where coral reefs, formed by living organisms, are home to a fascinating variety of fish and other sea creatures. These underwater habitats are formed by soft, saclike animals called polyps. Smaller than a pea, each polyp secretes an exoskeleton of limestone. A colony forms by polyps budding new polyps, with all the buds remaining connected. These tiny polyps, each living inside its own limestone cavity, feed mainly at night on floating plankton, which they trap with their extended tentacles. Microscopic algae grow within the polyp tissues and are collectively responsible for the coral colony's vivid colors. These symbiotic algae, called zooxanthellae, need sunlight and

Great Egret

clear water to take up carbon dioxide and photosynthesize, thus providing an internal supply of oxygen and organic nutrients to the polyp.

When coral colonies die, their surfaces are recolonized by new corals or other types of invertebrates, such as sponges or soft corals. Layers of skeletal materi-

Green Sea Turtle

Queen Angelfish

Moray Eel

Brain Coral

Sea Anemone

A CORAL REEF COMMUNITY

An abundance of life thrives in warm
Caribbean waters, where coral reefs
support schools of colorful fish and
other aquatic creatures.

Gray Angelfish

Trumpetfish

als gradually accumulate over time to form a coral reef. Although corals live in temperate as well as tropical waters, coral reefs are found only in tropical waters, within 30 degrees of the equator, where the water temperature remains above 70 degrees Fahrenheit year round.

Coral reefs that extend from shore are called fringing reefs, and those separated from shore by a wide lagoon are called barrier reefs. Barrier reefs rise like fortress walls from the sea floor and are habitat for tropical fish and large ocean-going predators, which feed here on the smaller fish. Fringe reefs, often within a few yards of the water's surface, serve as nurseries for hundreds of small tropical fish, as do mangroves which grow along shorelines. Their tangled roots and dense branches are saltwater tolerant, and they help stabilize coastlines by absorbing wave action. Coral reefs also deflect incoming waves, their porous

character allowing the absorption and dissipation of a pounding sea. In bays protected by strategically placed reefs, the steady shifting of particulate debris from the coral colony onto shore results in a beach of fine sand.

Adjacent to reefs are **seagrass beds**, where the sturdy stems and roots of underwater plants weave together to form a mat that stabilizes the shallow sandy bottom and provides food for sea turtles, manatees, conchs and reef fishes. A band of bare sand containing only the roots of seagrasses sometimes separates a reef from its adjacent seagrass bed. This is caused by grazing reef fishes which are reluctant to venture too far from the security of their reef, or by urchins which come off the reef at night to feed along the edge of the seagrass bed.

Seagrass beds also anchor sediments, helping maintain the water clarity required for a healthy reef which needs sunlight to survive. Excessive nutrients in the water, often caused by sewage and agricultural run-off, can trigger algal blooms that cloud the water and prevent sunlight from penetrating and activating photosynthesis in the corals' symbiotic algae. These unwanted blooms of algae can also attach to the surfaces of corals and grow until portions of the reef are smothered.

Protective measures are being taken in the Florida Keys and islands of the Caribbean, where environmental pressures in the

Golden Tube Sponge.

form of coastal development, water pollution, overfishing and increased recreational use have all threatened the survival of coral reefs. Preservation measures include the installation of mooring buoys so that no anchors are dropped from boats, and prohibiting snorkelers and divers from touching and taking pieces of coral. A number of marine parks contain sign-posted underwater trails guiding visitors past the colorful corals while providing an appreciation of their fragile environment. Artificial reefs in the form of sunken ships encrusted with corals and inhabited by schools of fish are one way of luring divers and snorkelers away from fragile natural reefs.

Most reef-forming corals belong to the stony or hard group of corals. There are many different types of hard corals, some branch-like, others rounded, their distinctive shapes determined by the budding pattern of the various polyp species. Corals are often named for their appearance and some common hard corals include **elkhorn**, with its thick stocky branches, and staghorn, which has smaller branches. Other branching colonies include flower, finger, pencil and ivory corals. Pillar and ribbon corals grow upright in clusters, and **brain corals** grow in rounded shapes. Soft corals also help build the reefs, their feathery forms including sea fans and gorgonians in a variety of vivid colors. Sea anemones, unlike the corals, do

A school of soldierfish in Belize.

not have a skeleton and often look like flowers when their feeding end is open and their tentacles are fully extended. Brilliantly colored sponges, another aquatic animal, attach themselves to coral reefs, often in colonies. They vary in shape and size, and show little movement.

The shimmering tropical fishes found along coral reefs come in an assortment of shapes, sizes, colors and markings, which often change as the juvenile fish matures. Angelfishes are among the most beautiful of the small fishes that inhabit shallow reefs, their flattened disc-like shapes allowing them to slip through nooks and crannies. Their elaborate markings are often blue and yellow, or black with yellow stripes. They feed on sponges and the ectoparasites of other fishes. Butterflyfishes are similar to angelfishes with yellow their dominant color. They travel in pairs, feeding on coral polyps, sea anemones, tubeworms and algae.

Blue tangs are another disc-like fish that live on the algae that grows on or among the coral. The juveniles are a lemon-yellow color, pre-adults are often part yellow and part blue, and adults are a blue to purplish gray. The size of reef fishes can vary, the butterflyfishes growing to about 6 inches, the angelfishes ranging from one to two feet in length, and the tiny cherubfish, which prefers deepwater reefs, reaching only 2 3/4" in size. **Parrotfishes** begin life as drably colored females, then turn into males with gaudy green and blue scales. They have molar-like teeth, which they use to grind algae off the corals, producing sand in the process.

Other members of the coral reef community include the **spiny lobster**, which hides in crevices by day and feeds at night, as does the **moray eel** – a snake-like fish

A reef shark looks for food along a barrier reef.

that is harmless unless provoked. The tiny **sea horse** (ranging in length from 2 to 8 inches) is usually found swimming upright among the seagrasses, using its tail to hold onto a seaweed when resting. Seahorses, which utter musical sounds during the mating embrace, belong to the same family as the **pipefishes**, with which they share a unique breeding habit. The female's eggs are forced into a pouch on the male's underside, where they are fertilized and nourished until expelled as miniature versions of the adult.

Coral reefs attract a variety of feeding creatures, including **sharks**, which are heavy fishes with skeletons made of cartilage. A shark must keep moving in order to breathe, by taking water in through its mouth and passing it over its gills, which form a line of slits down both sides of the fish. There are over 250 species of sharks, ranging in size from 2 feet to 50 feet. Abundant in warm waters, not all sharks are predato-

ry and few are interested in humans. Those considered harmless are the nurse shark, which grows to 12 feet in length, and the Caribbean reef shark, which grows to about 8 feet on a diet of reef fish, octopus, crabs and lobster. To detect their prey, sharks have electromagnetic senses on their snouts, which is why professional shark feeders wearing stainless-steel suits and gloves can hypnotize a reef shark with a gentle stroke of the hand. Not so placid are the hammerhead and tiger sharks, which are predatory and dangerous to humans.

Rays are flat-bodied fishes related to the shark. Shaped like kites with winglike pectoral fins that propel them through the water, rays also have long whip-like tails. There are three basic groups of ray: mantas, eagles and stingrays. Mantas are the largest, up to 22 feet in width and 3,000 pounds in weight. Mantas and eagles are active rays, whereas stingrays are bottom dwellers, lying like rugs on the sea floor as they dredge up shellfish and other small animals. The stingray's eyes and spiracles (breathing orifices) are on top of its head, its mouth and gill slits on the underside. Southern stingrays are common along Caribbean reefs, the females growing up to six feet in width. They have rows of spines along their tails which contain a poison that can inflict pain and be fatal to humans. Stingrays defend themselves against sharks by lashing with their tails but they rarely attack humans unless provoked or stepped on (shuffling your feet along the sea bottom will prevent this). They have no teeth, but their jaws are strong for grinding and sucking, which is why snorkelers at Stingray City on Grand Cayman will sometimes receive a hickey from a nuzzling stingray looking for food.

Turtles are the world's oldest surviving reptile, in existence since the time of the earliest dinosaurs some 200 million years

Southern stingrays are common in the Caribbean, living on the ocean floor near shores and in bays.

The loggerhead turtle grows to 450 pounds and nearly four feet in length.

ago. Equipped with toeless, oar-like legs, these ancient mariners can swim at speeds approaching 20 miles per hour, and some will travel thousands of ocean miles along warm-water currents to reach their nesting sites. Once a source of food for sailors, the endangered **green turtle** is now protected by law, as are the hawksbill, leatherback and **loggerhead**, the latter named for its large head (up to 10 inches wide) and powerful jaws used to crush clams and crabs. The **green turtle**, named for the greenish color of its body fat, is a plant eater and can be seen grazing on seagrasses or sleeping under reef ledges. The **hawksbill turtle**, named for its narrow, pointed beak with which it pries sponges from coral reefs, was hunted nearly to extinction for its beautiful tortoiseshell, used in making jewelry. The **leatherback** has a rubbery dark shell and is the largest of all tur-

tles, reaching lengths of eight feet and weighing up to 1,100 pounds.

The female nests on beaches where the warm sand incubates her eggs. She drags herself onto shore in the night, selects a site and digs a hole in which 100 or more eggs are laid. After covering them, she returns to the sea, having spent one to three hours on shore under cover of darkness. The two-inch-long hatchlings emerge two months later, again in the cool of the night, and crawl into the water. For years, the catching of females while they laid their eggs was a major factor in the marine turtle's decline, for as few as one in a thousand hatchlings survive to adulthood and it can take up to 20 years or more for some turtles to reach sexual maturity. Sea turtles spend their time feeding, sleeping under reef ledges and roaming the open ocean.

Caribbean waters host a range of marine mammals, including **Humpback whales** (average length, 45 feet) which migrate to warm tropical waters each winter to breed and calve. Other species sighted in the Caribbean include the small, toothed whales such as the **Killer Whale** (average length 25 feet) and the **Common Dolphin** (average length 8 feet), the latter often travelling in huge herds of more than a thousand and sometimes seen riding the bow waves of ships.

Wave riding is also a favorite pastime of the acrobatic **Bottlenosed Dolphin**, which averages 9 feet in length and weighs about 350 pounds. These playful creatures swim in large groups and can reach speeds up to 30 mph. They can dive 70 feet and are capable of remaining underwater for 15 minutes. They sleep at night just below the water's surface, rising for air every three or four minutes. Their days are spent within a socially organized hierarchy. If one of the group is injured or sick, the others will try to rescue it and hold it above the water for air. When a calf is born, after a gestation of 12 months, a female assistant bites the umbilical cord in two and pushes the newborn to the surface to breathe. Mothers nurse their young for two years and practice group babysitting, with one female watching over several calves while their mothers hunt for food. With a beak holding 200 teeth, the bottlenose feeds on small fish, crustaceans and squid. When pursued by a shark or killer whale, the dolphins will try to outswim their predator or, as a group, they will try battering it to death.

The average lifespan of a bottlenose is 25 years, and its brain is large and convoluted, capable of complex functions. These fascinating mammals communicate with an extensive array of sounds, using the air sacs and valves in their blowholes, allowing them to converse with one another and convey instructions. Each dolphin is identified by its signature whistle, and a calf quickly learns to recognize its mother's whistle. Clicking and rapid creaking sounds are used for echolocation (projecting a sound beam and listening to the echo) with which the dolphin locates prey and avoids predators.

The bottlenose frequents inshore waters and is friendly to humans, often approaching close enough to be touched, and tales of dolphins rescuing people from drowning date back to Greek mythology. However, man's fascination with these social creatures is now causing concern among animal-rights activists, who object to the recent proliferation of 'dolphin parks' in countries where there is little or no government regulation over the

Dolphins are highly intelligent, athletic and sociable.

dolphins' capture and care. Visitors to these parks can swim and interact with the captive dolphins, but Richard O'Barry, the dolphin trainer for the 1960s television show *Flipper*, has compared one of these operations to an animal cage. Conflicting studies are cited by both sides as proof or disproof of the dolphins' distress. Meanwhile, the U.S. National Marine Fisheries Service has developed rules to limit the ratio of swimmers to dolphins, restrict the time each dolphin spends with people and provide a refuge to which the dolphin can retreat when tired of interacting with humans.

In contrast to the gregarious bottlenosed dolphin is the reclusive **manatee**. Also called a sirenian or sea cow, this large marine mammal descends from the same primitive group of land mammals as the elephant. The manatee spends its entire life in the water, surfacing to breathe at least every 15 or 20 minutes through nostrils on the upper surface of its snout, which close tightly like valves when the animal submerges. Shy and completely harmless, manatees live in warm, shallow and sheltered waters, where they consume up to 100 pounds of vegetation daily. The manatee can grow to 12 feet in length and weigh over 500 pounds, its thick, heavy body covered with hairless grey-brown skin. A sluggish, nocturnal bottom feeder, it propels itself with two weak flippers and a beaver-like tail. The female gives birth to one calf every two to five years and uses her flippers to hold the nursing calf to her chest. Both parents care for their young, one holding it while the other dives for food. An endangered species, the Florida manatee has no natural predators but is vulnerable to injury from boat propellers, and is found in the coastal waters of Central America, the West Indies and Florida, where it's protected by law.

A pair of manatees surfaces in the coastal waters of Florida.

PART II

—— *THE VOYAGE AND THE PORTS* ——

Grand Anse, Grenada

The Caribbean, with its wide array of ports and easy access for American travelers, is the most popular cruise region in the world. Enhancing the Caribbean's accessibility is a growing selection of roundtrip cruises from drive-to U.S. ports such as Charleston, South Carolina; Norfolk, Virginia; and Baltimore, Maryland. But the biggest news is New York. The city's historic role as a transatlantic seaport has undergone a 21st-century renaissance and is once again a major port for the ship-traveling public. While the cruise liners pulling into New York Harbor still offer transatlantic crossings and round-the-world cruises, many now offer roundtrip cruises to the Caribbean from one of three terminals: the Manhattan Cruise Terminal, the Cape Liberty terminal in Bayonne, New Jersey, and the new terminal at the Brooklyn Naval Yard in Red Hook, Brooklyn.

New York Harbor

The **Manhattan Cruise Terminal** opened on Manhattan's west side as the New York City Passenger Ship

(Above) Manhattan Cruise Terminal. (Left) Statue of Liberty.

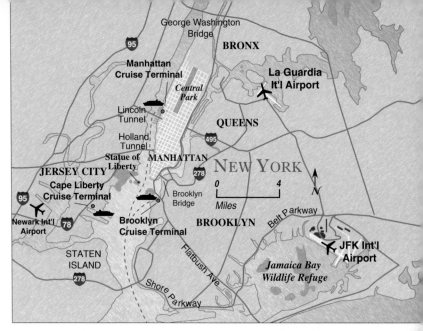

Terminal in the 1930s, its piers known as Luxury Liner Row. During World War II, thousands of GI's boarded the *Queen Mary* and *Queen Elizabeth* at its historic piers. Closed after the terror attack on September 11, 2001, to serve as an emergency command center, the Terminal reopened in January 2002 but is currently undergoing updates to its finger piers (piers for cruises are 88, 90 and 92), which were originally designed to accommodate ocean liners that were narrower than today's modern cruise ships.

The new **Brooklyn Cruise Terminal** – a converted cargo pier in Red Hook – opened in April, 2006. Its entrance is at the corner of Bowne and Imlay Streets, and its berths are designed to accommodate the Cunard liner *Queen Mary 2*, as well as other large ships. Its entrance is at the corner of Bowne and Imlay Streets. (For driving directions to these New York ter-

An NCL ship departs New York Harbor.

The Queen Mary 2 steams out of New York Harbor.

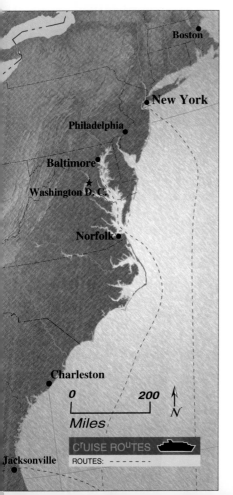

minals, go to: www.nycruiseter-minal.com/directions.html.)

Cape Liberty Cruise Port, located across the Hudson River from Manhattan in New Jersey, is situated on a 430-acre man-made peninsula originally built for a naval base. (For directions, go to www.cruiseliberty.com/dirpark.htm.)

Celebrity Cruises and Royal Caribbean International berth their Caribbean-bound ships at Cape Liberty. Carnival Cruise Line, Cunard, Holland America Line, Norwegian Cruise Line and Princess Cruises use the Manhattan or Brooklyn terminals. Long-term parking is available at all three terminals. Daily (24-hour) rates are: $25 at Manhattan; $20 at Red Hook; $12 (cash only) at Cape Liberty. Some cruise lines offer a motorcoach transfer service to New York from a variety of pick-up locations serving Massachusetts, Rhode Island, Connecticut, New York State, New Jersey, Pennsylvania and Maryland. For panoramic views of New York Harbor, visit Top of the Rock observation deck atop the GE Building (tickets sold at the entrance on West 50th Street, between 5th and 6th Avenues).

Baltimore

Historic Baltimore, seat of Johns Hopkins University and site of the famous Preakness thoroughbred horse race, is located on the Patapsco River estuary, an arm of Chesapeake Bay. The city's South Locust Point Cruise Terminal, located just off I-95 near Baltimore's famous inner harbor, is easily accessed by car. The cruise facility includes luggage drop-off and long-term parking within walking distance or a courtesy shuttle to the passenger building.

Norfolk

Norfolk's new cruise terminal, part of a waterfront park called Nauticus, opened in April of 2007 and is called the Half Moone Cruise and Celebration Center (named for a fort that once stood at this site). Next door is the Hampton Roads Naval Museum and the Battleship Wisconsin. Also at Nauticus is a maritime-themed science center with an aquarium and other attractions for kids. The cruise dock is a 20-minute taxi ride from the Norfolk Airport (an airport express shuttle is also available) and, depending on traffic, from 30 minutes to an hour from Newport News Airport. The Sheraton Norfolk Waterside and Marriott Norfolk Waterside are within walking distance of the cruise terminal. Long-term parking (about $10 a night) is available at the Cedar Grove parking area, with a complimentary shuttle to the ship. (For driving directions, go to: www.cruisenorfolk.org/parking.html.)

Charleston

Charleston's Cruise Ship Passenger Terminal (part of Union Pier) is located in downtown Charleston, in the heart of the historic district. Yellow A-frame signs guide motorists to the terminal entrance, where all cruise passengers enter through the main gate of the Union Pier Terminal at 32 Washington Street, then proceed to the Cruise Ship Terminal at 196 Concord Street. Long-term parking and a complimentary shuttle is available ($15 per day for standard vehicles; $40 per day for vehicles over 20 feet long; no reservations required; cash, traveler's checks and personal checks accepted).

Norfolk's new cruise terminal.

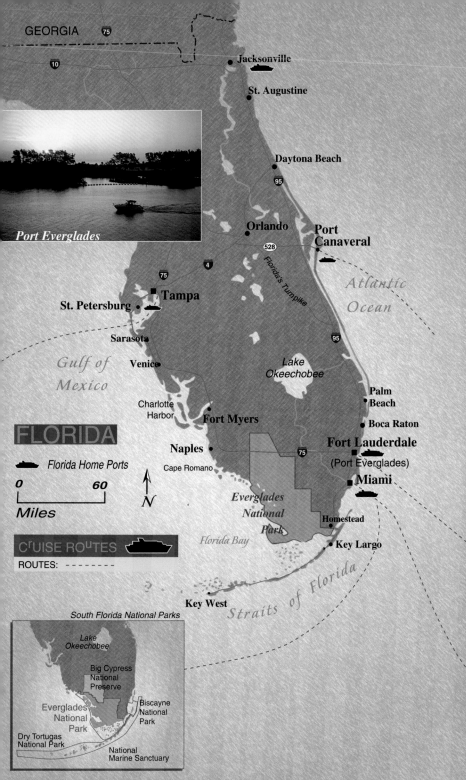

GEORGIA

75

10

Jacksonville

St. Augustine

Daytona Beach

95

Port Everglades

Orlando

Port
Canaveral

528

Florida's Turnpike

4

75

*Atlantic
Ocean*

Tampa

St. Petersburg

95

Sarasota

Venice

Lake
Okeechobee

*Gulf of
Mexico*

Charlotte
Harbor

Fort Myers

Palm
Beach

Boca Raton

Naples

75

Fort Lauderdale

Cape Romano

(Port Everglades)

FLORIDA

Miami

Florida Home Ports

0   60

*Everglades
National
Park*

Homestead

Miles

N

Florida Bay

Key Largo

CRUISE ROUTES

ROUTES: - - - - - - -

Straits of Florida

Key West

South Florida National Parks

*Lake
Okeechobee*

Big Cypress
National
Preserve

Everglades
National
Park

Biscayne
National
Park

Dry Tortugas
National Park

National
Marine
Sanctuary

CHAPTER ONE

FLORIDA

Florida is America's stepping stone to the Caribbean. Warmed by subtropical waters, cooled by trade winds, this southern state of swaying palms and coral cays has much in common with the history, culture and natural habitat of the West Indies. An international tourist destination, Florida is also a gateway to the Caribbean, and its cruise ports are among the busiest in the world.

Florida counts its visitors, and cruise passengers, in the millions. Every conceivable 'fun in the sun' attraction is here – palm-shaded swimming pools, championship golf courses, tennis camps, shopping malls, sporting events and theme parks galore.

A former trading post, Miami is the world's busiest cruise port.

Yet it is water more than anything that defines Florida. The sea is readily accessible from any point in the state and some of the best beaches lie on barrier cays that line much of the splendid coastline. And the water doesn't stop at the seashore. Rivers and canals meander past cypress stands and waterfront homes, linking many of the lakes, lagoons and wetlands that make Florida an angler's paradise.

Lake Okeechobee is the largest of these lakes and is a chief source of water (along with Big Cypress Swamp) for the Everglades – a marshy, tropical savanna extending southward to Florida Bay. Covering more than 4,000 square miles, the Everglades is a unique wilderness region of slow-flowing water. Sawgrass and hammocks (island-

like masses of vegetation) grow here in the solidly packed black muck, which has formed over millions of years from vegetation decaying in the nearly stagnant water. **Everglades National Park** includes Florida Bay and its many islets and islands, and contains a great variety of flora and fauna, including palms, pines and mangrove forests, as well as such endangered species as the crocodile, alligator, egret and bald eagle.

Bird life abounds in Florida, where critical wetlands are now protected as wildlife refuges. A shoreline of seemingly endless beaches and holiday resorts has become dotted with parks, preserves and recreation areas. These conservation measures follow a century of unbridled development in which men with a passion for building – be it hotels, railroads, planned communities or theme parks – were attracted to Florida's broad, untouched landscapes.

The first 'developer' to arrive on Florida's shores was Spanish explorer Ponce de Leon. Seeking the fabled Fountain of Youth, he landed near the site of **St. Augustine** in 1513 during the Easter season (Pascua Florida) and mistook the long peninsula for an island, which he claimed for Spain. Turning south, he explored the coast to Key West, then headed up the west side to Cape Romano before retracing his route to Miami Bay and returning to his settlement in Puerto Rico, where gold and slave labor had made him a wealthy man. The next year the Spanish king commissioned Ponce de Leon to colonize the

'isle of Florida' but it wasn't until 1521 that he returned with 200 men, farm implements and domestic animals, his two vessels landing in the vicinity of Charlotte Harbor.

The development-minded conquistador's plans were, however, thwarted by the Native Americans already living in the area. Called Caloosas, they built their dwellings on high rectangular mounds surrounded by waterways and boat basins. These terraced mounds were interconnected with ramps and shell-covered causeways and canals, some of which led to burial mounds and other midden mounds where waste was discarded. Temples, storehouses and leaders' homes were built on the tallest mounds. These people, their urban culture over 2,000 years old, did not take kindly to the sight of strangers attempting to sub-divide their land, and they attacked the Spanish party, fatally wounding Ponce de Leon with a poisoned arrow. The Spaniards retreated, sailing immediately for Cuba, where their leader died.

Spain abandoned any further plans to colonize Florida until the French began encroaching upon the area. St. Augustine was founded in 1565 to protect Spain's shipping route through the Straits of Florida, but Spain's tenuous hold on Florida ended in 1819 when it was ceded to the United States. Official U.S. occupation took place in 1821 with Andrew Jackson appointed military governor. The next year Florida became a territory, with settlers from other states soon establishing cotton and tobacco plantations around the new capital of Tallahassee. The resident Native Americans – the Seminoles – resisted being displaced and a small band fled to the Everglades, where their descendants live today on reservations near Lake Okeechobee.

Florida, a slave-holding state, was admitted to the state of the Union in 1845, but seceded from the Union in 1861 to join the Confederacy. After the war, Florida's new constitution provided for black suffrage and the state was readmitted to the Union in 1868. A decade later, New York financier Henry Flagler paid a visit to Florida's east coast. He envisioned the state as the perfect winter playground and proceeded to build a business empire of railroads, steamships and palatial hotels, while anonymously donating to the construction of schools, churches and hospitals. Another industrial tycoon, Henry Plant, built railroads and hotels on Florida's west coast. Sections of the Everglades were drained, starting in 1906, and land booms caused real estate prices to soar one year and plummet the next.

In the 1920s a ring dike was built around Lake Okeechobee to prevent water from blowing off the lake during hurricanes. This diking, along with land development in Big Cypress Swamp, disrupted the natural flow of water into the Everglades, and damaged plant and animal life. In the 1980s Florida instigated a massive conservation project which called for the reflooding of drained swampland and restoring to their natural state those areas previously cleared for agriculture and development. Sugar and vegetable farms have reduced the amount of phosphorus fertilizer

The original Breakers in Palm Beach was built by Henry Flagler in the late 1800s.

A Key Largo sunset.

discharged from their fields, and cleaner water is now running off their land into the imperiled Everglades ecosystem.

Miami

Named for an American Indian tribe, Miami was a trading post when Henry Flagler, having built grand hotels at St. Augustine and Palm Beach, set his sights on this southern port. He made Miami a railroad terminus in 1896, the year it was incorporated, then proceeded to dredge the harbor to accommodate his fleet of steamships. Set on a low ridge overlooking Biscayne Bay, Miami is now the transportation and business hub of south Florida. It is also the busiest cruise port in the world, receiving close to four million passengers a year.

Greater Miami encompasses the City of Miami, Miami Beach, Coral Gables, Hialeah and many smaller communities. About half of the City of Miami's population is Hispanic, many of Cuban descent, with hundreds of thousands of Cuban refugees moving here from the late 1950s to early 70s, settling in the city's Little Havana section. **Calle Ocho** (Southwest Eighth Street) is the main thoroughfare and scene of an annual Hispanic festival that's held in March and stretches the length of 23 lively blocks of music and dancing.

Miami Beach, located on a barrier island in Biscayne Bay, was a mangrove swamp until connected to the mainland by a wooden bridge in 1913. Opulent hotels and huge estates were soon built here, while the **South Beach** area was sub-divided into smaller lots and developed as a middle-class resort of modest hotels and apartments. Many of these buildings went up during the Depression, when visitors came to Miami Beach to temporarily escape their worries. The area suffered a decline following World War II. Then, in 1979, South Beach's square mile area of Art Deco structures, their style of smooth lines and white exteriors sometimes referred to as Tropical Deco, was declared a national historic district. During South Beach's revitalization in the late

1980s and early 90s, many of the run-down hotels were refurbished and repainted in pastel colors. Today the area is one of the trendiest in America, where a steady stream of pedestrian and car traffic along Ocean Drive includes movie stars and fashion models who frequent the stylish eateries and nightclubs. The **Art Deco Welcome Center** at 1001 Ocean Drive is a good place to start a tour of South Beach. Points of interest include the Cardozo Hotel at 1300 Ocean Drive, which was featured in the 1959 film *A Hole in the Head*, starring Frank Sinatra. The slain fashion designer Gianni Versace owned the gated palazzo at 1116 Ocean Drive.

Coral Gables, situated four miles south of downtown Miami, was founded in 1925 at the height of the Florida land boom, which sparked an explosion of growth in the Miami area. A planned city designed by George Merrick, its Mediterranean architecture includes such highlights as the Venetian Pool – a huge municipal pool set in a coral quarry with caves, waterfalls and arched bridges. Merrick's boyhood home, a gabled plantation house on Coral Way, is open to the public. His dream city of canals, plazas and tree-shaded streets is also home to the University of Miami, where the Lowe Art Museum houses a permanent collection of Renaissance and baroque art, as well as Spanish and American paintings and artwork by North American Indians. The Orange Bowl Classic & Festival has been a major annual event in Miami since 1933 when the University of Miami played the Manhattan University.

Coconut Grove, on the waterfront east of Coral Gables, was settled in the late 19th century by New England intellectuals and Bahamian seamen. The conical home of founding father Ralph Munroe, a New York yacht designer, is called the Barnacle and is open to the public at 3485 Main Highway. Also in Coconut

Miami Beach's popular Art Deco District in South Beach.

Grove is the **Vizcaya Museum and Gardens** (3251 S. Miami Avenue), a restored Italian Renaissance-style villa completed in 1916 as a winter residence for industrialist John Deering. The 34-room mansion, set in grounds of formal gardens and amid fountains overlooking Biscayne Bay, has been designated a National Historic Landmark. It contains Renaissance and baroque antiques and artwork, and has been visited by such dignitaries as Pope John Paul II and Queen Elizabeth, and President Clinton who hosted the 1994 Summit of the Americas at Vizcaya.

A toll causeway links the mainland with Virginia Key, location of the **Miami Seaquarium**, and Key Biscayne, where the late Richard Nixon had a presidential retreat. Both islands contain parks, with a golf course and tennis stadium located on Key Biscayne.

The bustling Bayside Marketplace is across the water from Miami's cruise port.

Getting Around

The Port of Miami's cruise port is a two-island complex in Biscayne Bay adjacent to downtown Miami. The port, consisting of numerous passenger terminals, is located eight miles from Miami International Airport (a $24 taxi ride). There is long-term parking at each terminal ($15 per day) and no reservations are required.

It's a short ($10) taxi ride from the cruise terminals to Bayside Marketplace, a bustling waterfront development of shops, restaurants and open-air entertainment. Tour boats depart daily from Bayside on 90-minute narrated tours of the port, affording passengers a view of the Miami skyline, waterfront mansions and other sights. Trolley tours of Miami and Miami Beach also depart regularly from Bayside, as do water taxis, which ply the waters of Biscayne Bay, stopping at various waterfront attractions. The elevated Metromover links downtown Miami's major hotels and shopping areas.

Where to Stay – The selection of hotels in Greater Miami is extensive and includes a plethora of luxury properties. Yesteryear's elegance can be enjoyed at the Biltmore Hotel, built in 1926 as the centerpiece of Coral Gables. In a lovely setting of waterways, tennis courts and golf links, this is a classic grand hotel with a vaulted lobby and an opulent swimming pool/bar area. Nearby in Coconut Grove, overlooking Biscayne Bay, is the Wyndham Grand Bay Hotel – a modern boutique hotel offering golf, tennis and deepsea fishing.

In downtown Miami, the Intercontinental Miami is within walking distance of Bayside. Its stunning lobby features a massive marble sculpture called *Spindle* by Henry Moore. Across the bay, in Miami Beach, the Casa Grande Suite Hotel at 834 Ocean Drive is highly touted, as are several boutique hotels in the high-energy Art Deco District of South Beach, including the Blue Moon Hotel. A few blocks up Collins Avenue, in North Beach, the restored art deco hotels are considerably less expensive.

Shopping & Dining.– The **Bayside Marketplace** is a great spot for visiting cruise passengers to soak in the local atmosphere while browsing the waterfront shops or enjoying an authentic Cuban sandwich to the sound of live Latin music. Other shopping/dining areas include bohemian-flavored Coconut Grove where interesting shops, open-air bistros and sidewalk cafes line CocoWalk on Grand Avenue. At Coral Gables the Miracle Mile (the main shopping thoroughfare on Coral Way between Southwest 42nd Avenue and Douglas Road) is lined with some of Miami's best restaurants. For a taste of Latin America and Miami's famous Cuban coffee, try one of the eateries on Calle Ocho in Little Havana.

Miami Beach has hotels, restaurants and sandy beaches.

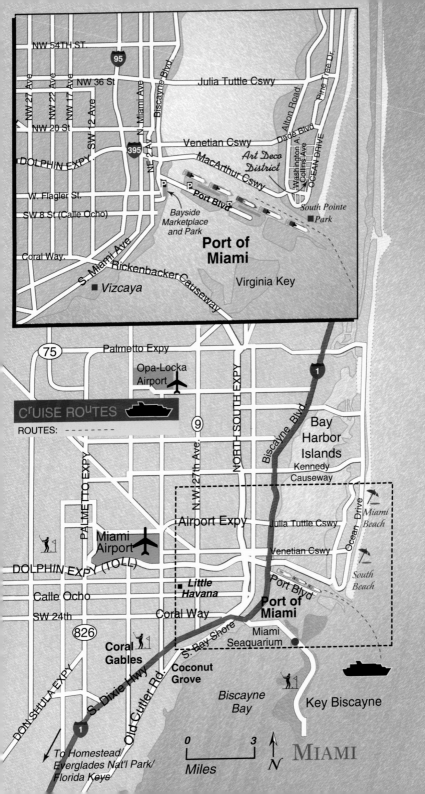

In South Beach, the family-owned Joe's Stone Crab Restaurant at 11 Washington Avenue (just off South Point Drive) is a legendary seafood restaurant and local favorite, established in 1913 by Hungarian-born Joseph Weiss. Also in South Beach is the popular Mango's Tropical Cafe, where lively beachfront dining can be enjoyed. For a sunset view of the Miami skyline, try The Rusty Pelican on Key Biscayne (at 3201 Rickenbacker Causeway).

Golf – The Doral Resort near the Miami International Airport, has four 18-hole courses including one of the most challenging courses in the Miami area. The Links at Key Biscayne, a top-ranked municipal course, is built around lagoons and contains four waterside holes with views of the Miami skyline. The city-owned Biltmore Golf Course in Coral Gables opened in 1925 and was recently refurbished, and the Golf Club of Miami offers three different courses.

South of Miami

Homestead, south of Miami, is the gateway to Everglades National Park, Biscayne National Park and the Florida Keys. The center of Florida's fruit and nursery production, one of its major attractions is **Coral Castle**, built from massive blocks of coral by a Latvian immigrant who labored alone from 1920 to 1940.

Biscayne National Park, nine miles east of Homestead on SW 328 Street, is an undeveloped underwater park containing miles of coral reefs. Its shallow waters are very clear and warm – a natural habitat for sponges, crabs, manatees and more than 500 different kinds of fish. The park is primarily accessible by boat, with tour boats operating out of park headquarters at Convoy Point.

Everglades National Park

The Everglades, a slow-moving 'river of grass', is about 50 miles wide and only a few inches deep, containing mangrove forests, sawgrass marshes, pinelands and hammocks. The tropical and subtropical foliage also includes six species of palm, and the park is a sanctuary for manatees, crocodiles, sea turtles and nearly 300 kinds of land and wading birds. Mosquitoes proliferate from May to November, and insect repellent is recommended year-round.

Parachute Key Visitor Center is located at the park's southeast entrance and another, the Royal Palm Visitor Center, is just inside the park. A road leads through the southern half of the Everglades to the Flamingo Ranger Station and Visitor Center on Florida Bay. In addition to canoe trails, boardwalks and nature trails in the Flamingo area, tours can be taken of Florida Bay and the backcountry for possible sightings of manatees, alligators and many varieties of birds, as well as the opportunity to disembark at a hammock to see Indian open-air dwellings. The Flamingo area has restaurants, accommodations, charter fishing boats and canoe rentals.

The 99-mile Wilderness Waterway winds between Flamingo and Everglades City, situated on the northwest side of the park, where airboat tours can be taken to the **Ten Thousand Islands** – a mangrove wilderness of islets, oyster bars and shell beaches.

The Keys

A chain of small coral islands extending 110 miles from the southern tip of Florida, the Keys are both exotic and all-American. Their tropical vegetation, steady trade winds and coral reefs are quintessentially Caribbean, while Key West's clapboard houses and white picket fences are reminiscent of a New England coastal town. The Keys' reef-riddled waters supported a thriving salvage industry in the mid-19th century before modern lighthouses and steam vessels brought an end to the steady stream of ships that were snared in the reefs off Key West.

Scenes from the 1940s film **Key Largo** *were shot inside the Caribbean Club at Key Largo.*

Key Largo, the largest of the islands at the 'top' of the Keys, is famous both as the setting for the 1940s film classic *Key Largo*, starring Humphrey Bogart and Lauren Bacall, and as the location of John Pennekamp **Coral Reef State Park** – America's first underwater park, established in 1960. Over time, adjoining sanctuaries were established to protect the threatened reefs from boats grounding on them or hitting them with their props and anchors. Then, in 1997, Florida's cabinet approved federal plans to establish Florida Keys National Marine Sanctuary, which encompasses the entire length of the Keys.

Key West

The southernmost point of the continental United States, and only 90 miles from Cuba, Key West is the largest center in the Keys, with about 25,000 residents. It was once a base of operation against pirates, who preyed on Spanish treasure ships as they sailed from Cuba to Spain via the Straits of Florida. When Florida was ceded by Spain to the United

States in 1819, Key West became a haven for exiled Cubans, including revolutionary leaders trying to rid their country of Spanish rule. The sinking of the battleship Maine in Havana harbor in 1898 led the U.S. to declare war on Spain, and some of the 266 men who died in that incident are buried in the Key West Cemetery.

In 1912 the Keys became linked with the mainland upon completion of Henry Flagler's railroad. The rail line was abandoned after sustaining hurricane damage in 1935, and was replaced a few years later with the 123-mile Overseas Highway that includes 42 bridges. Despite this well-travelled connection to the rest of Florida, the Keys have retained an island ambiance and sense of seclusion.

As a port of call, Key West holds many attractions. The cruise ship dock is located close to the downtown's tree-lined streets of shops, restaurants and colonial homes, a number of which are listed on the National Register of Historic Places. President Harry Truman had a presidential retreat in Key West, and other illustrious names associated with Key West include Haitian-born and French-educated John James Audubon, for whom one of the oldest and best-known U.S. environmental organizations is named, who visited Key West in 1832 to study and sketch the native birds.

Key West has long been an enclave for writers and artists drawn to the tiny island's exotic locale, including Winslow Homer, Robert Frost and Tennessee Williams. Of Key West's famous former residents, the one whose presence is most pervasive is Ernest Hemingway. For years Key West celebrated this Nobel Laureate with an annual Hemingway Days Festival, which included a writers' workshop, short-story contest, Caribbean street fair and a concert on the grounds of his former home. However, in 1997 Hemingway's sons denounced the festivities as tacky and threatened to sue if they weren't given control of the festival and a cut of the proceeds, prompting the festival's cancellation. However, Sloppy Joe's bar still stages its annual Ernest Hemingway look-alike contest.

Getting Around

The cruise ship docks are near Mallory Square, a bustling waterfront that attracts artists, entertainers and sunset watchers. Most major sights are within walking distance of the cruise pier but another option is to board either the Conch Tour Train at Mallory Square, or the Old Town Trolley at one of numerous stops, for a 90-minute narrated tour of Key West. Bicycles and mopeds can also be rented within the town.

Beaches & Watersports – Local scuba diving, snorkeling and sailing excursions are available. Departing just north of Mallory Square are glass-bottom boat rides to the nearby coral reef. The beach at Fort Zachary Taylor is popular for swimming and snorkeling along its artificial reef.

Shopping & Dining – Clinton Square Market on Front Street contains a number of shops selling handcrafted jewelry and Caribbean clothing. Key West Hand Print Fashions, located in the historic Curry Warehouse at 201 Simonton Street, is a good place to buy silk-screened fashions featuring original artwork. Sloppy Joe's, at the corner of Greene and Duval Streets, was Ernest Hemingway's favorite watering hole and this legendary bar, which opens at 9:00 a.m. also sells clothing and souvenirs in its retail shop. Live entertainment begins at noon.

Golf – The southernmost golf course in the continental United States, the Key West Golf & Country Club (Par 70; 6,500 yards) was designed by Rees Jones and features rolling fairways and dense mangroves.

Local Attractions

1 **The Key West Aquarium**, beside Mallory Square, presents sea life of the Atlantic Ocean and Gulf of Mexico.

2 **The Mel Fisher Maritime** Heritage Society, at 200 Greene Street, features artifacts and treasures retrieved from two Spanish galleons that sank off Key West in 1622. Beginning in the 1970s, Mel Fisher Enterprises, the legendary treasure hunters, recovered hundreds of millions of dollars in booty from these gold-laden ships.

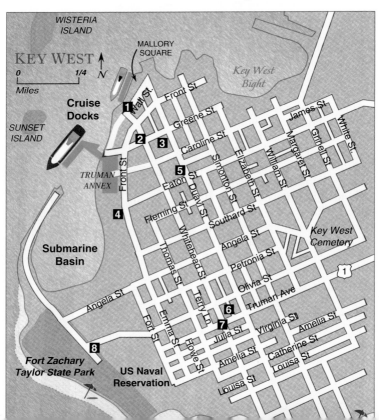

3 **The Audubon House &** Tropical Gardens at 205 Whitehead Street is housed in a restored 19th-century building. The museum commemorates John James Audubon's 1832 visit to Key West and contains a collection of his original engravings.

4 **Harry S. Truman Little White House** contains original furnishings and artifacts, which recreate the Truman era of the 1940s when the mansion was a presidential retreat.

At 322 Duval Street (near Eaton Street) stands Key West's oldest home, built in 1829 for a wrecker and sea captain. It now houses the **5** **Wreckers' Museum** with exhibits including marine artifacts and ship models. Other historic homes of note are the Curry Mansion (on Caroline near Duval) and the Donkey Milk House Museum, at 613 Eaton Street, a restored 19th-century mansion listed on the National Register of Historic Places. Named for the

Ernest Hemingway's Key West home is now a museum.

back alleyway along which donkeys used to pull milk delivery carts, the award-winning mansion features hand-decorated ceilings, Spanish tile floors and verandas off every room.

6 **The Ernest Hemingway Home & Museum** at 907 Whitehead Street is a Registered National Historic Landmark. The home was built in 1851 in the Spanish colonial style and contains furnishings and other items that Hemingway and his second wife, Pauline, collected in their travels to Spain, Africa and Cuba. Hemingway wrote some of his greatest works while living here in the 1930s and 40s, and his study in the loft of the pool house remains intact with his desk and typewriter on display. The home exudes Hemingway's forceful presence, and dozens of cats, descendants of those owned by the famous author, still wander the lushly landscaped grounds. Sloppy Joe's, Hemingway's favorite watering hole, was moved in 1937 from Greene Street to the corner of Duval and Greene. Its owner, Joe Russell, was Hemingway's boat pilot, fishing companion and a model for the character Freddy in *To Have and Have Not*, which was set in Key West and Cuba.

7 The **Lighthouse Museum** at 938 Whitehead Street features the keeper's clapboard house and the lighthouse itself, built in 1847, with a magnificent view of Key West at the top of its 98 steps.

8 **Fort Zachary Taylor State Historic Site** was part of Florida's coastal defence system. Built from 1845-66, the fort became a base for the Union blockade of Confederate shipping during the Civil War, with captured ships brought to its harbor. Artifacts, models and one of the largest collections of Civil War armaments are on display.

Fort Lauderdale

Situated on the New River, this retirement and resort city was settled around a fort built by Major William Lauderdale in 1838, during the Seminole War. Fort Lauderdale was incorporated in 1911, and the city grew rapidly during the Florida land boom of the 1920s. Its suburbs continue to expand, and today about 4.5 million people live in the metro area. Fort Lauderdale has one of the most popular beaches in the country, one of the largest marinas in North America, and a cruise port that is fast becoming one of the busiest in the world.

Fort Lauderdale's seaport was originally a small lake used by recreational boaters. Locally known as Bay Mabel Harbor, it came to the attention of a developer and businessman named Joseph Young, who moved to the area in the early 1920s, purchased 1,440 acres adjacent to the lake and created the Hollywood Harbor Development Company. On February 28, 1927, expectant spectators gathered to watch an explosion that would remove the lake's rock barrier to the ocean. At the appointed time, President Calvin Coolidge pressed a detonator in the White House, but nothing happened. Nonetheless, the harbor was officially opened that day and the rock barrier was removed a short while later. In 1930, the new seaport was named **Port Everglades** – chosen from submissions to a naming contest.

The port is located opposite the **John U. Lloyd Beach State Recreation Area**, situated on 251 acres of barrier island separating the Intracoastal Waterway from the Atlantic Ocean. The park is named in memory of a local attorney whose efforts helped bring about its creation. The park is entered at its south end via Dania Beach Boulevard, and its broad flat beach – popular for swimming and sunning – is also one of Broward County's most important sea turtle nesting beaches. A jetty at the north end is excellent for fishing and watching the comings and goings of cruise ships and small sailing craft.

The park also contains an open-air Environmental Education Facility. This timber structure and adjoining waterfront boardwalk were built by Port Everglades in 1991 as part of a wildlife protection/awareness project, which includes a comprehensive Manatee Protection Program. The Florida manatee is a protected species and in winter months these sluggish sea mammals frequent the Port, where they are attracted to the heated effluent from the Florida Power & Light plant. When calving mothers were found to be utilizing the FPL discharge canal, a section of it became designated a 'Manatee Nursery' and access to it was restricted. Manatees and other marine life also frequent the mangrove-lined tidal waterway that runs down the middle of the John Lloyd park.

Getting Around

Located south of downtown, Port Everglades is an artificial deepsea port with a short, straight entrance channel. Its passenger terminals are modern and efficient, with long-term parking available in nearby self-parking garages. Less than two miles from Fort Lauderdale / Hollywood International Airport (and 30 minutes from Miami International Airport via I-95), **Port Everglades** is serviced by a fleet of taxis and by several car rental companies that provide shuttle service between the port and their rental lots.

Water taxis and tour boats are a popular way to explore Fort Lauderdale's scenic waterways. Water Taxi picks up at most waterfront hotels and restaurants north of the Brooks Memorial Causeway. Call 467-6677 for a pick-up; the one-way fare between two points is $7.50, the round-trip fare is $14 and an all-day pass is $16.

Shopping & Dining
Las Olas Boulevard, the 'Rodeo Drive' of Fort Lauderdale, is lined with boutiques, galleries

Port Everglades is Florida's second busiest cruise port.

and several fine restaurants, including Mark's Las Olas and the Grill Room at the Riverside Hotel, a heritage property built in 1936. In Lauderdale-By-The-Sea, the Sea Watch serves superb seafood, and American cuisine can be enjoyed at Burt & Jack's, co-owned by movie star Burt Reynolds and situated on a scenic lookout near the passenger terminals of Port Everglades. The huge Sawgrass Mills Mall on Sunrise Boulevard contains more than a mile of shops and bills itself as the 'World's Largest Outlet Mall'.

Where to Stay – In recent years, Fort Lauderdale has shed its image as a spring break desti-

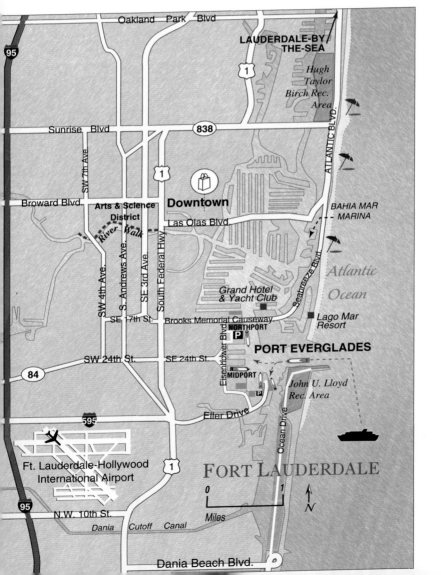

nation for college students and the opening of several luxury chain hotels, including a St. Regis and a W hotel, is bringing upscale sophistication to the city's selection of accommodations The Grande Hotel & Yacht Club (formerly the Marriott Marina) has undergone renovations by its new operator, Luxury Resorts, and is conveniently located across the street from Port Everglades. The beachfront Lago Mar Resort & Club, a four-diamond hotel located in the Harbor Beach neighborhood, offers an elegant atmosphere with its bougainvillea-bordered swimming lagoon; four restaurants, two swimming pools, tennis courts and miniature golf are among its extensive facilities. For a taste of 'Old Florida', the family-owned Riverside Hotel on Las Olas Boulevard is distinctly decorated with tropical murals and finely appointed rooms, with a pool area providing views of passing river traffic. North of downtown, in Lauderdale-by-the-Sea, the wide array of comfortable small hotels and motels includes A Little Inn By The Sea, with its bright and airy rooms overlooking a beach-side swimming pool.

Beaches – Fort Lauderdale's famous stretch of beach used to attract crowds of college students on spring break. They go elsewhere now, and the beach has been given a multi-million-dollar facelift. A wave-themed beachfront promenade consists of wide walkways, crested gateways and neon lamp posts.

The oceanfront boulevard proceeds north to Lauderdale-by-the-Sea, an inviting stretch of sand, restaurants and motels. Beyond is Pompano Beach, Hillsboro Beach and Deerfield Beach, and south of Fort Lauderdale are the beaches of John U. Lloyd State Recreation Area, Dania and Hollywood. There are 23 miles of beach in the Fort Lauderdale area, the shoreline punctuated by fishing piers.

Golf – There are over 50 golf courses in the Fort Lauderdale area. The

A pleasant stroll can be taken at Fort Lauderdale's Riverwalk.

Port Everglades viewed from John U. Lloyd Recreation Area.

Emerald Hills Golf Club in Hollywood, about two miles south of the airport, is one of many open to the public.

Local Attractions

Las Olas Boulevard is an upscale shopping street of boutiques and restaurants. The Greater Fort Lauderdale Convention & Visitors Bureau is located at 200 E. Las Olas Boulevard

At the western end of Las Olas is **Riverwalk**, a lovely promenade on the north bank of the New River. Attractions in the Riverwalk area – also known as the **Arts and Science District** – include Esplanade Park, which features outdoor exhibits on astronomy and navigation; the Museum of Art; a complex housing the Museum of Discovery and Science and Blockbuster IMAX Theater; the Broward Center for the Performing Arts; and the Fort Lauderdale Historical Society Museum.

Called the 'Venice of America', Fort Lauderdale is interwoven with more than 270 miles of natural and artificial waterways, and the eastern half of Las Olas runs through an exclusive residential area of canal-lined streets called The Isles, where both cars and yachts can be seen parked outside the palm-shaded homes. Nearby is the Bahia Mar Marina and the International Swimming Hall of Fame.

Across the road from Fort Lauderdale Beach is the **Hugh Taylor Birch State Recreation Area** with nature trails, picnic facilities and a museum. Directly south, on the other side of Sunrise Boulevard, is **Bonnet House**, the 35-acre estate of the late Frederic Bartlett and his wife Evelyn, who built their 1920s dream home on land given to him by his first father-in-law Hugh Taylor Birch. Now a wildlife preserve, the tranquil grounds feature a swan pond, and the house contains the Bartletts' own paintings and an extensive seashell collection.

North of Fort Lauderdale

The coastal drive north of Fort Lauderdale to Palm Beach follows a scenic highway, bordered by the Atlantic Ocean to the east and the Intracoastal Waterway to the west. **Spanish River Park**, in Boca Raton, provides access to an ocean beach and contains a lagoon, nature trails and picnic sites.

The **Arthur R. Marshall Loxahatchee National Wildlife Refuge**, located west of Boca Raton, is the last northernmost portion of the Everglades and is habitat for the American alligator and over 200 species of birds. Visitor facilities include walking and biking trails, a canoe trail, boat ramps and a fishing platform, as well as a visitor center, butterfly garden and observation towers.

Palm Beach is where you'll see some of Florida's most palatial estates along Ocean Boulevard, including the Kennedy compound (President Kennedy's Winter White House) at 1095 North Ocean Boulevard, which the family sold in 1995.

For a taste of Old Florida, visit The Breakers (on County Road) – a luxury grand hotel originally built by tycoon Henry Flagler in the late 1800s. Rebuilt in 1926, the resort's Italian Renaissance architecture includes vaulted ceilings, frescoes and Florentine fountains outside the main entrance. Nearby, on Cocoanut Row, is **Whitehall** – a mansion built by Flagler in 1901 and now a museum containing original furnishings and railroad exhibits.

Port Canaveral

Cape Canaveral is better known as a spaceport than a seaport, but Port Canaveral is increasingly busy as a staging area for cruise ships. Only 50 miles east of Orlando, Port Canaveral is ideally situated for passengers looking to combine a Caribbean cruise with a visit to Walt Disney World. Those fascinated with space travel can begin or end their cruise with a visit to Kennedy Space

Port Canaveral's excellent harbor and nearby beaches.

Center and the Cape Canaveral Air Force Station.

Since 1947, the low sandy promontory of Cape Canaveral has been the principal U.S. launching site for long-range missiles, earth satellites, manned space flights and space shuttle missions. John Glenn, the first American to orbit the earth in 1963, and Neil Armstrong, the first man on the moon in 1969, were launched from this cape. In 1982, operational flights of the space shuttles began here. Missile launches can be watched from Jetty Park right in Port Canaveral. Other popular viewing spots include Cocoa Beach and the Merritt Island National Wildlife Refuge, location of Spaceport USA, which features multimedia displays on the U.S. space program, including a moon rock and an actual spacecraft. In its IMAX theatre you can watch footage of astronauts in space on a 5-1/2-storey screen. Bus tours of the **Kennedy Space Center** and Cape Canaveral Air Force Station begin at Spaceport USA. Nearby is the **U.S. Astronaut Hall of Fame**. The **Wildlife Refuge** is home to bald eagles and turtles, which nest here, along with alligators, which live in lagoons bordering the shuttle's landing strip and occasionally have to be shooed away by workers at landing times.

The **Canaveral National Seashore**, north of the Kennedy Space Center, contains 25 miles of unspoiled barrier beaches and grassy dunes, with swimming beaches at each end. **Cocoa Beach**, south of Port Canaveral, features a downtown section called Olde Cocoa Village, in which restaurants and specialty shops are housed in heritage buildings along cobblestone lanes.

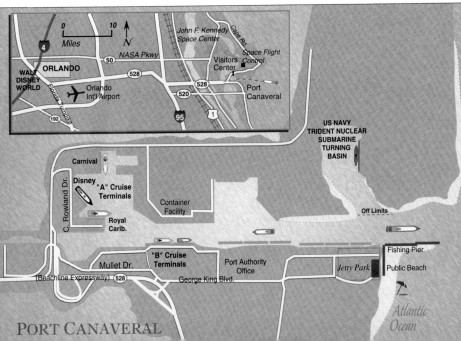

PORT CANAVERAL

Jacksonville

A major transportation hub situated near the mouth of the St. Johns River, Jacksonville is a major east coast port and a center of U.S. navy operations. It is also a relatively new cruise port, with Carnival Cruise Lines offering year-round cruises to the Bahamas and Key West from the **JAXPORT** Cruise Terminal in North Jacksonville. Long-term parking ($12 per day per passenger vehicle) is available next to the terminal (no reservations required), and the terminal opens to embarking passengers at 10:00 a.m. (www.jaxport.com).

Founded in 1816 and named for Andrew Jackson, Jacksonville is an appealing tourist resort offering ocean beaches and boating activities. Accommodations include The Inn at Oak Street, a luxury bed & breakfast located in historic **Riverside**, two miles from downtown Jacksonville. Outside Jacksonville, in **Ponte Vedra Beach**, is the Sawgrass Marriott Resort & Beach Club which features three outdoor pools, tennis courts and five 18-hole championship golf courses.

Tampa

Located on Tampa Bay, an inlet of the Gulf of Mexico, Tampa is the third largest city in Florida and one of the largest ports in the U.S. Incorporated in 1855, Tampa has long been a shipping and manufacturing hub on the Gulf Coast. First visited by Panfilo de Narvaez in 1528, the sole survivor of this Spanish expedition was rescued in 1539 by Hernando De Soto. He also negotiated a peace treaty with the Native Americans, on the present site of the University of Tampa, but they remained hostile and for two centuries Europeans avoided the area.

The first white settlement began in 1823 and Fort Brooke was built the next year. A farming and fishing town grew around the fort, which was taken by Union troops during the Civil War. The late 1800s brought a surge in development with the construction of railroads, the discovery of phosphate, an expanding fishing industry and the introduction of cigar making in **Ybor City**, the center of Tampa's Hispanic population. During the Spanish-American War, Tampa became a military base with Theodore Roosevelt training his Rough Riders there.

A commercial center, Tampa also has a thriving arts and culture scene, which includes the Florida Symphony Orchestra and the Tampa Ballet. It's also a sports-oriented city, and several major league baseball teams have spring training camps in area.

Tampa shares the shores of Tampa Bay with neighboring St. Petersburg and Clearwater. **St. Petersburg** is a popular resort and retirement community, its places of interest including a municipal pier, the **Salvador Dali Museum** and a **Museum of Fine Arts**, all located on the Bay waterfront. Clearwater's white sand beaches have supported a thriving tourist industry dating back to 1896, when railroad baron Henry Plant built a luxury resort called The Belleview on a bluff overlooking the water. The Bay Area's beaches are concentrated on the barrier islands of Clearwater and St. Petersburg, a popular one being Indian Rocks Beach on Sand Key.

Getting Around

Tampa International Airport, one of the top-rated airports in the U.S., is located 12 miles from downtown and the Garrison Seaport Center where the cruise ships dock. The Tampa-Ybor Trolley offers daily service around downtown Tampa, Ybor City and Garrison Seaport Center.

A Visitor Information Center is located downtown at the corner of Ashley and Madison streets.

Shopping & Dining – Old Hyde Park Village in the historic Hyde Park area of Tampa contains more than 60 shops, as well as restaurants and movie theatres. **Ybor Square** is another historic marketplace, consisting of three large brick buildings converted into shops and restaurants, including the popular Columbia Restaurant, which opened in 1905 and serves award-winning Spanish-Cuban

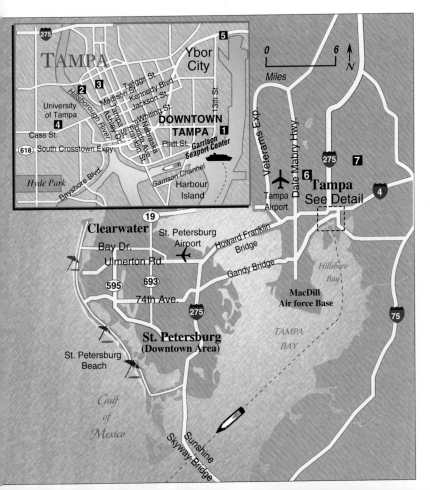

cuisine and features nightly flamenco dance performance. The Columbia's gift shop carries a wide variety of fine cigars and handcrafted ceramics from Spain. Other recommended gift ships are found in the Tampa Museum of Art in downtown Tampa and the Salvador Dali Museum in downtown St. Petersburg.

Where to Stay – Some of the Bay Area's best hotels are situated on the shores of Tampa Bay, such as the Hyatt Regency Westshore and the Renaissance Vinoy Resort and Golf Club, the latter a member of Historic Hotels of America and named to the National Register of Historic Places. Situated on a 14-acre site, the original Vinoy Park hotel was built in 1925 in the Mediterranean Revival style of architecture. Luminaries such as Babe Ruth and Jimmy Stewart stayed at this elegant hotel, but a decline in the 1960s was followed by its closure in the mid-1970s. Then, in the early 1990s, the dilapidated building was rebuilt as an exact replica of the original, but with modern amenities. Recreational facilities include a spa and fitness center, swimming pools, tennis courts and 18-hole championship golf.

Golf – There are over 90 courses in the Tampa Bay area, many of which are open to the public. Babe Zaharias Golf Course, Rogers Park Golf Course and USF Golf Course are all located north of downtown Tampa; the Rocky Point Golf Course is just west of the Tampa International Airport.

The Sunshine Skyway Bridge spans Tampa Bay.

Local Attractions

The **1** **Florida Aquarium** is located right beside the passenger terminals at Garrison Seaport Center. It features sea creatures in near-natural habitats, as well as a fascinating exhibit in which visitors follow the path of a water drop from its underground source to the open sea, viewing aquatic animals and plants native to Florida along the way.

The **2** Tampa Bay Performing **Arts Center** and **Tampa Museum of Art** are located downtown overlooking the Hillsborough River. East on Franklin Street is the Spanish-Mediterranean-style **3** **Tampa Theatre**, a restored 1926 movie palace.

Across the Hillsborough River, on the University of Tampa campus, is the **4** **Henry B. Plant Museum**, housed in a wing of an opulent building originally built as the Tampa Bay Hotel by Henry Plant in 1891. It's a striking example of Moorish-Revival architecture and is a city landmark with its domed spires.

Northeast of the downtown core is historic **5** **Ybor City**. Settled by Cubans, Spaniards and other Europeans, this designated national landmark district features Mediterranean-style buildings housing art galleries, cafes and antique stores. Popular attractions here include the Tampa Rico Cigar Company (a retail store with cigar-rolling demonstrations) and tours of the Ybor City Brewing Company, located in a 100-year-old cigar factory.

Animals in their natural habitats can be seen at **6** **Lowry Park** Zoological Garden, which also operates a manatee research and rehabilitation center. The **7** **Busch Gardens** theme park is famous for its large African zoo, tropical garden and rides, such as the inverted roller coaster. Another area attraction is the Florida Botanical Gardens, 250 acres of themed gardens forming the centerpiece of Pinewood Cultural Park.

Gulf Coast

A drive south of Tampa takes in historic Bradenton and nearby **Anna Maria Island**, with its public pier and numerous white sand beaches. Next is Sarasota, a cultural center of Florida, its bay protected by a string of keys connected by bridges. One of Sarasota's noted attractions is the **Ringling Museum of Art**, located on the circus baron's winter estate built in the Italian Renaissance style with fountains, courtyards and gardens. The art museum's huge galleries are lined with priceless paintings, including one of America's largest Baroque art collections.

Venice, to the south of Sarasota, is another upscale community of palm-lined streets, waterfront restaurants and the highly touted Ritz-Carlton resort on Vanderbilt

The Florida Aquarium is located beside Tampa's cruise terminal at Garrison Seaport Center.

Beach Road, where the Grill Room serves superb continental cuisine. Near Naples, off Route 846, is the **Corkscrew Swamp Sanctuary**, maintained by the National Audubon Society, where an easy-to-hike boardwalk winds through marshland which is habitat for great egrets, blue herons and alligators.

Fort Myers, about 50 miles south of Venice, was once a resort getaway for the wealthy. The winter estates of Thomas Edison and Henry Ford are now museums featuring daily guided tours of these restored homes, including Edison's laboratory. Ford bought his place in 1916 because it was next door to the winter home of his friend Edison, who spent working vacations here from 1886 until his death in 1931.

Nearby **Sanibel Island**, a barrier island joined by a causeway to Fort Myers, is famous for the hundreds of species of sea shells that wash ashore, and ardent collectors assume the 'Sanibel stoop' while scouring the sandy beaches. Each summer hundreds of loggerhead turtles drag their heavy bodies onto shore to dig a nest and lay eggs, their welfare overseen by a group called Turtle Time, based in Fort Myers, which monitors the beach to ensure the hatchlings are undisturbed as they thrash their way out of the nests and make a nighttime dash to the sea. Sanibel and its neighboring island of Captiva were devastated by Hurricane Charley in August 2004, but the area's native vegetation survived the onslaught of wind and water, as did the beaches – which are actually broader now, due to sand being washed ashore. Local resorts, boutiques and galleries have been rebuilt, and Sanibel's laid-back character, reflected in the absence of neon signs or stop lights, remains intact.

The coastal drive south of Tampa to Fort Myers takes in numerous beaches and scenic towns.

CHAPTER TWO

GULF OF MEXICO PORTS

New Orleans

Louisiana's largest city, New Orleans was built on subtropical lowlands within a great bend of the Mississippi. Lying below sea level between the river and the shores of Lake Pontchartrain, the city was long protected from flooding by a system of levees. Then, in August 2005, Hurricane Katrina swept ashore. The city's storm-damaged levees and drainage pumps were unable to contain the rising flood-waters, and several drainage canals flowing into Lake Pontchartrain were breached. Water inundated the city, flooding entire neighbor-hoods, although some areas – such as the historic French Quarter – were undamaged. Amid the ensuing chaos and human suffering, Carnival Corporation provided three cruise ships for the housing of evacuees and emergency personnel at New Orleans and at Mobile, Alabama. The city's tourism infrastructure is up and running, and it's business as usual at the Port of New Orleans with several cruise ships once again home-porting here. The port's new Erato Street terminal (adjacent to the existing Julia Street terminal) opened in September of 2006. The allure of New Orleans may have been tarnished in the aftermath of Hurricane Katrina, but the the city's colorful history and unique Creole culture continue to draw visitors. One of America's oldest cities, New Orleans was founded in 1718 by the Sieur de Bienville. A strategic port in the struggle for control of the Mississippi, New Orleans soon became the new cap-ital of the French colony of Louisiana but was transferred to Spain in 1762, then briefly returned to France before transfer-ring to the United States with the Louisiana Purchase of 1803. The French-speaking Cajuns of Acadia arrived in 1763, and the westward movement of the 1800s brought growth and prosperity to New Orleans.

Louisiana Literature

As the queen city of the Mississippi, this thriving port earned a lasting reputation for elegance and extravagant living. **Mark Twain** arrived in New Orleans in 1857, on his way to South America to make his for-tune, and ended up working as a Mississippi River pilot. The Civil War marked the end of the golden era of river steamboats and sump-tuous balls, but the city's exotic flavor lives on in its music, cui-sine and literature. **William Faulkner** worked on his first novel, *A Soldiers' Pay*, while liv-

New Orleans' Julia Street Cruise Terminal.

ing in the city's French Quarter at 624 Pirate's Alley (then called Orleans Alley) which runs parallel with the west side of St. Louis Cathedral. Faulkner's former residence is now a bookstore called Faulkner House. **Tennessee Williams**, whose Pulitzer-prize-winning play, *A Streetcar Named Desire*, was set on a tenement street of New Orleans, also spent time in the French Quarter, living at 722 Toulouse Street in 1938. The playwright **Lillian Hellman** was born in New Orleans and lived in the stately Garden District, which is where **Anne Rice** – author of a series of best-selling vampire books – once owned a Victorian mansion. This district of elegant old homes also contains a cemetery of graves and crypts built above ground. **F. Scott Fitzgerald** rented an apartment overlooking this graveyard while reviewing the galleys of his first novel, *This Side of Paradise*. Jazz was born in New Orleans, among the city's black musicians in the late 19th century, and a park is named for native son Louis Armstrong.

Getting Around

Louis Armstrong International Airport is about 17 miles from the city core and location of the cruise ship terminals. Travel time is about 45 minutes, and an airport shuttle (kiosks in baggage area) is available for $13 per person. Limousine rates start at $35 for one or two passengers. Taxis charge a flat rate of $28 for two passengers; $12 per person for three or more. Long-term parking is available at the **Erato Street Cruise Terminal** (adjacent to the Julia Street Cruise Terminal) at a cost of $14 per day (cruise tickets are required to enter the lot). The **Convention Center** is beside the cruise terminals, and the **Julia Street Terminal** is located within the same building as the Riverwalk Shopping Mall. The historic French Quarter is within walking distance and in between are a number of waterfront attractions – Riverwalk Marketplace, World Trade Center, Harrah's Casino, and Aquarium of the Americas. In the other direction from the cruise terminals is the Garden District, one of the city's oldest residential neighborhoods of grand homes and leafy oaks.

Walking tours are available of the French Quarter, the Garden District, and local cemeteries. Gray Line, its ticket office located beside the Jackson (Jax) Brewery in the French Quarter, offers a variety of tours. The Regional Transit Authority (RTA) operates three streetcars, and at least two of these are back in operation – the red Riverfront Streetcar and the Canal Streetcar. The Riverfront Streetcar runs between the Convention Center and the French Market. The Canal Streetcar travels from the French Market to the Mid City, with a spur line terminating at the New Orleans Museum of Art.

Paddle wheel steamboats, which dock on the waterfront between the cruise pier and Jackson Square, offer local river tours. A ferry runs between the foot of Canal Street and Algiers, on the other side of the river.

Shopping & Dining – Canal Street is famous for its shopping, as is the French Quarter, with its fashion boutiques, museum shops and antique dealers selling everything from rare furniture to objets d'art. Canal Place features designer fashions, and the Jackson Brewery, which opened in 1984, is a shopping / dining / entertainment complex located beside Jackson Square in a renovated turn-of-the-century brewery. The French Market is an open-air produce and handicraft fair overlooking the river, and the Riverwalk Marketplace is a retail center located adjacent to the riverboat piers, just downstream of the cruise terminal.

(Top) The Riverfront Streetcar runs between the cruise pier and the French Quarter. (Bottom) St. Louis Cathedral.

Dining in New Orleans is done in the Continental style, its Creole and Cajun cuisine served with leisurely elegance in world-famous restaurants. The sophisticated sauces of Creole cooking are what distinguish it from the more robust Cajun dishes, but the two traditions – citified Creole and country Cajun – are often blended together and referred to as Louisiana cooking. Legendary dining establishments in the French Quarter include **Galatoire's Restaurant** at 209 Bourbon Street, which was founded by a French chef named Jean Galatoire in 1905. Still family-owned and operated, Galatoire's serves classic French Creole cuisine and maintains a dress code requiring jackets for gentlemen during dinner. Internationally renowned **Antoine's** at 713 Rue Saint Louis was established in 1840 by the French chef Antoine Alciatore, whose son Jules invented Oysters Rockefeller. Presidents, popes and movie stars have savored the French-Creole cuisine at Antoine's, where a jacket (tie optional) is required at dinner. For excellent Cajun cooking, K-Paul's Louisiana Kitchen at 416 Chartres Street serves up blackened redfish and crawfish etoufee in a casual setting.

Where to Stay – Historic boutique hotels in the French Quarter include the Holiday Inn Chateau Le Moyne on Rue Dauphine, which is built around an inner courtyard. The beautifully restored Historic French Market Inn on Rue Decaur was built in the 1800s for Baron and Baroness Joseph Xavier de Pontalba. Recommended hotels near the French Quarter include the InterContinental New Orleans at 444 St. Charles Avenue.

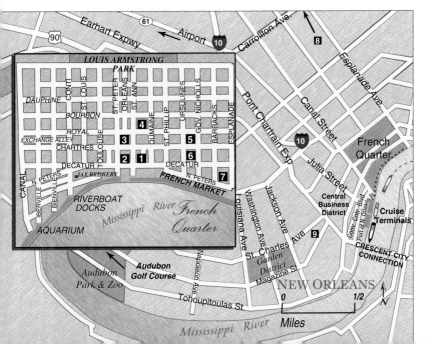

Local Attractions

The **French Quarter** (Vieux Carre) is the heart of New Orleans. It is a vibrant neighborhood of restaurants, hotels, jazz clubs, shops, museums and art galleries housed in 19th-century townhouses. The French Quarter burned twice in the late 1700s, and was last rebuilt by the Spanish, their Mediterranean influence reflected in ornamental cast-iron balconies and fountain courtyards. Most famous of the French Quarter's narrow streets and cobblestone alleyways is Bourbon Street, an entertainment strip packed with revelers during Mardi Gras, held each February or early March, depending on when Easter falls.

A **1** **Visitor Center** is located at 529 St. Ann Street, opposite Jackson Square, a popular starting point for a tour of the French Quarter. **2** **Jackson Square** (formerly the Place d'Armes) is the centerpiece of the French Quarter. Public meetings, celebrations and the welcoming of heroes have long been held in this square, its focal point a bronze equestrian statue of Andrew Jackson. Fronting the square is the magnificent **3** **St. Louis Cathedral**, completed in 1794, its Spanish style modified in 1851. On one side is the Cabildo, built by the Spanish in 1795, which now houses part of the Louisiana State Museum. The Presbytere, on the other side of the Cathedral, is also part of the Louisiana State Museum, as is the 1850 House, which is an authentic re-creation of an antebellum townhouse.

Numerous other attractions are found in the vicinity of Jackson Square. These include the **4** **Voodoo Museum** at 724 Dumaine Street and the **5** **Beauregard-Keyes House** at 1113 Chartres Street, which was built in 1826 and resided in by Confederate General P.G.T. Beauregard in the 1860s, then later restored by author Frances Parkinson Keyes. Also on Chartres is the **6** **Old Ursuline Convent**, built in 1752.

Museum exhibits on jazz and Mardi Gras are housed in the **7** **Old U.S. Mint** at the foot of Esplanade, backed by a courtyard in which stands the 'Streetcar Named Desire'. Beyond the French Quarter, major attractions include the **8** **New Orleans Museum of Art** at City Park (open Wednesday through Sunday, 10 a.m. to 4:40 p.m.), and the **9** **Confederate Museum**, at 929 Camp Street, which is the oldest museum in Louisiana and contains Civil War memorabilia.

Mobile, Alabama

Situated at the mouth of the Mobile River and a year-round base port for Caribbean cruises, this southern Alabama city and important seaport has a long and eventful history. Founded in 1710 by the Sieur de Bienville as the capital of French Louisiana, Mobile was eventually held by the British, then taken by the Spanish before being seized for the Americans by General James Wilkinson in 1813. Two forts stand at the entrance to Mobile

Galveston's beach-lined shores.

Bay, and the city's colonial past is reflected in its many beautiful antebellum homes, azalea-filled gardens and colorful Mardi Gras, an annual event dating to the early 1700s. Mobile's cruise terminal opened in 2004, and is accessed off Water Street, south of the George C. Wallace Tunnel.

Galveston, Texas

Situated on an island at the entrance to Galveston Bay, this city of some 60,000 is connected by causeways to the Texas mainland and the city of Houston. Although Houston has a larger port, accessed from Galveston Bay by a ship channel, Galveston remains a key port of entry and industrial shipping center, as well as a growing base port for cruise ships servicing the Western Caribbean. The Port of Galveston provides long-term parking (about $10 per day; Visa and MasterCard accepted) and free shuttles to the cruise terminals.

The Spanish were the first Europeans to discover Galveston Island, when Cabeza de Vaca was likely shipwrecked here in 1528. Settlement began in the 1830s but the natural port was plagued by hurricanes, including one that ruined the city and killed thousands of people in 1900. A 10-mile-long seawall was built against future hurricanes, and the city's beach and sportfishing

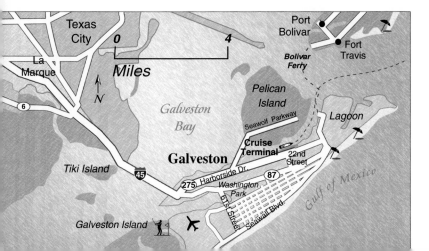

resorts now thrive alongside its traditional shipbuilding yards and commercial fishing fleets.

Stately old homes grace many of Galveston's streets, their gardens brightened with the blooms of bougainvillea, pink oleander and other subtropical flowers. Of local interest is the Texas Heroes monument, and halfway between Galveston and Houston (about 50 miles away) is the Johnson Space Center and NASA headquarters.

Houston

Named for Sam Houston, the 19th-century frontier hero and statesman of Texas, the city of Houston began in 1836 as a muddy town on Buffalo Bayou and became a major deepwater port in 1914, after a ship channel was dug on Buffalo Bayou and Galveston Bay, linking Houston to the Gulf of Mexico. Phenomenal growth followed, with the city's suburbs spreading outward across the wide prairie, its expanding wealth based on oil, chemical production, shipbuilding and the aerospace industry.

Cruise ships dock at Barbours Cut, a 15-mile-long complex of port facilities situated at the head of Galveston Bay. Houston International Airport is a 50-minute drive north of the port, while William P. Hobby Airport is about half the distance to the south.

Visitor attractions in Houston include Hermann Park (with a zoo and planetarium), the Sam Houston Coliseum and Music Hall, the Jesse H. Jones Hall for the Performing Arts (home of the symphony orchestra) and the National Space Hall of Fame. Other places of interest include the Galleria (a massive mall filled with luxury stores), Old Market Square, Sam Houston Historical Park with its restored homes, and the Astrodome and adjacent 'Astroworld' amusement center.

Horse-drawn carriages take visitors along the historic streets of Galveston.

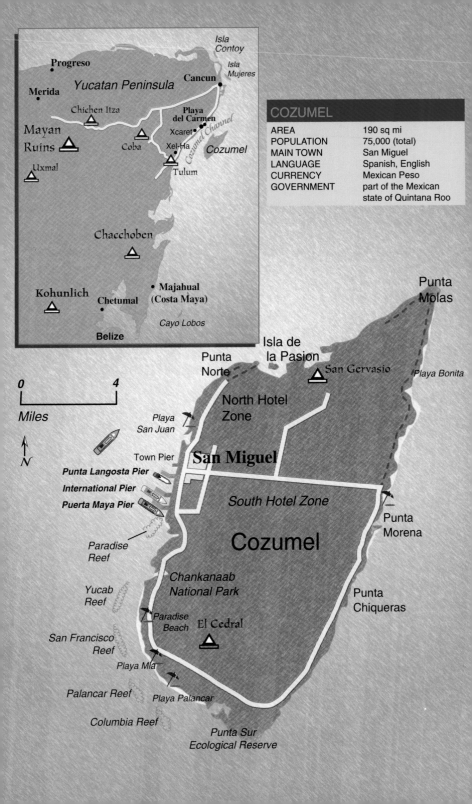

Isla
Contoy

Progreso

Yucatan Peninsula

Isla
Mujeres

Cancun

Merida

Chichen Itza

**Playa
del Carmen**

Mayan
Ruins

Xcaret

Coba

Xel-Ha

Cozumel Channel

Cozumel

Uxmal

Tulum

Chacchoben

Kohunlich

Chetumal

**Majahual
(Costa Maya)**

Cayo Lobos

Belize

COZUMEL

AREA   190 sq mi
POPULATION   75,000 (total)
MAIN TOWN   San Miguel
LANGUAGE   Spanish, English
CURRENCY   Mexican Peso
GOVERNMENT   part of the Mexican
                    state of Quintana Roo

Punta
Molas

Isla de
la Pasion

San Gervasio

Playa Bonita

Punta
Norte

North Hotel
Zone

0   4

Miles

N

*Playa
San Juan*

Town Pier

San Miguel

Punta Langosta Pier

International Pier

South Hotel Zone

Puerta Maya Pier

Punta
Morena

*Paradise
Reef*

Cozumel

*Yucab
Reef*

*Chankanaab
National Park*

Punta
Chiqueras

*San Francisco
Reef*

Paradise
Beach

El Cedral

Playa Mia

Palancar Reef

Playa Palancar

Columbia Reef

*Punta Sur
Ecological Reserve*

CHAPTER THREE

COZUMEL & COSTA MAYA

The coral-fringed island of Cozumel was a sleepy hideaway when Jacques Cousteau paid it a visit in the early 1960s and introduced the world to one of the Caribbean's top dive sites. The documentary Cousteau filmed here captured the brilliance of Cozumel's extensive coral reefs, which thrive in crystal-clear waters teeming with tropical fish and other marine life. The clarity of the water is unsurpassed anywhere in the Caribbean, and the underwater caves and spectacular sponges are considered some of the best in the world. The island is also popular for its beautiful beaches and fascinating Mayan ruins which have attracted such notable visitors as Jacqueline Kennedy, who came to Cozumel in 1968 while touring the area's archaeological sites.

The ancient **Maya**, from which Cozumel's inhabitants descend, named the island 'Land of Swallows' and dedicated it to Ixchel, the moon goddess of fertility. Remnants of temples and religious artifacts have been found throughout the island which lies 12 miles off the **Yucatan Peninsula**. The Yucatan, low and flat like Cozumel, is a limestone tableland covered with thin topsoil which supports subsistence crops as well as tobacco and corn. It is also one of the world's most important henequen-growing regions, the leaves of these tropical plants containing a strong fiber used for making binder twine. The uncultivated areas are covered with a dense growth of scrub, cactus, sapete wood and mangrove thickets. No rivers run through this area and the light rainfall is absorbed by the porous limestone where it collects in underground rivers and wells (cenotes), and in surface pools called *aguadas*.

Scattered throughout the low hills are thousands of pre-Columbian archaeological sites, for the Yucatan was once the seat of the great Mayan civilization that flourished for three millennium, beginning in about 1500 B.C. **El Mundo Maya** (The Maya World) extended from the Yucatan peninsula, which encompasses modern Belize and northern Guatemala, into parts of El Salvador and Honduras. An advanced society with an understanding of astronomy and engineering, the Maya built their pyramidal structures oriented to the spring and fall equinoxes. Each city state had its own internal structure of dynastic status and power, and their civic centers followed a pattern in which pyramidal structures and temples were built around a central plaza. Kilns were used to reduce the region's limestone into lime, which was mixed with white earth and water to create the mortar used in constructing the walls, corbelled arches and roof combs of these massive stone temples – often decorated with elaborate carvings and ceramic paintings. A common feature of the civic centers was a ball court with stone hoops. Opposing teams played with a heavy rubber ball that players kept in the air by bouncing it off any part of the body except the hands and feet. It's believed these games were sometimes used as a peaceful means to settle disputes between leaders, with the loser giving up his land and followers to be assimilated with the winning team's people. Another theory is the losing team offered a human sacrifice – often the team captain.

Mayan civilization reached its height during the Classic period (300 to 900 AD), followed by a rapid decline during which the population plummeted. In the Yucatan, however, settlement persisted due to the arrival of the Toltec from Central Mexico. Also an advanced civilization, Toltec society was based on a warrior aristocracy. These master builders dominated the Yucatan's Maya from the 11th to the 13th century, at which time the nomadic Chichimec brought about the fall of the Toltec empire, soon to be followed by the rise of the Aztec. Toltec art depicts male nobility in feathered headdresses inspired by the brilliant plumage of the quetzal. A chief god of the Toltec and Aztec was Quetzalcoatl, who was iden-

tified with the wind and air, and was symbolized by a feathered serpent.

The first Europeans to arrive at the Yucatan were most likely a pair of survivors from a 1511 Spanish shipwreck. One man joined the Maya, the other was rescued by Hernan Cortes in 1519 and became his interpreter. Spanish battles with the Maya began in 1527, with Cozumel used as a staging base, and continued until 1546 when a Mayan revolt was crushed. The Spanish colonialists tried to impose their own religious and political organization on the Mayan population but assimilation was far from complete, especially among the rural peasants. Spain held limited interest in the Yucatan due to its lack of mineral wealth and export crops. The islands of Cozumel and Isla Mujeres also were of little value to the Spaniards, but they did attract pirates such as Henry Morgan and Jean Lafitte who hid in coves to lie in wait for passing ships laden with gold and other treasures.

In the late 18th century, a growing world demand for cordage prompted the establishment of huge henequen plantations throughout the northern Yucatan. The local Maya's village lands were expropriated and, as the plantations grew in size, former land owners were pressed into labor. Tensions reached a boiling point in the mid-1800s and sparked a rebellion in which the Maya tried to drive all Europeans off the Yucatan peninsula. They were unsuccessful, but the Spanish were never able to completely suppress the indigenous population, and isolated pockets located outside the plantation zone remained autonomous throughout the 19th century.

Mexico gained independence from Spain in 1821, but widespread political turmoil continued. The social order inherited from Spanish colonialists consisted of two groups: Spanish-speaking whites and ladinos who resided in the major towns and maintained control of the region's commercial interests, and the much larger group of Mayan-speaking farmers who lived in rural villages. Following the Mexican Revolution of 1910-17, a land redistribution program guaranteed the rural Maya would no longer have their village lands expropriated.

In the early 1970s, flush with oil revenue, the Mexican government decided to build a world-class resort and once again the Yucatan became the focus of outside interests. The location for a master-plan resort – carefully chosen for its white sand beaches, Caribbean climate, clear waters and access to Mayan ruins – was Isla Cancun, lying off the northeast coast of the Yucatan Peninsula. Cancun and Cozumel were battered by Hurricane Wilma in October 2005, but rebuilding began immediately and within weeks cruise ships were again calling at Cozumel.

Cozumel

Cozumel is a flat island, its highest point only 35 feet above sea level, and is covered with scrub

Chacmool statues represent reclining idols.

jungle. The majority of islanders live in the town of San Miguel, located on the island's sheltered west coast overlooking Cozumel Channel. While no longer the quiet seaside town that greeted visitors back in the 1950s, San Miguel has retained much of its early charm. Safe and compact, the port is laid out in a grid pattern with streets running parallel and perpendicular to the waterfront. The locals, of Mayan descent, are generally shorter than the average Mexican and most speak Spanish as well as some English. The Mexican peso is the official currency but American currency is widely accepted.

Getting Around

The three cruise ship piers are located south of San Miguel. The closest, **Punta Langosta**, is a short walk from the town center. The **International Pier** and **Puerta Maya Pier** are a 10-minute taxi ride from town (about

COZUMEL
& the YUCATAN

(Above and right) San Miguel's charming museum features a replica Mayan home. (Below) Tulum was an ancient trading center of the Maya-Toltec.

(Top) Chichen Itza is an important Maya-Toltec site on the Yucatan peninsula. (Middle, right) San Miguel's main shopping street is lined with lively restaurants. (Middle left) A Mayan family sells crafts outside the walls of Tulum. (Below) A cruise ship off Cozumel.

30 minutes on foot). Ships that anchor off San Miguel transport their passengers by tender to the town pier, opposite the central plaza. A taxi ride from San Miguel to Chankanaab Lagoon is about $8, to Paradise Beach – $12, and to Playa Mia – $15. Cozumel taxi drivers are also certified as tourist guides. A passenger ferry runs between Cozumel and Playa del Carmen on the mainland (a 45-minute trip), where cruise passengers disembark on organized shore excursions to the Yucatan's Mayan sites and other attractions.

Shopping – Cozumel offers excellent shopping, and there are malls located at Puerta Maya and at Punta Langosta. The local flea market is located off 5th Avenue between Calles 2 and 4, while the town's upscale boutiques and restaurants are located on the waterfront's Avenue Rafael E. Melgar. Mexican handicrafts are among the finest in the world and include

Cozumel's Punta Langosta cruise pier is within easy walking distance of San Miguel's shops and attractions.

ceramics, tiles, pottery, copperware, glassware and whimsical hand-painted wooden animals. Quality leather goods include wallets, belts, sandals and cowboy boots, while hand-woven products range from baskets, rugs and hammocks to embroidered blouses, fine beaded tapestries and colorful woolen shawls called serapes. Gold and silver filigree (intricate ornamental work) is another Mexican specialty, creating exquisite earrings, necklaces and bracelets. Mayan craftsmanship includes elaborate weavings, decorative stitching and ceremonial masks. All Mexican-made products are duty-exempt and good buys are available in products made of silver, onyx and leather. Small discounts are often given for cash purchases and most stores accept U.S. dollars. Passengers visiting the mainland will also have an opportunity to buy local Mayan crafts at outdoor markets.

Beaches – The majority of sheltered beaches lie south of San Miguel, starting with **Chankanaab Bay** where a full-service beach offers water sports and a restaurant.

Shore Excursions

Cozumel

The following is a sampling of shore excursions offered by the cruise ships calling at Cozumel. Most ships also offer tours to the Yucatan peninsula, to visit various Mayan sites and parks, but these will vary from ship to ship. For more detail, log onto each cruise line's website or, if you have booked your cruise, refer to the shore excursion booklet provided.
• Adventure Park, Zip Line & Snorkel Combo
• Jungle Adventure by ATV or Bike
• Certified Two Tank Dive

• Clear Kayak & Snorkel Adventure
• Cozumel Golf & Country Club
• Deep Sea Fishing
• Sail, Snorkel & Beach Party
• Isla Pasion – beach, kayak or jeep adventure
• Playa Mia Beach Break
• Dolphin Encounter / Swim
• Sunset Catamaran Cruise
• Night Dive

YUCATAN EXCURSIONS -
• Mayan ruins of Tulum
• Mayan ruins of Coba
• Cenote Cavern Dive
• Cenote Snorkeling, Zip Line & Biking
• Xcaret Eco-Archaeological Park

Next is **Paradise Beach** (one of three beach clubs lying along a lovely three-mile stretch of sand formerly known as San Francisco Beach) which features a bar and restaurant as well as beach chairs and umbrellas; kayaks and snorkel gear can be rented.

South of Paradise Beach is **Playa Mia** (formerly Playa Del Sol) which is the island's party beach, its pier used by a local tour boat which provides live music and tropical punch for its beach-bound passengers. Snorkel tours to Palancar Reef, watersports equipment, lockers and beach umbrellas are available here.

Continuing south, you will come to **Mr. Sancho's Beach** where facilities include an array of watersports rentals, beach palapas, a bar and restaurant, and an open-air shopping arcade. Other activities here include horseback riding and ATV jungle touring.

Playa Mia, south of San Miguel, is one of Cozumel's best beaches.

One of the island's southernmost beaches, **Playa Palancar**, is quieter than those closer to the cruise terminals. Divers and snorkelers come here to explore the famous Palancar Reef (see next section), and facilities include a bar, restaurant, beach chairs and umbrellas.

Good beaches north of San Miguel include **Playa San Juan**, just north of the Melia Mayan Hotel, offering shade and calm water. Several hotels offer day passes for cruise ship passengers, starting at $45 per person, which provide access to the resort's private beach and guest facilities.

The east coast beaches are pounded with surf and less crowded than the sheltered west side. **Punta Morena** is an excellent beach with palapas, a beach bar and restaurant, and souvenir stand.

Dive & Snorkel Sites – A strong current flows through Cozumel Channel, so drift diving is how the offshore reefs are explored. The continual current carries food to the reefs, which is why the sponge growth is so spectacular. Many of these sponges and soft corals were torn when Hurricane Wilma pounded local waters, but the hard corals and sea life are doing fine. Some of the shallower reefs suffered damage, but reefs at 35 feet and deeper were unscathed and the local dive community spent three months clearing away bags of debris deposited on the sea floor by Hurricane Wilma. One of Cozumel's most famous dive sites is three-mile **Palancar Reef** at the southern tip of the island, with seven different dive sites ranging from 35 to over 80 feet. Other good dive sites include: Columbia Reef; Punta Sur with caverns and steep drop-offs; Santa Rosa Reef with its huge coral mounds; San Francisco Reef's valleys and vertical wall; and Yucab Reef, an extensive and shallow dive site encompassing a wide variety of coral formations and fish species.

Cozumel's reefs were protected by presidential decree in 1980, so construction of a new cruise pier near Paradise Reef in the late 1990s was greeted with protests from several environmental groups, as well as local residents and dive operators. Paradise Wall

DOWNTOWN SAN MIGUEL

begins at a depth of 50 feet and contains an abundance of marine life including giant sponges.

The best **snorkel sites** are the shallow reefs at Paradise Beach (a.k.a. Playa San Francisco) and the reefs of Chankanaab Bay.

Cozumel Golf & Country Club features a championship 18-hole golf course.

Local Attractions

1 Main Square, located opposite San Miguel's town pier, is pleasant for strolling with its shaded areas, large gazebo, clock tower and a monument to motherhood.

2 Museum de le Isla de Cozumel, located on the waterfront between Calle 4 Norte and Calle 6 Norte, is a welcome retreat from the busy street and bustling boutiques. For a small admission charge, you can enjoy exhibits ranging from Cozumel's natural habitat to its Mayan and colonial history. A highlight is the replica Mayan house, set in a courtyard, with a garden outside and authentic tools and furnishings inside. A Mayan host demonstrates the various stone tools, identifies foodstuffs on display and generally brings to life the workings of a typical village home. An open-air restaurant on the museum's second floor provides a lovely view out to sea.

3 Cozumel Archaeological Park contains full-size replicas of Mayan and Toltec stone carvings set in a jungle setting. A guided walking tour is included in the admission fee.

Chankanaab Park ($12 admission) is part of Isla Cozumel's Reefs National Marine Park and contains a natural underwater preserve connected to the sea by underground channels (*chankanaab* means 'small lake' or 'little sea' in Mayan). This beautiful lagoon is filled with bright corals and surrounded by a botanical garden, where visitors can stand and watch the colorful fish. The lagoon itself is off-limits to snorkeling and swimming to protect the marine life from harmful suntan lotions, but there is good snorkeling among the reefs of Chankanaab Bay. Other attractions include Dolphin Discovery (visitors can swim with dolphins), a sea lion show, and a reproduction of a Mayan village. Atlantis Submarine operates daily tours of Chankanaab Bay's underwater coral heads and tropical fish, with passengers transported to the dive site by ferry from various pick-up points, including the cruise piers.

Punta Sur Light House is an ecological park and nature reserve featuring mangrove forests and white sand beaches where sea turtles come ashore between June and August to lay their eggs. Crocodiles can be viewed from a look-out tower, while the old lighthouse and navigation museum are rich in nautical history.

Although there are numerous archaeological sites on Cozumel, none reach the scale and architectural significance of those found on the Yucatan peninsula. The most important island site is the Mayan temple of Ixchel located at San Gervasio, about 10 miles from San Miguel.

Yucatan Peninsula

Progreso – The lure of Mayan ruins and dazzling white beaches has prompted the construction of several cruise ship ports on the Yucatan Peninsula. Progreso, a tiny fishing village on the north coast, is now home to a cruise pier providing access to Merida (22 miles) and the Mayan sites of Uxmal (49 miles) and Chichen Itza (72 miles). Other shore excursions feature nearby caves and cenotes, dune buggy sightseeing or a visit to a flamingo reserve where these birds nest and feed among the mangroves. Spanish colonialism is revisited at the area's haciendas and the town of Izamal. Maya-themed excursions include a visit to the ruins at Dzibilchaltun, or to the Mayan community of Dzemul with its thatched roof palapa houses. Golf can be enjoyed at La Ceiba Golf & Country Club's 18-hole championship course (par 72, 6,528 yards) which was designed by Jack Nicklaus.

Merida – Once called the White City for its clean streets of gleaming white buildings where rooftop windmills are used to pump water from underground wells and streams, this Spanish colonial town was founded in 1542 by Francisco de Montejo, who conquered the Yucatan peninsula after his father withdrew due to fierce resistance. Built on the site of a ruined Mayan city, Merida became the cultural center of the Yucatan peninsula, its Cathedral of San Ildelfonso completed in 1599. Today, as the Yucatan state capital with a population exceeding 1/2 million, Merida's colonial heritage endures in its public buildings and the elegant old mansions of Paseo Montejo.

Uxmal – Situated in the Puuc hills (and pronounced *oosh-mal*), this important center of education flourished between 600 and 900 and is considered one of the finest examples of the Maya's Late Classic architecture. The site's impressive structures include the unique Pyramid of the Magician; the Governor's Palace, its facade decorated with some 20,0000 carved stone elements; and the Nunnery Quadrangle, the equivalent of a modern university.

Chichen Itza – This well-restored and popular Mayan site was founded around two large cenotes (deep, natural wells) in circa 514 by the Itza – the last strong, independent Mayan tribe. A political and religious center, the site was occupied at various times until 1194 when it was abandoned for the last time. The buildings span two periods of Mayan civilization. The Classic style is reflected in massive structures and heavy, decorative sculpture; the Post-Classic period, with a strong Toltec influence, produced plainer buildings, columns and sculpture based on the Mexican feathered serpent motif. The site's highlights include the Castillo temple, a ball court and, unusual among Mayan buildings, a round tower called the Caracol (snail shell) which was built in the Post-Classic period, probably as an astronomical observatory. Offerings, including human sacrifices, were thrown into Chichen

Itza's sacred well which was a mecca for pilgrimages by other Mayan tribes of Central America and Mexico.

Cancun – Originally a Mayan settlement, its name meaning 'vessel at the end of the rainbow', Cancun consisted of a few hundred inhabitants before an international holiday resort was built on its offshore island in the early 1970s. Long and narrow, the island is lined with powdery white beaches and connected to the mainland by a bridge at each end. Its hotel zone contains first-class hotels and recreation facilities that draw over two million visitors annually, mostly from the U.S. The L-shaped island forms a lagoon where water sports can be enjoyed, and the outer beaches are sheltered by coral reefs. Isla Mujeres is a short ferry or water taxi ride from Cancun, and this tiny island (5 miles long and 1 mile wide) of secluded beaches and lagoons contains the National Marine Park El Garrafon at its southern tip – a snorkeling and diving paradise.

Coba – Dozens of stone roads and causeways once led to Coba – a commercial hub of the Maya, which flourished from 400 to 1100. The largest settlement found to date, much of this site is still overgrown but those structures that have been excavated include the 80-foot-high Iglesia temple-pyramid, the Crossword pyramid, and the Nohochmul pyramid, which is the tallest on the Yucatan peninsula with 120 steps climbing to the top of its 138-foot-high face.

Calica is a cruise terminal located about five miles south of Playa del Carmen. Two natural parks are in the vicinity, the nearest being **Xcaret** ('little inlet'), which is an eco-archeological park built around the ruins of a Mayan ceremonial center. Visitors can don life vests and ride the gentle currents along an underground river, through caves illuminated by shafts of sunlight. The grounds include a botanical gardens, butterfly pavilion, turtle farm, swimming lagoons and restaurants.

Further south (about 15 miles) along the coast is **Xel-Ha**, touted as the world's largest natural aquarium. The park's limestone shoreline has been sculpted by the sea and freshwater springs, forming turquoise lagoons filled with tropical fish that can viewed from wooden platforms above the rocky shore. Snorkelers can swim in the lagoons and along the Xel-Ha river. A footpath also leads to the river and into the jungle where two cenotes and the Cave of Miracles, a massive underground cavern, can be viewed.

One of several temples at Coba.

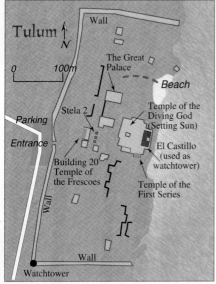

Visitors explore the site of Tulum, shown on map at left.

be 16 feet thick in places. Tulum, 'City of the New Dawn', was the only Mayan city still occupied when the Spanish arrived in the early 1500s. The protected cove at the base of this site is ideal for swimming and snorkeling off its white sand beach.

Costa Maya

This cruise port at Majahual was designed exclusively for cruise ships and features a shopping center, a beach and saltwater pools, restaurants and an amphitheater where Mexican folkloric shows are staged. Majahual is a mostly modern city, rebuilt after its destruction by a hurricane in 1955. Excursions from Costa Maya highlight the area's beautiful beaches, lagoons and coral reefs, which can be

Tulum – The only known walled city of the Maya, this ancient trading center is a stunning sight perched on the edge of a bluff overlooking the sea. Its stone buildings are surrounded on three sides by a stone wall that dates from 1200 AD and is said to

explored in clear-bottom kayaks and on guided scuba dives and snorkel expeditions. **Banco Chinchorro**, a huge coral reef the size of Cozumel Island, lies offshore and provides diving and snorkeling opportunities. Land-based tours include dune buggy rides, 4X4 safaris, horseback riding and bicycling. The area's notable Mayan ruins include **Chacchoben** (City of Red Corn), which dates to the 4th century and is surrounded by low-lying jungle. **Kohunlich**, which also dates from the Classical Period,was discovered in 1912 and named for a nearby palm-harvesting camp. Its major structure is the Temple of Masks, its staircase lined with stucco masks adorned with features of the Sun God.

(Above) A lovely swimming beach lies at the base of Tulum. (Below) Costa Maya's modern cruise terminal.

CHAPTER FOUR

CENTRAL AMERICA

C entral America is a verdant, mountainous region encompassing seven small nations and a variety of ecosystems – from coastal mangroves to volcanic summits. It was once part of El Mundo Maya (The Maya World), which thrived for 3,000 years and encompassed a territory extending from Mexico's Yucatan peninsula down through Belize and Guatemala into areas of El Salvador and Honduras. Several Central American ports are featured on various Caribbean cruise itineraries, including Belize City, Roatan Island (Honduras), Santo Tomas de Castilla (Guatemala), Puerto Limon (Costa Rica) and Colon (Panama).

Belize City, Belize

The tiny country of Belize, squeezed between Guatemala and the Caribbean Sea, was part of the Mayan civilization before the arrival of Europeans. The Spanish paid the region little notice, but British buccaneers preying on Spain's treasure ships began hiding out in the white-sand cays that dot the coast. When British settlers from Jamaica started colonizing the area, several battles ensued between Spain and England until a decisive defeat of the Spanish at St. George's Cay in 1798 settled the matter. Known as British Honduras until gaining independence in 1981, Belize had

been claimed by Guatemala since 1821 as part of its inheritance form Spain. Finally, in 1991, Guatemala officially recognized Belize's sovereignty.

Belize City, devastated by three hurricanes in the last century, was the country's capital until 1970 and it remains the commercial center and major port for Belize, the only Central American country with English its official language, although Spanish is widely spoken along with Creole and Maya. The Belize Dollar is worth 50¢ US, and American currency is accepted almost everywhere. The city is situated at the mouth of the Belize River and has retained the air of a British colonial port with its canals, wooden houses and fishing boats. Offshore the cays (low islands) are sheltered by the

The snorkeling is excellent along the reefs of Belize.

longest unbroken reef in the Western Hemisphere. **Dive and snorkel excursions** can be taken to several of these cays where the underwater attractions include Shark Ray Alley, which is part of Hol Chan Marine Reserve and an area where southern stingrays and nurse sharks congregate.

Shore Excursions

Belize

Escorted shore excursions include snorkeling, scuba diving, cave tubing, kayaking, canoeing and reef bottom fishing. Land-based options include traversing jungle trails by bicycle, 4X4 or jungle buggy. Horseback riding and canopy tours are also offered, as are tours to several Mayan sites. Belize City tours often include a visit to the Belize Zoo or Baboon Sanctuary. Golfers can enjoy a round at Caye Chapel Golf Resort's 18-hole course.

In addition to dive trips and fishing charters, **shore excursions** can be taken from Belize City to the nearby Mayan ruins, such as the sprawling site of **Altun Ha**. There, amid hundreds of mounds, archaeologists discovered the Green Tomb, so named for its stash of jade treasures that included a carved head representing the Mayan sun god, now one of Belize's national symbols. Nearby **Lamani**, still occupied when Spanish conquistadors sailed up the New River, is an immense site of some 700 structures standing on high ground that is now home to howler monkeys. An excursion to Lamani still requires a boat trip up the river, past mangroves, crocodiles basking on the banks, and a variety of birds and tropical flowers.

In between these two Mayan sites is the **Crooked Tree Wildlife Sanctuary**, its guided tours touted as one of Belize's best nature experiences. Established by the Belize Audubon Society in 1984, the sanctuary is habitat to a wealth of bird life and encompasses the fishing and farming village of Crooked Tree, a lagoon upon which boat trips can be taken, a system of trails, observation towers and an elevated boardwalk. South of Belize City is the 98,000-acre **Cockscomb Basin Wildlife Sanctuary**, where the world's highest concentrated population of big cats roam, including the puma, gaguarondi and jaguar, the latter numbering about 200 of the world's remaining 15,000 jaguars.

Santo Tomas de Castilla, Guatemala

Guatemala's chief Caribbean port, Santo Tomas de Castilla was built in the 1960s by the Guatemalan government to replace Puerto Barrios, a few miles to the north, which was controlled by foreign commercial interests. Most of the country's population (which is evenly divided between Maya Indians and mestizos) lives in the southern highlands. The northern half of the country is covered by a vast tropical forest, called El Peten, where the magnificent temples of Tikal, the largest and possibly oldest of the Maya cities, rise above the surrounding jungle.

Tikal was built during the Classic Period (AD 300-900) and is a United Nations World Heritage Site. These ruins were once a hub of the Mayan world, where traders would bring fish and shells from the Caribbean Sea and Pacific Ocean. Built on limestone hills, Tikal's nine groups of courts, plazas, pyramids and temples were interconnected with bridges and causeways. At its height in the 8th century, Tikal was home to 100,000 people before falling into decline at the end of the 9th century. When the Spaniards marched past Tikal in 1525, they did not see the abandoned city concealed behind the tropical foliage, and not until 1848 was this magnificent site discovered.

The great Maya site of Tikal is situated in Guatemala.

Guatemala's official currency is the quetzal, but US dollars are widely accepted. Mayan crafts to look for include ceremonial masks and intricate decorative stitching on cotton blouses and fabric handbags.

Roatan Island, Honduras

The sultry Bay Islands, lying off the Caribbean coast of Honduras, were once a 17th century hideout for the Welsh pirate Henry Morgan who established his base at Port Royal on Roatan Island, the largest of the three main islands making up this archipelago. Two centuries later, shortly after Britain relinquished the Bay Islands to Honduras, the American fillibuster William Walker sought refuge here amongst the English-speaking islanders until forced to surrender to the Royal Navy.

Today, Roatan Island is a popular tourist resort of powdery white beaches and clear turquoise water protected by a reef that surrounds the island. Seaside towns hug the coastline of this long, narrow island, home to about 15,000 seafaring inhabitants who are as like-ly to hop into a boat as a car to get somewhere on the island. Taxis, however, are plentiful and visiting cruise passengers – who are tendered ashore at Coxen Hole – should agree on a fare before setting out (riding colectivo is the cheapest way to go, which means the driver can pick up more fares along the way).

The **best beaches** are at the island's western end, about five miles from Coxen Hole. West Bay Beach is considered the island's most beautiful, with good snorkeling and diving along the protected reef, especially in the Blue Channel. Half Moon Bay is also good for snorkeling, and semi-submersible glass-bottomed boat tours operate out of both bays. Anthony's Key Resort, which offers scuba lessons and escorted boat dives, also owns and operates the Roatan Institute of Marine Sciences, where visitors can swim with dolphins who reside in a natural lagoon and are trained in the open ocean. Other excursions include a forest canopy ride along cables leading from a mountain ridge into Gumbalimba Park where the tropical forest is home to monkeys and a variety of birds.

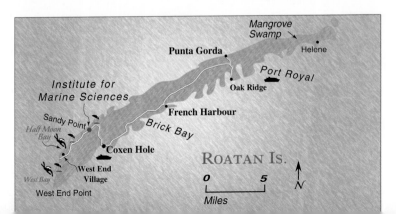

Puerto Limon, Costa Rica

Costa Rica ('rich coast') may be a tiny country (about the size of West Virginia) but it holds three mountain ranges and supports such an abundance of flora and fauna that nearly one quarter of its total land area is preserved by national parks or private reserves. Costa Rica's 3.5 million citizens are mainly of Spanish descent and the country's public health system is considered one of the best in the world, with an average life expectancy of 79.8 years for women. The literacy rate is over 90% and although Spanish is the

Costa's Rica's Puerto Limon.

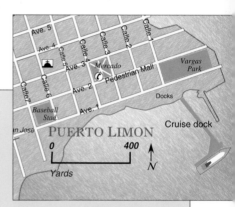

Shore Excursions

Costa Rica

The country's natural beauty and protected parkland have made it one of the world's premier eco-tourism destinations. There are 80 national parks, protected zones, and biological and forest reserves in Costa Rica, and several of these can be visited by ship-organized shore excursions – a recommended way to view a tropical forest, for it's not advisable to hike into the jungle without an experienced guide who is able to spot and identify the flora and fauna as well as watch out for everyone's safety.The **Rain Forest Aerial Tram** whisks visitors over the forest canopy in open tram cars suspended from a moving steel cable supported by converted ski lift towers. This unique attraction was the brainchild of American biologist Donald Perry and is located on a privately owned reserve bordering Braulio Carillo National Park, which protects a virgin forest ranging from the summit of Barva Volcano to the Caribbean lowlands.

Tortuguero Park is situated on the Caribbean coast, about 50 miles north of Limon, and is an important nesting site for green sea turtles, which arrive from July to early October. The leatherback and hawksbill turtles also nest here, but in much smaller numbers, and the park is home to three species of monkey and over 300 species of birds. Sightings can be made on the park trails or during boat trips on the river, which is home to caimans (similar to alligators), crocodiles, basilisk lizards and freshwater turtles.

official language, English and French are taught in schools. Voting is compulsory and the president, upon completing a four-year term, cannot be immediately reelected.

Puerto Limon, on the Caribbean coast, is the country's leading port from which bananas, cocoa and timber are exported. Although not considered a tourist town, it does have a pleasant waterfront park (Parque Vargas) and a colorful market. The offshore island of Uvita is where Columbus landed in 1502, and Columbus Day (October 12) is celebrated in Limon with street parades and other festivities. Popular dishes in Costa Rica include rice and black beans accompanied by corn tortillas and fried plantains.

Best Beaches – Many of Costa Rica's beaches consist of black volcanic sand. On the Caribbean side, some beautiful swimming beaches can be found at Cahuita, 27 miles south of

Two Pacific-bound cruise ships emerge from Gatun Locks.

LImon, where a long black-sand beach lies at the north end of the village and a white-sand beach lies at the other end within a national park.

Shopping – Costa Rica is considered the Bordeaux of coffee-growing countries, and its most famous brand is Cafe Britt, grown and roasted on a plantation near Heredia on the country's central plateau, which lies several thousand feet above sea level where the climate is perennially spring-like. Wooden handicrafts include salad bowls and jewelry. Costa Rica's official currency is the colon, but the US dollar is widely accepted. The approximate exchange is: $1 US = 520 colons; $1 Cdn = 490 colons.

Colon, Panama

(For complete cruise information on Panama Canal cruises see Panama Canal By Cruise Ship by Anne Vipond.)

The Panama Canal changed the face of the earth. Upon its completion, the world's two great oceans were joined and a safe maritime route, sought after for centuries, was created. Built by the United States, this monumental engineering project was completed under budget, in both time and money, and has operated successfully ever since. Since the locks first opened on August 15, 1914, nearly a million vessels have transited the 50-mile-long canal.

With its handover by the United States at the end of 1999, the Panama Canal became an inalienable patrimony of the nation of Panama – it can't be

Miraflores Locks located at the
west side of Panama Canal.

sold, assigned, mortgaged or transferred, and the permanent neutrality of the Canal is guaranteed. The United States has retained the right to defend the waterway in the interest of national security, but Panama has assumed full responsibility for the administration, operation and maintenance of the Canal.

Panama has made some changes to the former Canal Zone, which is now called the Canal Area, where investment in tourism has soared. With improvements in pier facilities and numerous companies now offering local tours, the cruise lines have come to regard Panama as more than just a canal. Most ships stop at one of two dock facilities in Colon, which is situated on a swampy island near the Caribbean entrance of the Panama Canal. Cruise Terminal Pier 6, on the west side of the town, is adjacent to Cristobal (a Colon suburb). The newer Colon 2000 pier, located on the west side of Colon just outside the Free Zone, features a shopping mall with duty-free products and tours to local attractions.

Panama's monetary unit is the balboa (equal to the U.S. dollar) and is interchangeable with U.S. paper money. Coins are identical in shape and value to American coins. The country's official language is Spanish, although English is widely understood in urban areas.

Shore Excursions

Panama

Shore excursions from Colon include a ride on the railroad that crosses the Isthmus of Panama to the Pacific Ocean. Other excursions feature a visit to the observation areas at Gatun Locks where the workings of the locks can be viewed up close. This is often combined with other local attractions, such as a tour of Portobelo (which was the main shipping port for Spanish gold during the days of piracy) or of San Lorenzo (a Spanish fort captured by Henry Morgan in 1671). Nature tours include the Gamboa aerial tram for viewing some of the most renowned rainforest canopy in Central America, and boat tours and kayaking expeditions on Gatun Lake, the largest man-made lake in the world. Tours of an Embera native village are also offered.

GRAND CAYMAN ISLAND

AREA	76 sq mi
POPULATION	40,000
CAPITAL	George Town
LANGUAGE	English
CURRENCY	Cayman Islands dollar, U.S. dollar
GOVERNMENT	British overseas territory

N

0   2

Miles

Gun Bay

▲ 43 ft

East End

Blow Holes

Old Man Bay

Queen Elizabeth
Botanic Park

Frank Sound Rd

Frank Sound

North Side

Mastic Trail

Pearse Bay

North Side Rd

Bodden Bay

Rum Point

Cayman Kai

Little Sound

Booby Cay

Bodden Town

Beach Bay

Savannah

Pedro St. James Castle

North Sound

Caribbean Sea

Stingray City

Governor's Harbour

The Links at SafeHaven

Taxi Stand

Hyatt Britannia Golf Course

Crewe Rd

Prospect Point

South Sound

Conch Point

Cayman Turtle Farm

West Bay

Hell

West Bay

Seven Mile Beach

Governor's Residence
Westin Casuarina
Beach Club Colony

West Bay Road

Walker's Rd

South Church St

George Town

Smith Cove

CHAPTER FIVE

GRAND CAYMAN

Grand Cayman, an international center for offshore banking, is one of the best-rated dive locations in the world. A person needn't even get wet to enjoy some of the island's remarkable aquatic sights, for a variety of vessels and observatories allow visitors to see the reefs, wrecks and marine life for which the Cayman Islands are famous.

Grand Cayman is the largest of a three-island group which includes Little Cayman and Cayman Brac – a Gaelic word for cliff. The name Cayman is derived from a Carib word for crocodile, although the Caymans were first called Las Tortugas by Columbus when he observed, in 1503, the hundreds of turtles living on these uninhabited islands. The Spanish paid these flat coral outcrops little attention as the soil was poor and there were no precious metals to mine, but English, Dutch and French ships pulled in regularly to take on fresh water and salted turtle meat. Today, the green sea turtle is an endangered species and in 1978 the United States banned the import of all turtle products, even those raised at the Cayman Turtle Farm, which releases young turtles into local waters.

Sea turtles are not the only species protected in the Cayman Islands. In 1978 a marine conservation law was passed, and four preservation zones were established in 1986. The Replenishment Zones provide year-round protection of conch and lobster breeding grounds, as well as every other kind of marine life. Line fishing from shore or beyond the drop-off are the only forms of harvesting allowed. Permanent moorings have been installed to protect the reefs

Stingray City is a highlight for visitors to Grand Cayman.

George Town's tender pier is centrally located.

which were becoming damaged by the anchors of dive boats. These progressive conservation measures have extended onto land with the establishment of animal sanctuaries and the opening of a botanical park by Queen Elizabeth. Grand Cayman's indigenous animal species include iguanas and parrots. Bird watching is popular here, with more than a hundred species of birds observed, including those on spring and fall migrations.

The Cayman Islands, a British Crown Colony since 1670, were settled by a motley collection of British army deserters, shipwrecked sailors, retired pirates and African slaves who gained freedom when ships carrying them foundered on Cayman reefs. Slavery was abolished by Britain in 1833, a year after a representative government was established on the Cayman Islands. When Jamaica opted for independence from Britain in 1962, a debate ensued among Cayman residents who eventually voted to remain a British Crown Colony. About 30,000 people live on the three islands, the majority on Grand Cayman. Of mixed origin and free of racial tensions, they descend from the English, Irish, Scottish and Africans who first settled the islands. With few natural resources on these mangrove-covered islands, the Cayman men traditionally made their living from the sea – turtle fishing, ship building and serving in the merchant marine. As recently as the 1950s, those working on foreign-owned ships were sustaining the local economy with the money they sent back home.

Grand Cayman remained an isolated backwater until 1954, when an airfield was built. But it wasn't until the island's troublesome mosquitoes were brought under control in the 1970s that tourists began arriving in droves. The climate is ideal, the beaches are beautiful and the marine life prolific due to the varied underwater terrain which ranges from shallow coral reefs to submarine canyons. Meanwhile, Cayman's political stability and attractive tax laws make it an ideal environment for offshore banking interests. Some 70 financial institutions, six of which are clearing banks, operate on Grand Cayman where local services include offshore incorporation, company management and private banking. This thriving financial industry, which includes major accounting firms, is subject to strict government controls – which apply to both its banks and its customers.

Grand Cayman was devastated by **Hurricane Ivan** in September 2004. With winds gusting to 200 miles per hour, Ivan was the worst storm to hit the island in 86 years. There was no direct loss of life but property damage was extensive.

Getting Around

The cruise ships anchor off George Town and tender their passengers ashore. A visitor information booth and telephones are located at the north tender pier. The town's sights and stores are all within easy walking distance of the waterfront, and **shuttle vans** transport visitors between George Town and Seven Mile Beach for a fee of $4 per person. A regular **taxi** ride between Georgetown and Seven Mile Beach is $12. The Holiday Taxi Stand is located at the Westin Casuarina Resort. Ship-organized excursions cover most of the island's attractions, concentrating on the western end of the island where Stingray City and Seven Mile Beach are located. Passengers interested in touring the island independently can hire a taxi (about $40 US to East End) or rent a car (approximately $40 a day plus $7.50 for a temporary driving permit) as well as mopeds, motorbikes and bicycles. Driving is on the left.

Shopping – A free port, Grand Cayman carries an assortment of duty-free goods. George Town, where the majority of shops are located (many of which are closed on Sundays), is

A cruise ship anchors off George Town where shore excursions include snorkeling and scuba diving.

(Above) Seven Mile Beach.
(Below) The Cayman Islands
National Museum is housed in a
former courthouse.

very clean and orderly with no roadside pedlars. Local items to look for include numismatic jewelry, crafted from old coins retrieved from sunken vessels and featured in exquisite gold-and-diamond settings. Unique to the Cayman Islands are sculptures and jewelry made of an earth-toned, hard dolomite stone called caymanite that was discovered at East End. Another island specialty is Tortuga Rum Cake, baked according to a century-old family recipe and coated with an aromatic syrup made with specially blended, five-year-old Tortuga Gold rum stored in oak barrels.

The Cayman Island dollar equals about $1.25 US, but American currency is accepted throughout the islands. American and Canadian visitors should be aware it is against customs regulations to import turtle products into their countries.

Local Sights – Overlooking the pier area is the **1 Cayman Islands National Museum**, housed in the former courthouse and containing displays on the islands' natural and cultural history, including artifacts of pirate lore. Cardinal, one of the main shopping streets, leads to the post office and the adjacent **2 Elizabethan Square**. A few blocks north on Edward is the Public Library. Across the street is a small park containing a massive fig tree. At the intersection of Edward and Fort Streets is **3 Clock Tower**, a monument to Britain's King George V. Fort Street leads down to the waterfront where the remains of Fort George can be seen, built in the

17th century to protect the island from pirate attacks. Nearby, on Harbour Drive, is the restored 19th-century **4 Elmslie Memorial Church**.

Best Beaches – The natural choice for cruise passengers is **Seven Mile Beach**, one of the finest in the Caribbean, which starts just north of George Town and stretches for about five miles along the island's western shore. Lined with hotels, this beautiful white-sand beach is ideal for swimming, snorkeling and other water sports. The cruise lines often arrange with one of the hotels for their passengers to utilize its beach-front facilities for a small fee. Sailboards and other equipment can be rented at a sports center beside the public beach which is usually uncrowded. Government House, the Governor's official residence, is near the public beach area.

Dive & Snorkel Sites – Grand Cayman is the top of a submerged mountain and its offshore coral reefs form the famous 'Cayman Wall'. An estimated 60 miles of drop-offs encircle Grand Cayman where the underwater visibility extends to depths of 150 feet. There are more than a hundred dive sites surrounding the island, and they include numerous shipwrecks as well as coral gardens, grottos, caves and canyons which are habitat for rays, turtles, tropical fish and huge, colorful sponges. Whether snorkeling, shore diving or deep diving, Cayman Island offers crystal clear water, an abundance of marine life and a variety of underwater terrain.

This fascinating marine world can also be viewed from vessels that operate out of George Town, including a glass-bottom boat, a semi-submersible and a submarine. There are reefs and wrecks to explore right in Hog Sty Bay, such as Cheeseburger Reef and the wreck of the Cali. Other easily accessible dive sites include

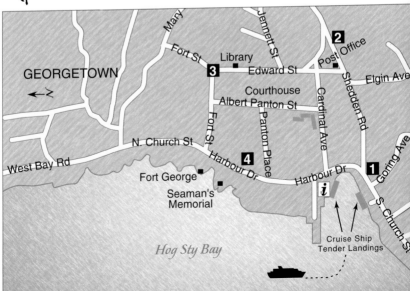

A diver swims with the tropical fish in George Town's harbor.

Eden Rock and Devil's Grotto, just south of George Town, as well as those along Seven Mile Beach. Dive boats take certified divers to the island's incredible drop-offs, such as the West Wall which lies about nine miles offshore. Atlantis Submarine operates out of George Town and offers non-divers the opportunity to view the famous Cayman Wall. Several dive and snorkel shops are located within walking distance of the tender pier, and the cruise lines also offer snorkel and dive excursions.

Golf – There are two golf courses on Grand Cayman, both a few miles north of George Town along West Bay Road. Closest to town is the Hyatt Britannia Golf Course, designed by Jack Nicklaus and offering three courses in one: a nine-hole championship course, an 18-hole course and one played with a special Cayman ball. The Links at SafeHaven is an 18-hole championship course and is reminiscent of those in Scotland.

Island Attractions

Stingray City, located in the protected waters of North Sound, has been described in National Geographic as "one of the most rewarding experiences in the undersea world." Visitors are taken by boat to this shallow sandbar where for decades fishermen used to clean fish, their discarded entrails attracting stingrays who would arrive at the sound of a ship's motor. In 1987 some divers began frequenting this spot, bringing squid for the normally shy stingrays who gradually got used to the divers' presence. Now 30 to 50 stingrays show up daily to be hand fed, stroked and held by humans. Visitors can watch from an observatory or snorkel with the stingrays.

Cayman Turtle Farm is situated in a tidal creek of North

Sound. Originally established in 1968 to raise and market turtle products, the farm now concentrates on research and breeding. Green sea turtles and hawksbill turtles are bred, hatched, raised and tagged before being released into Cayman waters. Tours of the facility are self-guided. While many visitors like to stop at nearby **Hell** so they can send a postcard, the real attraction is the weathered outcrop of iron shore which, although said to look like the charred remains of a hell fire, is actually made of black limestone about 1.5 million years old.

East of George Town the attractions include **Pedro St. James Castle**, an 18th-century great house beautifully situated on landscaped grounds atop a bluff. **Bodden Town**, with its legendary Pirate Cave, is where pirates are said to have hidden their loot in a series of tunnels. Nearby is the Meagre Bay Bird Sanctuary and further east is the **Botanic Park**, officially opened by Queen Elizabeth in 1994. The park's 60 acres of grounds include a floral garden and an interpretive trail that winds through woodlands, wetlands, swamps and thickets. Adjacent to the park is the **Mastic Trail**, a restored 200-year-old footpath that winds for two miles through primary woodlands and mangrove swamps. The island's eastern shores contain **The Blow Holes**, saltwater geysers spouting from the coral rock as waves crash onto shore. East End is the oldest town on the island, founded in the late 17th century.

Shore Excursions

Grand Cayman

Grand Cayman's shore excursions include driving tours to various attractions, such as the Botanic Park, Butterfly Farm, Pedro St. James, Hell, Turtle Farm and Stingray City. Boat excursions range from two-person, self-operated craft to catamaran rides. Marine life can be viewed from an Atlantis submarine, a semi-submersible, snorkeling tours, dive expeditions and walking on the sea bottom with a Jules Vern type helmet resting on your shoulders. Beach breaks, kayaking safaris and horseback riding are also offered.

Viewing young sea turtles at the Cayman Turtle Farm.

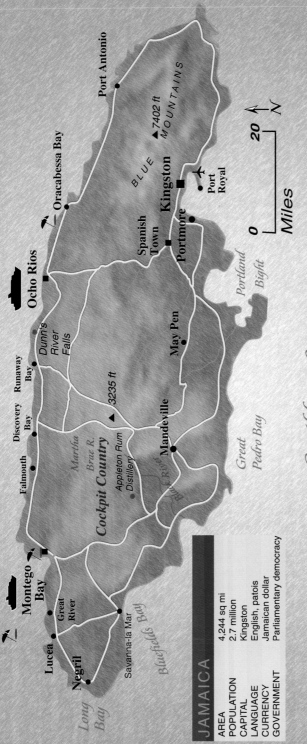

Port Antonio

BLUE ▲ 7402 ft
MOUNTAINS

Oracabessa Bay

Kingston
Port Royal

Ocho Rios

Spanish Town

Portmore

Dunn's
River
Falls

Runaway
Bay

May Pen

Portland
Bight

Discovery
Bay

▲ 3235 ft

Martha
Brae R.

Appleton Rum
Distillery

Mandeville

Black River

Great
Pedro Bay

Falmouth

Cockpit Country

Montego
Bay

Great
River

Savanna-la-Mar

Bluefields Bay

Lucea

Negril

Long
Bay

Caribbean Sea

N

20

0

Miles

JAMAICA

AREA	4,244 sq mi
POPULATION	2.7 million
CAPITAL	Kingston
LANGUAGE	English, patois
CURRENCY	Jamaican dollar
GOVERNMENT	Parliamentary democracy

CHAPTER SIX

JAMAICA

Jamaica, third largest island of the West Indies after Cuba and Hispaniola, is one of the most beautiful in the Caribbean. A lush and mountainous island, Jamaica has long attracted a diversity of peoples to its shores, from famous buccaneers to accomplished artists. The country's official motto is "Out of many, one people" – acknowledging the range of races and nationalities that have colonized this island nation. Its history is turbulent and social problems still exist, but a 'No problem mon' attitude sums up the buoyant spirit of Jamaicans.

Arawaks, an agricultural people, were the first to inhabit the island about a thousand years ago. The Spanish began colonizing Jamaica in 1509 under licence from Christopher Columbus's son, and the Arawaks soon died out under Spanish occupation. Captured by the British in 1655 and formally ceded to England in 1670, the island was a haven for buccaneers before becoming a major sugar producer in the 18th century

The island is a limestone plateau more than 3,000 feet above sea level, its mountainous backbone rising at its eastern end to the Blue Mountains. Fertile slopes and broad river valleys lead down to narrow coastal plains and support large plantations of sugarcane, bananas and other crops, including the famous Blue Mountain Coffee.

Rainfall, abundant in the mountainous regions, diminishes westward across a rugged plateau of streams and subterranean rivers. The heart of this plateau, called the Cockpits, is used for livestock grazing. During Jamaica's colonial days, escaped or freed slaves – called maroons – fled to Cockpit country where they lived in villages and organized frequent uprisings against the European landowners.

Half of Jamaica's population is still rural, with much of the work force employed in agriculture. However, the continuing trend is one of migration to the cities. Of the country's 2.6 million residents, about 600,000 live in the capital of Kingston. Situated on a deep, landlocked harbor, Kingston was established in 1692 after an earthquake destroyed Port Royal at the tip of the peninsula that forms the harbor. This British outpost and pirate haven suddenly sank 33 feet into the sea, taking 2,000 inhabitants with it. When a subsequent tsunami swept ashore, a British naval frigate was carried across the sunken townsite and deposited inland.

Plans are now underway to recreate 17th-century Port Royal, which wasn't properly excavated

Jamaica's scenic north coast.

until 1965, although some of its treasure was salvaged at once. The most famous name associated with Port Royal is Sir Henry Morgan, a Welsh privateer whose daring exploits included the sacking of Portobelo in 1668 and the capture of Panama in 1671. He was eventually arrested on charges of piracy and sent to England where, with war against Spain threatening once more, he was knighted and returned to Jamaica as deputy-governor.

The entire north coast, from Negril at its western end to Port Antonio at its eastern end, is dotted with beach-lined bays and palm-shaded resorts, including some of the most exclusive in the Caribbean. It also contains Jamaica's two main cruise ports – Ocho Rios and Montego Bay.

Many a famous person has spent time living or vacationing in Jamaica, beginning with Christopher Columbus who first stepped ashore in 1494 at Rio Bueno. On his fourth voyage to the West Indies in 1503, Columbus beached his damaged ships on the island's north shore and spent a year on Jamaican soil awaiting rescue. In more recent times, the swashbuckling movie star Errol Flynn pulled into Port Antonio in his private yacht to escape a storm and ended up building a home there on Navy Island.

For a relatively small country, Jamaica has had a far-reaching impact on the rest of the world with its music, dance and art. Jamaicans are international in outlook and many of its citizens have migrated to other countries, most notably Britain. Over 90% of Jamaicans are of West African descent with Asians and Europeans adding to the cultural tapestry of this dynamic island nation. Yet, the country's rich social fabric has at times appeared to be unraveling, with political tribalism resulting in election violence.

The People's National Party (PNP) was founded in 1938 by Norman Manley. His cousin, Sir Alexander Bustamante, founded the Jamaica Labour Party (JLP). These two parties, their roots in rival trade unions, have dominated Jamaican politics since 1944 when universal adult suffrage was introduced. Jamaica gained its independence from Britain in 1962 but remains a member of the British Commonwealth. The country's economy is one of the more prosperous in the West Indies, despite a recession that persisted throughout the 1970s and 80s. After embracing socialism in the 1970s, Jamaica now has a free market economy based on tourism, agricultural products and the export of bauxite, from which alumina is extracted.

Hurricane Gilbert caused widespread devastation when it swept the length of the island in 1988 and the country's tourism industry was crippled. The island has since regained its prominence as a popular Caribbean destination but many tourists stay at all-inclusive resorts. The government is trying to counter this insular attitude with a Meet the People program in which the tourist board will arrange for a visitor to spend time with a Jamaican host who shares a common interest.

Cruise passengers who might be apprehensive about venturing ashore can simply book a shore excursion. Those who prefer to strike out on their own will find the Jamaican people, despite their reputation for aggressively selling their wares (including narcotics), are an outgoing and friendly people who will respond to a polite but firm 'No thank you' with a 'No problem mon' wave of the hand. Most Jamaicans have a good sense of humor and this is usually the best way to fend off persistent advances.

Reggae & Rastafarianism

Rastafarianism is a religious-cultural movement that began in Jamaica in the 1930s when Haile Selassie (also named Ras Tafari) became Emperor of Ethiopia, as predicted by Jamaican hero Marcus Garvey. Selassie was hailed as the movement's messiah, Ethiopia was the promised land, and Garvey was considered a major prophet and early leader in creating black awareness and unity.

Reggae, which originated in the 1960s among the poor blacks of Kingston, is the protest music of the Rastafarian faith. Its sound is characterized by an off-beat rhythm that draws on American

Bob Marley, the 'King of Reggae Music', died at age 36.

soul and traditional African and Jamaican folk music. Reggae's most famous performer is the late Bob Marley, a Jamaican singer, songwriter and guitarist to whom a museum is dedicated in Kingston.

Born in 1945 and deserted by his white Jamaican father, Marley was raised by his mother in Nine Miles village on Jamaica's north coast. As a youth, he and his mother moved to the poor shanty area of Kingston where he worked in the welding trade while seeking success as a musician. Fame finally came to Marley in the 1970s when his new group began playing reggae and their songs soared in the charts. When Marley died of cancer at the age of 36, he had achieved international stardom and received his country's highest public honor, the Order of Merit. The worldwide popularity of reggae is attributed in large part to Marley, whose songs supported his belief in non-violence and the Rastafarian religion.

Rastas, who object to shaving and cutting hair, wear their hair in long braids called dreadlocks – a symbolic connection with the Ethiopian lion. They are vegetarians who prefer natural foods and many of them smoke ganga, locally grown marijuana. Not everyone wearing dreadlocks is a Rasta and most 'real' Rastas are congenial, generally preferring the country to urban areas.

Ocho Rios

The original Spanish name for Ocho Rios was Las Chorreras –

The Waterfalls – an appropriate name for a port situated at the base of lush mountains where rivers and streams spill into the sea. A former fishing village, Ocho Rios has been developed as a tourist destination with high-rise hotels and condominiums lining the beaches to the east of Ocho Rios Bay. The local population numbers about 11,000 and residents speak an English-based patois. Ocho Rios Bay contains two piers – the Reynolds Pier and the new cruise ship pier which is joined by a jetty to shore where telephones, tourist information and a handful of shops are located.

Getting Around

The cruise lines offer organized excursions to the major attractions, or you can hire a taxi. A visitor information booth is located in the terminal building and the taxi fares to various destinations are posted nearby. A dispatcher is also stationed there and, upon telling him where you want to go, he will hail you a driver whose car will carry the red Public Passenger Vehicle (PPV) license plates. If you want to visit a number of destinations, negotiate the fare with your driver before getting in. The fare is per taxi, so travelling in groups of four is the most economical. Some sample taxi tour rates for one to four persons: Dunn's River Falls – $20; Prospect Plantation – $30.

Shopping – Jamaica offers good buys in duty-free goods and great bargains in locally produced clothing, wood carvings, coffee and rum. Beautiful, hand-carved walking sticks can be bought for $15 and tee shirts screened with unique Jamaican designs sell for as little as $5. More expensive are the beautiful batik cottons and silks. The exchange rate is approximately 70 Jamaican dollars for 1 US dollar, but there's no need to exchange money because American currency and credit cards are widely accepted.

Within walking distance of the cruise ship pier are the **1 Taj Mahal Centre** and **2 Soni's Plaza**, or you can take a shopping shuttle which costs $2 per person. In between are the **3 Old Market Craft Shoppes** and **4 Craft Park**, where local artisans sell their wares. Excellent arts and crafts can also be bought at the Dunn's River Falls marketplace, and paintings by acclaimed Jamaican artists are on display at the **9 Harmony Hall Gallery**, five miles east of the cruise port.

Best Beaches – Beautiful white sand beaches line the shoreline east of Ocho Rios Bay. Most of these are backed by hotels and have controlled access to pro-

(Above) A hotel resort at Turtle Beach. (Below) The waterfront at Ocho Rios.

tect tourists from pedlars. The admission fee is usually $1.00 per person. Closest to the pier is Turtle Beach, and an excellent beach lies on the other side of The Point at Mallards Bay.

Dive & Snorkel Sites – excursions are available out of Ocho Rios to nearby shallow coral gardens, some of which have been damaged in recent years by hurricanes. Serious divers recommend going deeper to see an abundance of coral and sponge life. Wall diving is popular at Runaway Bay.

Sandal's Golf & Country Club, overlooking Mallards Bay, is considered one of the most scenic in Jamaica, situated 700 feet up into the mountains. This 18-hole par-71 course was designed by P.K. Sanders and totals 6,500 yards.

Turtle Beach is a short walk from the cruise pier.

Local Attractions

A botanical garden and bird sanctuary, **5 Shaw Park Gardens'** hillside location provides panoramic views in a tropical setting. The Coyaba River flows through **6 Coyaba Garden** where riverside paths and boardwalks lead past waterfalls and pools filled with koi carp and turtles. The museum contains pre-Columbian artifacts and the gallery displays creative works by Jamaicans.

Area Highlights

7 Fern Gully, a former riverbed that went dry following an earthquake, is a three-mile stretch of road that winds into the Blue Mountains and leads, eventually, to Kingston on the other side of the island. The many species of fern that grow in this gully form a lush canopy for vehicles passing beneath it.

One of Jamaica's most popular attractions, **8 Dunn's River Falls** consist of clear mountain water flowing seaward across a tiered limestone bed. Visitors are charged $5 US to enter the park area, which includes a guided climb up this stunning set of falls. Guides lead visitors, in single file, along a known route. Operators of the park are fairly insistent you remain part of a guided climb to prevent personal injury. For an additional $5, a guide will hold your camera and other belongings as you scramble up the falls. A pair of running shoes or aqua socks (which can be rented) are recommended for the climb over slippery stones and rushing, knee-

Shore Excursions

Ocho Rios &
Montego Bay

Ocho Rios and Montego Bay are located about 50 miles apart on Jamaica's north coast, and several area attractions are covered by ship-organized excursions from either port, namely Dunn's River Falls, Dolphin Cove and river rafting on the **Martha Brae**, which lies between Montego Bay and Ocho Rios. On bamboo rafts carrying two people, the raft man uses a pole to guide the raft gently downstream past bamboo groves and chirping birds. The drive from Ocho Rios to Martha Brae takes 1.5 hours along the winding coastal highway, and the river ride is just over an hour in length. An organized shore excursion lasts about five hours, often with a stop at Columbus Park, near Discovery Bay, where Columbus first landed at Jamaica. Other notable places along this stretch of coastline include Nine Miles village, the birthplace and gravesite of Bob Marley, and the 18th-century Georgian town of Falmouth near the mouth of the Martha Brae, about 20 miles east of Montego Bay.

Excursions specific to **Ocho Rios** include visits to Prospect Plantation and Coyaba Gardens. Other organized excursions include ocean and river kayaking, and biking expeditions.

Montego Bay excursions include tours of Appleton Rum Estate or of a local great house (see box on page 183). Beach time can be enjoyed at nearby Negril's Margaritaville, which features a 100-foot waterslide, or at Doctor's Cave Beach, the latter included with snorkeling excursions at Montego Bay Marine Park.

Both ports feature party boat excursions, horseback riding, river tubing and a rainforest canopy adventure.

deep water. Dunn's Falls are about 1.5 miles by road from Ocho Rios and can also be reached by boat, a popular excursion being one of the party cruises that depart the cruise pier for a relaxing yacht ride to the mouth of Dunn's River and back, with time allowed for climbing the falls. Mountain biking excursions are also popular and involve an uphill drive followed by a downhill bike ride from Murphy Hill to Dunn's River Falls. Dolphin

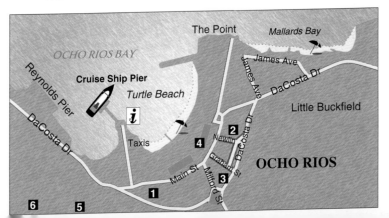

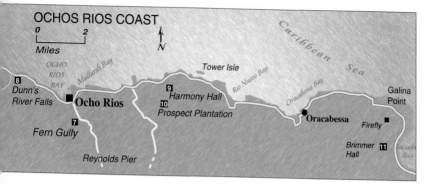

OCHOS RIOS COAST

0   2

Miles

N

Caribbean Sea

Tower Isle

Rio Nuevo Bay

Oracabessa Bay

OCHO RIOS BAY

Mallards Bay

8 Dunn's River Falls

Ocho Rios

9 Harmony Hall

10 Prospect Plantation

Oracabessa

Galina Point

Firefly

7 Fern Gully

Reynolds Pier

Brimmer 11 Hall

Saccabus Bay

Cove, located beside Dunn's River Falls, is a new attraction where visitors can feed, pet and swim with dolphins.

Anyone interested in Jamaican folk art will enjoy a visit to **9 Harmony Hall**, a restored Victorian great house. Set on a small plantation estate four miles east of Ocho Rios, it contains an art gallery, craft and book shops, boutique and restaurant.

10 Prospect Plantation is a working plantation estate where guides take visitors on tractor-drawn jitneys past various flora and agricultural crops including bananas, sugarcane and coffee, as well as the White River Gorge and Sir Harold's Viewpoint, where Cuba, about 100 miles due north, can be seen on a clear day. Horseback tours are also available on each of three varied trails that traverse the 900 acres of grounds, which also contain a miniature golf course and a gift shop selling local crafts and souvenirs.

About 10 miles east of Prospect Plantation, **11 Brimmer Hall Plantation** is another working plantation providing tours by tractor-drawn jitney. The beautiful grounds contain an 18th-century great house open for viewing, as well as a swimming pool, bar and shops.

Firefly, Noel Coward's "earthly paradise" set atop a plateau with a dramatic view of the surf pounding into Saccabus Bay, was the famous playwright's home for the last 25 years of his life and the place where he wrote some of his most celebrated works. Screen stars and British royalty would

River rafting on the Martha Brae.

The tiered falls at Dunn's River.

come to visit, but when Coward died in 1973 he asked that no fuss be made, and the site of his grave was where he often sat with friends sipping a pre-dinner cocktail while looking out to sea. Coward's home and contents were bequeathed to Jamaica in 1975 and restored as a museum run on behalf of the National Heritage Trust by Island Outpost, which is owned by Chris Blackwell, the multi-millionaire founder of Island Records. However, Firefly failed to attract enough visitors and in early 2000 plans were made to auction many of Coward's belongings and rent the property out for private receptions.

At **Oracabessa** ('Golden Head' in Spanish), the road winds past Goldeneye, an estate overlooking a private cove. This was the former winter retreat of the late Ian Fleming, who wrote his James Bond novels at this idyllic location. Noel Coward referred to Fleming's rather plain U-shaped house as the, "Goldeneye, nose and throat clinic," while describing the cove's crescent beach of dazzling white sand as "unbelievable." Chris Blackwell's Island Outpost now owns the property and has converted it into a boutique-style luxury resort.

Montego Bay

Jamaica's second-largest city, Montego Bay is one of the Caribbean's most popular resorts, beautifully situated on a beach-lined bay surrounded by green hills. A commercial center and shipping port, it's a growing city of over 70,000 residents, many of whom live in shanty towns on the outskirts. On the lower slopes of the Miranda Hills are luxury hotels set in manicured grounds.

Getting Around

The cruise ships dock at Freeport, about three miles from downtown. An information booth and telephones are situated on the dock. Nearby is the Montego Freeport duty-free shopping area. The taxi fare into town is about $12 for up to four people, and only JUTA (Jamaica Union of Travellers Association) taxis and mini-vans should be rented.

Best Beaches – Montego Bay Marine Park encompasses all of Montego Bay, its office located at Pier 1. Beautiful beaches and good snorkel sites lie within the park's boundaries. **Doctor's Cave Beach**, located just north of the town center, is Montego Bay's most celebrated beach. Named after Dr. Alexander McCatty who donated the beach to a local bathing club, the beach was originally accessible through a small cave, destroyed by a hurricane in 1932. Today it's Montego Bay's most popular beach, with an entry charge that includes change facilities. Other good stretches of sand are found at **Walter Fletcher Beach**, south of Doctor's Cave, and at **Cornwall Beach**, which lies directly north of Doctor's Cave . Coral sea gardens can be viewed by glass-bottom boat in the clear, sheltered waters of Doctor's Cave, which offers good snorkeling for beginners. Unity

Famous beaches lure cruise visitors to Montego Bay.

Hall at the eastern end of Montego Bay Marine Park, is another premier snorkel site with plenty of coral and juvenile fish inside the reef that lies in front of Sahara De La Mer Hotel.

Golf – A championship golf course (7,130 yards, par 72) is located at the **Half Moon Golf Course**, near the sea on the eastern outskirts of Montego Bay. The White Witch course (6,820 yards, par 71) is part of the Ritz-Carlton Rose Hall Resort.

Local Sights & Shopping – The city's business district includes a few historic landmarks, most of them situated on or near **1 Sam Sharpe Square** – named for a Jamaican hero who was hanged in 1831 for leading a slave revolt. On the southwest side of the square stands the Court House, an early-19th century colonial building. The Cage, a small building of the same period on the square's northeast corner, was used for detaining runaway slaves. Nearby, on Church Street, are a number of restored Georgian

Shore Excursions

Montego Bay

Shore excursions from Montego Bay include visits to Dunn's River Falls, Dolphin Cove and river rafting on the Martha Brae (see page 179), as well as other attractions, such as Greenwood Great House and Rose Hall Great House. **Greenwood Great House**, located 16 miles east of Montego Bay, was built by relatives of poet Elizabeth Barrett Browning, and the stately mansion is furnished with antiques and contains a rare-book library. A tour of Greenwood gives visitors an inside look at the privileged lives once enjoyed by plantation owners.

Rose Hall, a British mansion built in 1770, lies about 10 miles east of Montego Bay and is Jamaica's most famous great house thanks to a legendary mistress by the name of Annie Palmer. She lived here around 1820 and is said to have murdered three husbands and numerous slave lovers whom she controlled through witchcraft. According to one version of the legend, she was finally murdered by a lover who felt he was destined to be next on Annie's hit list.

buildings including St. James's Parish Church which was rebuilt after suffering major damage in a 1957 earthquake. South of Church Street, near the water, is the colorful **2 Crafts Market**. A few blocks to the north, along the waterfront, stand the remains of Fort Montego which was built by the British in 1752. From here Gloucester Avenue, the main shopping thoroughfare, wends north past the hotel strip.

Area Attractions – **3 Rockland Bird Sanctuary**, nine miles south of Montego Bay, is popular with visitors, as is the **4 Appleton Estate Express**, a train that departs daily from Montego Bay and heads into Cockpit Country, location of the famous Appleton Rum Distillery and the Ipswich Caves with their limestone stalagmites and stalactites.

East of Montego Bay are Rose Hall, Greenwood Great House and the Martha Brae River (see box above).

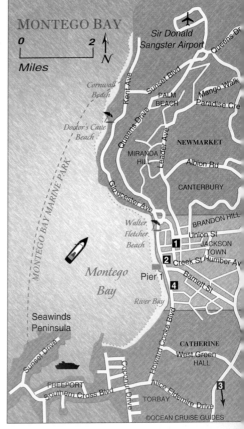

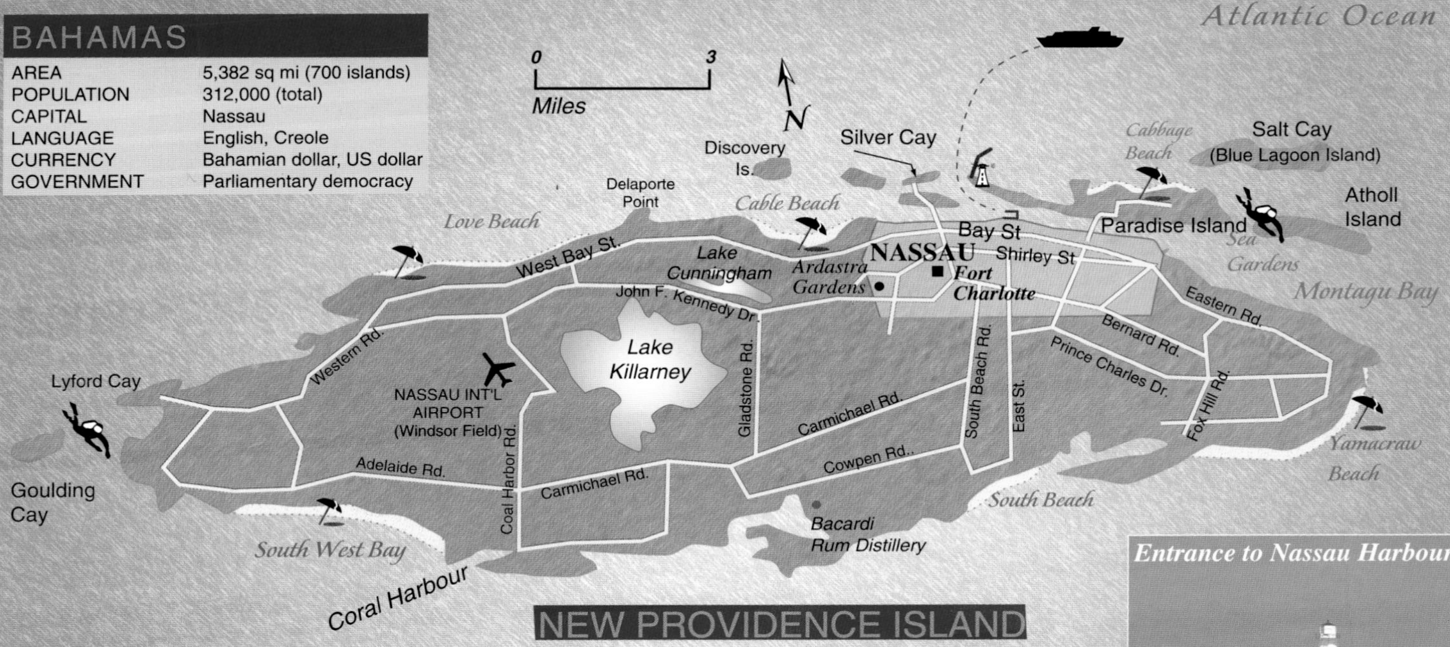

Entrance to Nassau Harbour.

NEW PROVIDENCE ISLAND

Atlantic Ocean

Salt Cay
(Blue Lagoon Island)

Atholl Island

Montague Bay

Sea Gardens

Cabbage Beach

Paradise Island

Yamacrau Beach

Eastern Rd.

Fox Hill Rd.

Bernard Rd.

Prince Charles Dr.

South Beach

Bay St.

Shirley St.

East St.

South Beach Rd.

NASSAU

Fort Charlotte

Silver Cay

Ardastra Gardens

Carmichael Rd.

Cowpen Rd.

Bacardi Rum Distillery

Discovery Is.

N

Cable Beach

Lake Cunningham

Gladstone Rd.

John F. Kennedy Dr.

Lake Killarney

Carmichael Rd.

Delaporte Point

West Bay St.

Coal Harbor Rd.

Love Beach

NASSAU INT'L AIRPORT
(Windsor Field)

Adelaide Rd.

Coral Harbour

Western Rd.

South West Bay

Lyford Cay

Goulding Cay

0   3
Miles

BAHAMAS

AREA	5,382 sq mi (700 islands)
POPULATION	312,000 (total)
CAPITAL	Nassau
LANGUAGE	English, Creole
CURRENCY	Bahamian dollar, US dollar
GOVERNMENT	Parliamentary democracy

CHAPTER SEVEN

BAHAMAS
& GRAND TURK

Once a haven for pirates, the Bahamas seem the perfect setting for actor Johnny Depp, a.k.a. Captain Jack Sparrow, who owns a private island off Exuma. There are some 700 islands and islets in the island chain, which lies 50 miles off the coast of Florida and extends for 600 miles in a southeasterly direction toward Haiti. The **Turks and Caicos Islands**, lying southeast of the Bahamas, are geographically part of the archipelago but have been separately administered by Great Britain since 1848. Small and snakelike in shape, these limestone islands lie low on the horizon and are surrounded by clear turquoise seas filled with coral gardens and sunken wrecks. A diver's delight, they were treacherous waterways in the days of piracy when buccaneers, intent on pillage, would lure passing ships into these shallow reef-strewn waters. Spanish galleons laden with gold and silver had to pass through the Straits of Florida and around the top end of the Bahamas on their way back to Spain, so they became easy prey for pirates like the notorious Blackbeard who would escape Spanish convoys by retreating to the port of Nassau on New Providence Island.

Two centuries earlier these far-flung islands were home to a much different breed of seafaring people – a tribe of Arawaks called Lucayans who lived here in fishing villages. Travelling by canoe, the Lucayans had migrated from South America to these remote and riverless islands to avoid the aggressive Carib tribes. Their solitude was shattered in 1492 by the arrival of an unexpected visitor.

The Bahamian island of Guanahani was where Christopher Columbus first stepped ashore in the New World after crossing the Atlantic into the unknown. Relieved to have reached what he assumed were the islands of Asia, Columbus called the island San Salvador and claimed it for Spain. The Spanish, whose goal was to find gold and other treasures, were not interested in colonizing these islands situated in what Columbus called a baja mar (shallow sea). They did, however, enslave the Lucayans to work in the gold mines on Hispaniola, and the first inhabitants of the Bahamas were soon exterminated.

The islands remained deserted until the mid-17th century when a group of English Puritans arrived from Bermuda. They settled at Preacher's Cave on Eleuthera and tried to scratch out an existence, but conditions were harsh. The Bahamas rise from a vast submarine plateau, their brackish lakes connected with the ocean by underground passages, and rainfall or desalinization are the main sources of fresh water. The settlers on Eleuthera slowly cultivated the thin soil for growing cotton, tobacco and vegetables. Others moved to the Turks and Caicos and began extracting salt, which supplied the cod-fishing fleet of New England. Another settlement was established on New Providence Island. Originally called Charles Towne, it was renamed Nassau in 1695 for England's King William III, a member of Europe's Orange-Nassau dynasty. The town became a pirate haven and in 1718 the British government dispatched Captain Woodes Rogers to Nassau to restore order. The town was so squalid he chose to live on board his ship while overseeing the cleaning of streets and the manning of local forts. Woodes Rogers also restructured

the island government and issued a proclamation guaranteeing freedom for runaway slaves fleeing the American colonies, who would stow away on Bahama-bound merchant ships. When the American Revolutionary War broke out in 1776, hundreds of loyalists also fled to the Bahamas. Over time, the islands' inhabitants developed a unique culture of Goombay music, Junkanoo dance and straw crafts, but the influence of British colonialism remained strong, with English nobility maintaining beautiful homes and gardens on New Providence Island. Wealthy Americans also began vacationing in the Bahamas in the 1860s, arriving by steamship from New York. In 1900, the Florida railroad baron Henry Flagler built the huge Colonial Hotel in Nassau and offered steamship service from Miami, but it wasn't until after World War II that tourism flourished, as did social activism. Black Bahamians began to challenge the ruling white party and in 1972 a newly elected Bahamian government began negotiating independence from Britain. The following year, Britain's Prince Charles presented the new Constitution of the Bahamas to Prime Minister Pindling and the British crown colony became the Commonwealth of the Bahamas. The Turks and Caicos, which had been linked to the Bahamas since 1962, became a separate crown colony of Britain.

Fort Fincastle has overlooked Nassau Harbour since 1793.

Nassau

Nassau, one of the busiest cruise ports in the world, is a vibrant city with a population of about 150,000. Its pink buildings and white gloved bobbies are part of the British colonial charm of this bustling port.

Getting Around

Nassau is fairly compact and the major historical sights can be seen on foot, although there is some uphill walking. Another option is to see the local sights by horse-drawn buggy. These can be hired in Rawson Square and the usual fare is $10 for a half-hour ride, but settle on a price before climbing in.

Jitney buses to Cable Beach leave from the British Colonial Hilton every 10 or 15 minutes and the fare is $1 per person. A one-hour island tour by taxi costs $30 to $40. The water taxi to Paradise Island is $3 each way and takes about half an hour (plus a ten-minute walk if you're heading to the Atlantis Resort). A cab ride, which is much faster, costs $4 per person each way, plus a $2 bridge toll. Taxi drivers expect a tip.

Rental cars and scooters are available in Nassau. Driving is on the left and helmets are mandatory for people on scooters.

Nassau is one of the Caribbean's busiest cruise ports.

Shopping – Nassau and Hong Kong have been touted as the two best places in the world to buy watches. Other duty-free items to look for in Nassau include jewelry, crystal, china, leather and liquor. Bay Street (from East Street to the British Colonial Hilton) is where the majority of shops are located, as is the famous Straw Market where handcrafted baskets and other items are sold. The Bahamian Dollar is on par with the U.S. dollar and the two currencies are used interchangeably. When paying with American money, ask for your change in the same currency or you'll receive Bahamian currency. Travellers checks and credit cards are widely accepted.

Beaches – Closest to the cruise pier and within easy walking distance is the beach in front of the British Colonial Hilton. West of downtown is lovely Cable Beach (which can be reached by jitney bus), while a few miles farther along Bay Street is secluded Love Beach, which offers ideal snorkeling about a mile off the shore. Among the excellent beaches on Paradise Island is popular

Horse-drawn buggy is a popular way to tour the streets of Nassau.

Cabbage Beach, which can be accessed by a public walkway, but this beach can be busy and on windy days the seas can get rough (the seas are calmer and the crowds fewer at Cable Beach). The beautiful beaches of Blue Lagoon Island can be reached by 30-minute boat shuttles from Paradise Island (Dolphin Encounter provides a shuttle for its clients) .

Dive & Snorkel Sites – Excellent snorkeling and diving can be enjoyed in the waters off Nassau, and several dive operators are located on Paradise Island and in Nassau at the foot the Paradise Island bridge. Local snorkeling sites include Athol Island's Sea Gardens (see page 185) and Love Beach, where a reef lies about a mile offshore. Divers can explore numerous wrecks immediately north of Paradise Island. About 10 miles east of Nassau is the famous Lost Blue Hole – a massive oceanic hole which begins at 45 feet and contains coral heads, moray eels and other creatures.

The southwest coast also has great snorkeling and diving, and many a filmmaker has shot underwater footage here. The shallow reef areas at Goulding Cay contain magnificent elkhorn coral – featured in such movies as 20,000 Leagues Under the Sea and Splash. A number of James Bond flicks have also been filmed in these waters, including *Thunderball, For Your Eyes Only* and *Never Say Never Again*. Sunken movie props include the Vulcan Bomber and Tears of Allah freighter, both of which are popular dive sites. Natural attractions include Tunnel Wall, Southwest Reef and Shark Wall, a drop-off along the edge of a deep-water abyss called Tongue of the Ocean.

Golf – There are plenty of golf courses to choose from in the Nassau area, a popular one for cruise passengers being the par-72 course at the Dick Wilson-designed Paradise Island Golf & Country Club (par 72, 6,776 yards). The new course at

Shore Excursions

Bahamas

Shore Excursions – Ship-organized tours include a 25-minute boat ride across Nassau Harbour to the private island of Blackbeard's Cay for a beach break with swimming and snorkeling. Other snorkeling excursions head to Pearl Island and include a stingray encounter. City tours are offered, as are visits to Ardastra Gardens or to Atlantis on Paradise Island.

Sheraton Cable Beach Resort (formerly Radisson) was designed by Jim McCormick (par 72).

Local Attractions

The **1 Tourist Office** is located right beside the cruise pier on the edge of **2 Rawson Square**, named for a former governor. Horse-drawn buggies wait here for hire.

Clustered around a statue of Queen Victoria in **3 Parliament Square** are the Houses of Parliament, built from 1805 to 1813. When facing Queen Victoria's statue, the House of Assembly is to the right, the Senate Building is straight ahead and the old Colonial Secretary's Office and Treasury is to the left. South of these buildings are the Supreme Court and Garden of Remembrance with a cenotaph.

The octagonal-shaped **4 Public Library**, once used as a prison and complete with dungeons, stands at the corner of Parliament and Shirley Streets.

5 The **Royal Victorian Gardens** offer a shady spot to rest before tackling the **6**

Queen's Staircase where 66 steps, cut into a limestone gorge by slave laborers in the 18th century, lead up the hill to **7 Fort Fincastle**. The fort was built in 1793 to ward off Spanish invasions. Nearby is a water tower where visitors can take the stairs or an elevator (for a small charge) to the top for a commanding view of the fort and harbor beyond.

8 Government House is one of Nassau's most photographed buildings with a statue of Columbus standing on the steps leading to its front entrance. The building isn't open to the public and sentry guards man the gates on either side of the grounds, but they will allow visitors to walk through. Edward, Duke of Windsor, resided here when he was governor of the Bahamas from 1940 to 1945. A former King of England who renounced his throne to marry American divorcee Wallis Warfield Simpson, the Duke was suspected of either inadvertently or inten-

The beach in front of the British Colonial Hilton.

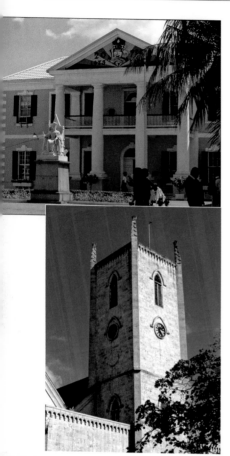

tionally leaking Allied secrets to the Nazis. To keep him a safe distance from the war raging in Europe, the British government sent him to the Bahamas in July, 1940.

9 **St. Andrew's Presbyterian Church**, begun in 1810, stands at the corner of Duke and Market streets, and **10** **Christ Church Cathedral** at the corner of George and King streets was built in 1837. Across the street is the **11** **Pirates of Nassau Interactive Museum** where exhibits include dioramas depicting pirates battling on the high seas.

Dominating the waterfront, the British Colonial Hilton stands on the former site of Fort Nassau and was built soon after the original Colonial Hotel was destroyed by fire in 1929. Since acquired as a Hilton property, this historic landmark has undergone a $68-million restoration and renovation.

(Top) Parliament Square.

(Left) Christ Church Cathedral.

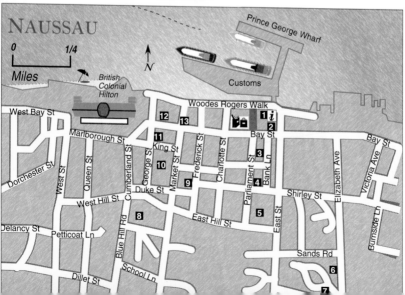

12 **Vendue House**, which stands on the site of a former slave market, dates back to 1769 and was rebuilt in the early 1900s. It now houses the Pompey Museum of Slavery and Emancipation, opened in 1992 as part of the Columbus Quincentennial. The museum is named after a slave and Bahamian hero who lived on Exuma.

The **13** **Straw Market**, in the heart of Nassau's shopping district, is a traditional Bahamian market where shoppers bargain with the vendors for items which include jewelry, t-shirts, carvings and, of course, an array of straw woven products. Most of the more-than-500 vendors are women whose stalls and craft skills have been passed down through generations. In fall 2001, a fire swept through the Straw Market and a temporary market was opened on the block between the Pompey Museum on Bay Street and Woodes Rogers Walk.

(Above) The main entrance to Government House.

(Below) The Queens Staircase leads to Fort Fincastle.

Island Attractions

About a mile west of downtown Nassau stands **Fort Charlotte**. Built on a hilltop from 1787-94, this imposing fort features a moat and dungeons, and provides impressive views. Nearby are **Ardastra Gardens and Zoo**, a 5-1/2 acre nature park which is home to nearly 300 animals in a tropical garden setting. Amid the lush foliage there live peacocks, parrots, monkeys and some famous marching flamingos, featured here since the 1950s. They were initially trained by a Jamaican horticulturist, and sub-

sequent trainers have simply introduced a few young flamingos at a time who follow the veteran members of the group and quickly learn the maneuvers.

Beach-lined **Paradise Island** was once a playground for the wealthy, and the Astors, Rockefellers and Vanderbilts all built winter residences here in the 1920s. Called Hog Island, its name was changed to Paradise Island when Huntington Hartford bought the island and developed it into a holiday resort. A unique attraction is the Versailles Gardens and French Cloister, a ruined 14th-century Augustinian

monastery transported from France. The island's modern resorts include Atlantis, a huge water-themed resort owned since 1994 by the South African developer Sol Kerzner, which features a spectacular water park for the exclusive use of the resort's guests. The Atlantis casino, shops and lobbies are open to the public, and a $29 ticket will get you into Digs Underground Aquariums.

Thirty-minute boat shuttles are available from Paradise Island ($20 round trip) to **Blue Lagoon Island**, popular with day trippers and where Dolphin Encounters offer participants the chance to pet and hug an Atlantic bottle-nose dolphin in a controlled setting.

The waters surrounding **Athol Island**, lying east of Paradise Island, are referred to as the Sea Gardens, for they are filled with shipwrecks, coral colonies and schools of tropical fish. Seaworld Explorer's tours begin at Captain Nemo's Dock (just east of the cruise pier) with a 20-minute boat tour of Nassau Harbor en route to Athol Island, where passengers transfer to an observatory vessel in which they sit five feet beneath the water's surface for a submarine-like viewing experience.

Atlantis Submarine, based at the west end of New Providence Island, departs from West Bay near Lyford Cay for deep-water viewing of the area's renowned reefs and wrecks.

(Above left) Vendue House.
(Left) A sentry at Government House.

Freeport

The cruise port of Freeport/Lucaya, located on Grand Bahama Island, was developed as a tourist destination and world-class dive resort in the 1950s and '60s. The island, 75 miles long by 15 miles wide, is an exposed portion of the Little Bahama Bank, where a combination of shallow waters and deep chasms creates a diver's paradise of shallow, medium-depth and deep reefs as well as dramatic drop-offs.

Beaches, nature parks, golf courses, gambling casinos, duty-free shopping and every conceivable water sport await visitors to Freeport. Cars, mopeds and bicycles can be rented, and metered taxis are available at the cruise terminal which is about five miles from town. Local attractions include the Garden of the Groves, an 11-acre botanical garden containing the Grand Bahama Museum, and the Rand Memorial Nature Center, 100 acres of natural woodland containing trails and a bird sanctuary. Lucaya National Park, 25 miles west of Freeport, contains an underground system of limestone caverns, shady trails, pine forests, a mangrove creek and ocean beach.

Shopping can be enjoyed at the International Bazaar & Strawmarket and at the Port Lucaya Marketplace & Marina. At the Perfume Factory, a restored 18th-century Bahamian mansion located next to the International Bazaar, shoppers can mix, bottle, label and name their own fragrance.

Beaches abound on Grand Bahama and they line the shores of Freeport and Lucaya. Those with hotels and facilities include Xanadu Beach (about five miles from the cruise pier) and Lucaya Beach, located across the street from the Port Lucaya Marketplace.

The Underwater Explorers Society (UNEXSO), a famous scuba diving school, is located at Port Lucaya. Their organized dives include a daily trip to Shark Junction, where a dozen or more Caribbean Reef Sharks often appear and feed on bait. Also popular is The Dolphin Experience at Sanctuary Bay, the

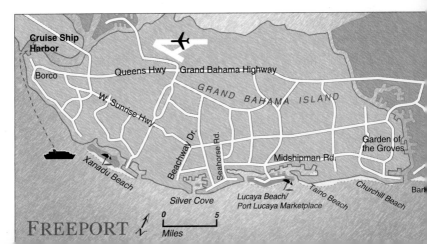

world's largest dolphin sanctuary, where Atlantic Bottlenose dolphins swim with divers both in a sheltered lagoon and in open water along an offshore coral reef. For wild dolphin encounters, White Sand Ridge off the northwest point of the island is a good place to interact with a resident pod of Spotted Dolphins that frequent these waters. A number of local dive boats offer snorkel trips to this area.

Shore excursions include scuba diving, snorkeling, dolphin encounters, bottom fishing and a glass-bottom boat ride. Kayaking in Lucaya National Park, biking, and touring by jeep are also offered.

Golfers can choose from three PGA-rated courses – Princess Ruby Golf Course, Princess Emerald Golf Course, and the Dick Wilson-designed Lucayan Golf & Country Club (one of the top three courses in the Caribbean and the oldest club in the Bahamas).

Grand Turk

The capital of the Turks and Caicos, which consist of more than 30 cays and islands (six of which are inhabited), Grand Turk is home to a new cruise port that opened in 2006 at the island's south end. The island, six miles long and a mile wide, was chosen for its deepwater port, colonial charm and natural attractions of sugary beaches and fabulous snorkeling and diving. The cruise terminal provides direct access to a private beach and a supersized swimming pool with changing

Shore Excursions

Grand Turk

Shore Excursions include a trolley train ride to Governor's Beach for a beach break with snorkeling. Scuba diving (both beginner and certified) are offered, as are stingray encounters, blue water fishing, aqua boats, power snorkel, snuba, semi-submersible glass-bottom boat rides and sea trek helmet diving (walking on the sea floor). Guided bike tours, horseback riding, horse-and-buggy rides, and 4X4 safaris are also featured.

rooms and watersports equipment for rent. Facilities at the terminal's welcome center include the newest outpost of Jimmy Buffet's Margaritaville restaurant, as well as duty-free shopping, an internet cafe, and car, jeep and bicycle rentals. The local buses provide a continuous loop service around the island, and you can jump off and on at several stops.

Cockburn Town has been the seat of government since 1766 and its colonial architecture includes the **Turks & Caicos National Museum** with displays of artifacts recovered from the **Molasses Reef Wreck** (1513) – one of the oldest known shipwrecks in the New World. Some locals claim that Christopher Columbus made his first landfall on Grand Turk (a stone monument attests to this), while most historians believe that Ponce de Leon was the first to visit these islands in 1512. One historic landing that is not open to debate is that of John Glenn, the first

What's In A Name?

Some say the Turks & Caicos were named for the indigenous Turk's Head cactus (which resembles a fez) and for *caya hico*, which means 'string of islands' in Lucayan. Others say the name Turk often meant 'pirate' during the days of the Ottoman Empire. Mail sent to the islands is sometimes misdirected to Turkey but eventually arrives at its destination, even when mistakenly addressed to the Turks & Tacos!

American astronaut to orbit the earth, whose space capsule splashed down in local waters on February 20, 1962. From the early 1950s until 1984, a U.S. Air Force tracking station operated on the island's west coast, and the remains of a U.S. Navy base are located at the island's northeast point, where a lighthouse stands. Modern-day tourism began on the Turks & Caicos in the 1960s, when several millionaires (including Teddy Roosevelt III) leased land from the British government and built a small airstrip for their private planes and a

Grand Turk's cruise terminal has a beach and other facilities.

deep-water anchorage for their yachts. Count Ferdinand Czernin of the Austro-Hungarian empire acquired Pine Cay, which after his death became the exclusive Meridian Club resort.

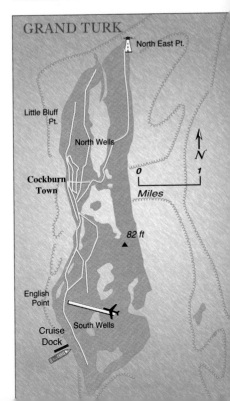

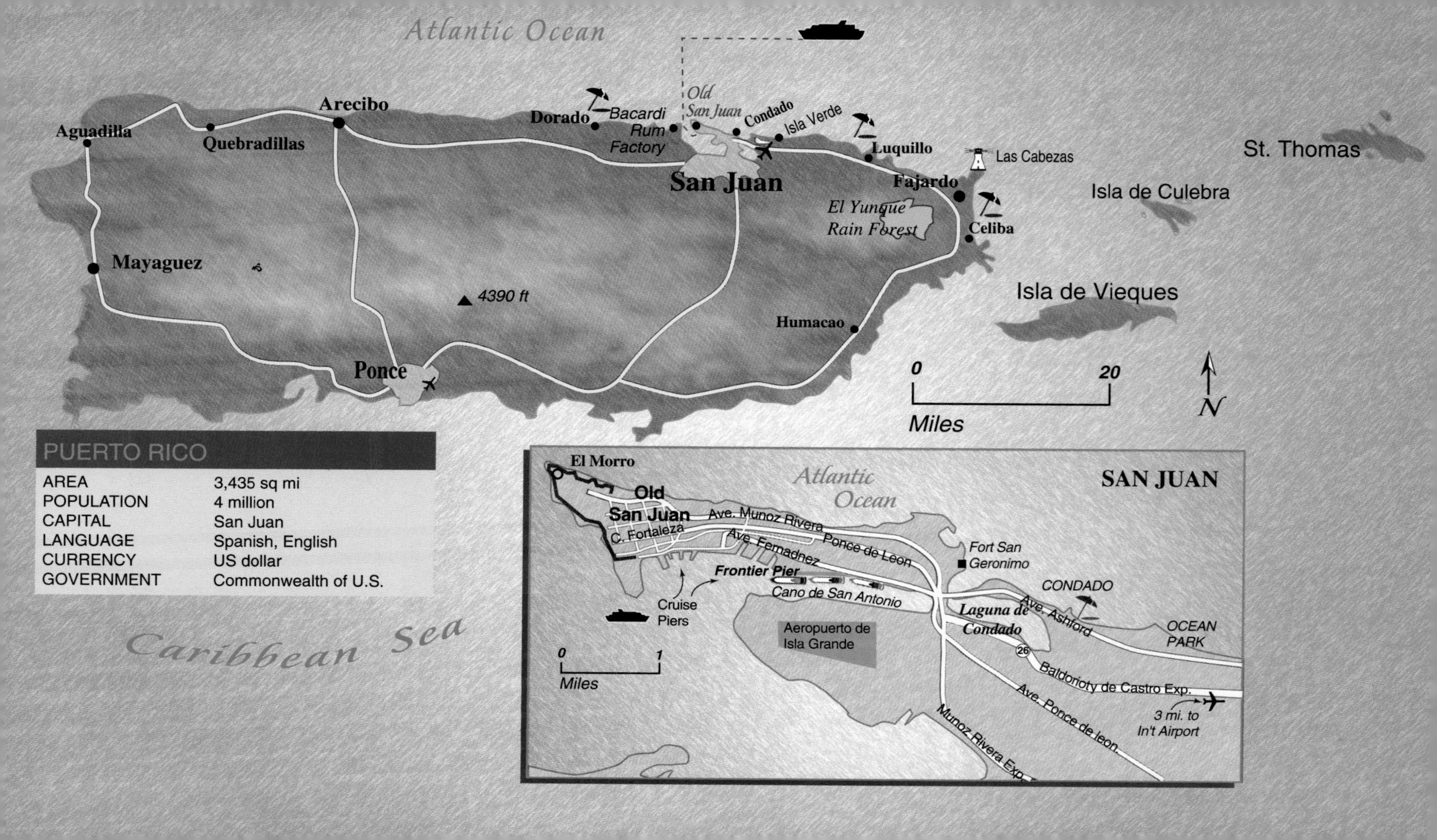

Atlantic Ocean

St. Thomas

Isla de Culebra

Isla de Vieques

Las Cabezas

Ceiba

Fajardo

Luquillo

Isla Verde

Condado

El Yunque
Rain Forest

Old
San Juan

San Juan

Dorado

Bacardi
Rum
Factory

Humacao

Arecibo

Quebradillas

Mayaguez

Aguadilla

▲ 4390 ft

Ponce

Caribbean Sea

N

Miles

0   20

PUERTO RICO

AREA	3,435 sq mi
POPULATION	4 million
CAPITAL	San Juan
LANGUAGE	Spanish, English
CURRENCY	US dollar
GOVERNMENT	Commonwealth of U.S.

SAN JUAN

OCEAN
PARK

3 mi. to
Int Airport

CONDADO

Ave. Ashford

Baldorioty de Castro Exp.

Laguna de
Condado

Ave. Ponce de Leon

Fort San
Geronimo

Munoz Rivera Exp.

Atlantic
Ocean

Ave. Munoz Rivera

Ave. Ponce de Leon

Ave. Fernandez

Frontier Pier

Cano de San Antonio

Aeropuerto de
Isla Grande

Old
San Juan

El Morro

C. Fortaleza

Cruise
Piers

Miles
0   1

CHAPTER EIGHT

SAN JUAN

San Juan, a busy base port for Caribbean cruises, is also one of the best-preserved ports of colonial Spain. The walled city of Old San Juan, the oldest Spanish settlement under American sovereignty, is a World Heritage Site. Its cobblestone streets are paved with ballast from Spanish galleons and the impenetrable citadel of El Morro was once a symbol of Spanish domination in the Caribbean. In contrast to the historic feel of Old San Juan is the nearby Condado area, where modern high-rise hotels line the beaches and a sizzling night life can be enjoyed in the night clubs and casinos.

Puerto Ricans number about four million and they refer to their Connecticut-sized island as the 'continent' of Puerto Rico due to its geographical diversity. Mountains here soar to over 4,000 feet and vegetation ranges from lush rainforests to low-lying mangrove swamps. Beautiful beaches line much of the coastline and, in the northwest, an extensive system of caves has been carved by one of the world's largest underground rivers.

Puerto Rico is a self-governing Commonwealth of the United States and its infrastructure includes a major airport, well-maintained roads, luxury resorts and championship golf courses.

Industrialization came to Puerto Rico in the 1940s when Operation Bootstrap was introduced and its tax exemptions promoted American investment. Manufacturing, pharmaceuticals and the production of high-tech equipment are now major industries, along with agriculture and tourism.

While Puerto Rico's per capita income is only $8,000 a year (the highest in Latin America), Puerto Ricans say they are among the happiest people in the world thanks to their extended family ties and a readiness to celebrate life, with an easy warmth among even strangers. Few deny that the island's ties to America are beneficial and worth preserving, but an ongoing debate revolves around the 'statehood versus status quo' issue. The electorate is fairly evenly divided, with those supporting the status quo concerned about preserving their Spanish culture. Those supporting statehood accuse their opponents of wanting to have their cake and eat it too. A small minority support independence, a movement that began in the last century when Puerto Rican statesman and journalist Luis Munoz Rivera led a growing demand for self government, which resulted in Spain granting its Caribbean colony some autonomy in February 1898. However, the

The massive fortress El Morro looms at the entrance to San Juan Harbor.

Spanish-American war began a few months later and American troops soon occupied the island. By December, Spain had ceded Puerto Rico to the United States.

Puerto Rico remained under direct military rule until 1900 when Congress passed the Foraker Act, setting up a local administration with a U.S. Governor, an elected house of delegates and an upper chamber appointed by the U.S. President. In 1917 the Jones Act pronounced Puerto Rico a U.S. territory, granting its occupants U.S. citizenship and increased internal self-government. In 1948 Puerto Ricans elected their governor for the first time, and in 1952 the Commonwealth of Puerto Rico was proclaimed.

Puerto Rico was originally inhabited by Taino Indians who called the island Borinquen. Christopher Columbus visited in 1493 and named the island San Juan Bautista (St. John the Baptist) but sailed on to Hispaniola to establish a settlement. Juan Ponce de Leon began the Spanish conquest of Borinquen, after finding gold there in 1508. He established a settlement on the shores of San Juan harbor, calling it Puerto Rico – rich port. The names were eventually switched, and rich is what Ponce de Leon became as governor of the island, with the lure of new conquests drawing him away from Puerto Rico from time to time. By 1513, disease and Spanish massacres had eliminated the Tainos and they were replaced with African slaves.

Once the island's placer gold deposits were depleted in the

1530s, the Spanish turned their attention to sugar plantations. Distractions came in the form of raids by Carib Indians and by British, French and Dutch pirates and roving corsairs, all of whom were attracted to this important outpost of the Spanish empire.

Twice a year two armed convoys were sent from Spain to collect precious gems, gold and silver at Veracruz and Cartagena. To protect her treasure fleets, Spain established several military fortifications in the Caribbean, the most strategic being San Juan harbor, which Spain's King Philip II called "the key to the West Indies." The famous El Morro fortress was built at the east side of the harbor entrance. It began as a round masonry tower which, over time and following various enemy assaults, was strengthened and expanded until it was a massive citadel. The main purpose of this fortification was to prevent Spain's European enemies from gaining possession of the port and using it as a base for attacks on Spanish settlements and trading ships.

Britain's Sir Francis Drake, justly feared by the Spanish and emboldened by his successful sackings of Santo Domingo, Cartagena and St. Augustine, was the first to test El Morro. In 1595 he forced the entrance to the harbor but was repulsed, with heavy losses suffered by the Spanish defenders. Three years later Britain's Earl of Cumberland successfully besieged El Morro, his brief occupation cut short by an outbreak of dysentery. The Dutch were next, in 1625, sacking and burning the town before being driven off by the Spanish.

In response to these attacks, Spain built several fortresses, making San Juan virtually impregnable. Massive walls of sandstone, some 50 feet high and 20 feet thick at the base, were raised around the town. A redoubt named San Cristobal was built about a mile east of El Morro to protect the town from a land-based attack. But it wasn't until the end of the Seven Years War (1756-1763), which left Spain and Britain the two powers in the Caribbean, that San Juan was transformed into the stronghold we see today. Thomas O'Daly, an Irish-born military engineer, was hired by Spain's King Charles III to oversee the completion of the wall, expand San Cristobal into the largest fortress built by Spain in the Americas, and turn El Morro into an impenetrable citadel. Hundreds of workmen were employed in this massive undertaking which took 20 years to complete. San Juan remained impregnable for more than a century and was one of Spain's last remaining holdings in the Americas when a revolution in Cuba sparked the Spanish-American War. A United States naval flotilla, in search of the Spanish war fleet, bombarded San Juan in May of 1898, and two months later American troops landed on the south coast of Puerto Rico. As soldiers advanced to the outskirts of San Juan, an armistice was signed. Spain's four-century rule of Puerto Rico had come to an end.

Getting Around San Juan

Along the El Malecon.

San Juan's main cruise port is located adjacent to the walled city; its secondary cruise pier (**Frontier Pier**) is two miles east of the main port. In between the airport and the cruise piers lie the hotel-lined beaches of Isla Verde, Ocean Beach and Condado, where the majority of passengers stay if spending extra time in San Juan before or after their cruise.

Two **hotels** located right in Old San Juan are the El Convento (a former convent) and the Sheraton Old San Juan Hotel, a modern building that opened on the waterfront as a Wyndham hotel. Tourist taxis are painted white and they offer fixed rates (per car) to and from tourist zones. The fare from the airport to Isla Verde is $8, to Condado is $12, and to the cruise piers in Old San Juan is $16. From Isla Verde to the cruise piers the fare is $16 and from Condado, $10. From Frontier Pier to Old San Juan is about $10.

Parking is limited in Old San Juan and its streets are best explored on foot or by using the free trolley service which originates at the Covadonga parking lot, a block up from the cruise ship piers. Five trolley buses, equipped with wheelchair ramps, operate daily and cover two routes: a central one to Plaza de Armas and a northern route to the grounds of El Morro. Passengers can hop off and on at any stop.

To see some of the city's outlying districts and area attractions, such as the El Yunque National Forest, **tours** can be booked through the cruise lines' shore excursion office or at the tour desks of the major hotels. Another option is to rent a car. Rental agencies are numerous in the San Juan metropolitan area, including Avis, Budget and Hertz.

Spanish and English are the official languages. Spanish is predominant, but English is taught in school and is widely spoken. Long-distance phone calls can be made at 'Phones & More' located inside Pier 6 and other phones are opposite Pier 4. A post office is located opposite Pier 1 where San Justo intersects with Comercio.

Dining – San Juan has become  a restaurant town, serving both traditional creole cuisine and the new Puerto Rican cuisine, which has taken traditional recipes featuring native Indian, Spanish and African foods, and enhanced them with new seasonings and presentation. A good place to sample some local fare is Amadeus, a popular bistro-style bar and restaurant across from the Plaza San Juan.

Shopping – San Juan has dutyfree shopping at its airport and at several factory outlets in Old San Juan. The main shopping streets are Cristo, Fortaleza, San Francisco and Cristo, where a Pusser's Store and Polo/Ralph Lauren Factory Store are located. Numerous art galleries are situated in the shopping area and on San Jose Street. Traditional items include *cuatros* (handmade guitars), bobbin lace (*mundillo*) and small wood carvings of religious figures called *santos*. Other local crafts include straw work, ceramics, hammocks and carnival masks. The Institute of Puerto

The cuatro is a traditional handmade guitar.

Rican Culture operates the Popular Arts and Crafts Center, located at the bottom of Cristo Street near the Capilla de Cristo, where a variety of island crafts are displayed and offered for sale Monday through Saturday. On weekends, local crafts can be purchased at an outdoor market beside La Casita information center and along La Princesa promenade. This market is a popular venue for local musicians.

(Below) Sheraton Old San Juan Hotel.
(Right) El Convento, a heritage hotel building.

Rum is another Puerto Rican specialty, with free tours and samples provided at the **Bacardi Rum Factory** – reached by harbor ferry from the cruise ship pier. Gourmet coffee drinkers may want to purchase a pound or two of flavorful Puerto Rican coffee. If you're looking for fine cigars, there's a boutique catering to connoisseurs at El San Juan Hotel on Isla Verde. Shoppers looking for interesting books and souvenirs should check out the museum gift shops, such as the one at El Morro, where visitors can purchase replica gold and silver coins of the 16th century.

Beaches – Good beaches in the metropolitan area include Escambron Beach and Isla Verde Beach, both of which are *balnearios* (government-run beaches with facilities, lifeguards and security personnel). About 20 miles east of San Juan is highly popular and beautiful Luquillo Beach – rated one of the world's top ten by National Geographic. A favorite with children is Seven Seas in Fajardo at the northeast

San Juan's Isla Verde Beach.

> ## Shore Excursions
> *San Juan*
> Shore excursions include a variety of Old San Juan walking tours, and horseback riding in El Yunque National Forest. Kayaking, biking and shopping tours are also offered. The Bacardi Rum Factory is featured in several excursions.

end of the island. More beautiful beaches lie west of San Juan at Dorado where a public beach is located near the hotel and golf resorts.

Golf – Puerto Rico boasts a dozen public golf courses, including four at the Hyatt Resorts west of San Juan. Designed by Robert Trent Jones Sr., the par-72 East course at Dorado Beach contains a par-5 thirteenth hole, rated by Jack Nicklaus as one of the top ten in the world.

Local Attractions

The cruise ships dock right at the doorstep of Old San Juan, a seven-block area packed with historical and cultural sights which include Gothic churches, restored

colonial buildings, townhouses with inner courtyards and wrought-iron balconies, museums, art galleries, boutiques, plazas, fountains and gardens. An information center **i** is conveniently located beside Pier 1 inside **1** **La Casita (The Little House)** and is an ideal starting point for a self-guided walking tour of these historic streets and fortifications. Refreshments can be enjoyed along the way at various restaurants and sidewalk cafes, or from street vendors who sell bottled water and soft drinks. *Piraguas* (fruit-flavored snow cones) and *helados* (coconut and pineapple ices) are popular with the locals. **2** **Aduana**, the beautiful pink building overlooking the harbor, is a U.S. Customs House. Nearby **3** **El Arsenal** was built in 1800 as a base for patrol boats and houses Divisions of the

Institute of Puerto Rican Culture. Three art galleries are located within the grounds. An elegant promenade, **4** **Paseo La Princesa**, runs parallel with the city wall and is where Spanish gentry of the 19th century once strolled. Restored for the Columbus Quincentennial, the esplanade is lined with palms and ornate street lamps, and features a large bronze fountain titled Raices (Roots), its human figures representing Puerto Rico's Indian, African and Spanish founders.

Paseo La Princesa leads past **5** **La Princesa**, a former jail, which has also been restored to its former colonial grandeur and is now the headquarters for the Puerto Rico Tourism Company, the island's official tourism body. The promenade curves along the waterfront at the base of the city

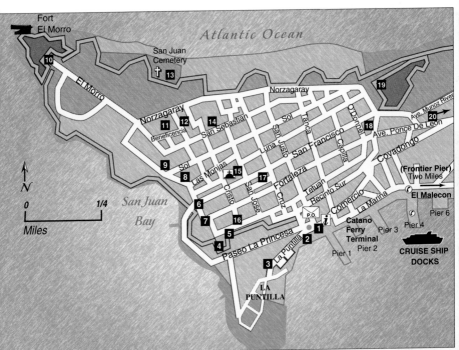

Viejo San Juan

(Right) Pablo Casals Museum. (Below) Paseo La Princesa.

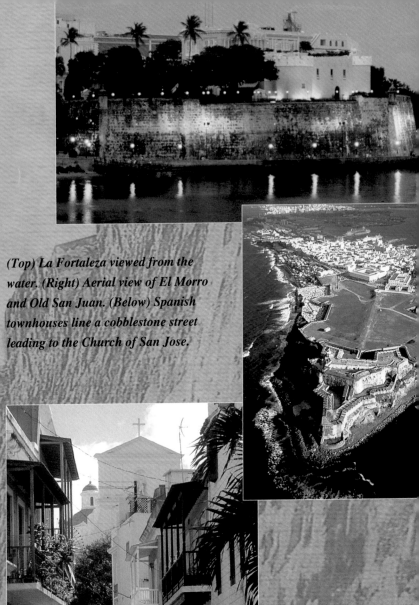

(Top) La Fortaleza viewed from the water. (Right) Aerial view of El Morro and Old San Juan. (Below) Spanish townhouses line a cobblestone street leading to the Church of San Jose.

(Above) The waterfront promenade leads to San Juan Gate. (Opposite) Children play in Plaza of the Religious Procession.

wall, called La Muralla, which is guarded at strategic points by *garitas* (sentry boxes). **6** **La Puerta de San Juan (San Juan Gate)** is one of six heavy wooden doors once positioned along the wall and which, for centuries, were bolted shut at sundown to secure the fortified city from enemy attack.

Pass through this gate and make an immediate right on Recinto Oeste Street for a look at **7** **La Fortaleza (The Fortress)** which overlooks San Juan Bay. Built as a fort in 1540, its location proved poor for military defence and its role reverted to that of governor's mansion – the oldest one in use in the Western Hemisphere. The grounds are open weekdays to organized tours that start every hour in a small plaza beside the building.

A turn to the left upon passing

through the San Juan Gate will take you to the top of a hill where **8** **Plazuela de la Rogativa (Small Plaza of the Religious Procession)** is a popular gathering place for local residents and the staging of children's puppet shows. A bronze sculpture here depicts an event of 1797 when Old San Juan was under attack by British ships. In desperation, the residents of San Juan, led by their bishop, marched through the streets one night carrying lit torches and praying for their safety. The British apparently mistook this parade of lights for Spanish reinforcements and retreated from the harbor. Opposite the Plazuela de la Rogativa is the Museo Felisa Rincon de Gautier (the former home of a popular mayor) and behind it the Museo del Nino (Children's Museum).

North of Plazuela de la Rogativa you will come to a fork in the road. On the left is Casa Rosada (Pink House) which was built in 1812 for the Spanish army. To the right an upper road

leads past a plant-decked wall to a doorway from which steps lead into the lovely gardens of **9 Casa Blanca (White House)**. Built in 1521 as the city's original fortress, this is the oldest Spanish colonial building in Old San Juan and has been modified over the years. It was a gift from Spain's monarch to Ponce de Leon for his settling of Puerto Rico. Ponce de Leon died the year the original wooden house was built, but his family resided there until 1779, when it was sold to the Spanish government. Following the Spanish-American war in 1898, the Commander of the U.S. Army lived at Casa Blanca until 1967. It was declared a National Historic Monument in 1968. Recently restored and furnished with authentic 16th- and 17th-century pieces, the mansion now contains two museums – the Juan Ponce de Leon Museum and the Taino Indian Ethno-Historic Museum. They are open Tuesday through Sunday, 9:00 a.m. to noon and 1:00 p.m. to 4:30 p.m.

Between Casa Blanca and the grounds of El Morro stand two impressive colonial buildings. Asilo de Beneficenica, its facade consisting of wrought-iron fencing and green shutters, contains the headquarters of the Institute of Puerto Rican Culture and several galleries which are open Wednesday through Sunday. The red-domed building beside it was built in the 1800s and now houses a school of fine arts.

One of the most popular attractions in Old San Juan is the dramatic fort of **10 El Morro**, open daily from 9:00 a.m. to 5:00 p.m. Admission is free and a brochure map is available at the entrance. Administered by the National Park Service, El Morro's full name is Castillo de San Felipe del Morro or 'Castle St. Philip of the Headland'. The fort is reached by a long, straight path which leads across a broad grassy area called a glacis. This cleared land was smoothed and sloped by the Spanish so that attacking troops had no shelter from the fort's cannon fire. Beneath the ground are tunnels in

(Above) A cruise ship heads to San Juan Harbor. (Below) Visitors approach El Morro from its landward side.

which kegs of gunpowder were planted should enemy troops try to lay siege to the fort.

From this landward approach, the fort strikes a surprisingly low profile, so engineered to make it a small target for enemy troops approaching by land. This was achieved by a dry moat which was dug along its length so the main wall could be sunk into the ground, yet still present a formidable height for scaling. The ocean side of the fort, in contrast to the landward side, consists of six tiers of batteries that loom above the water, protecting the fort from sea attacks. The lowest gun platform, the Water Battery, is washed by ocean swells while the uppermost ramparts – the Ochoa and Austria Bastions – stand 145 feet high. Inside the fort, its entrance guarded by a drawbridge, are storerooms, gun rooms, troop quarters, a chapel and prison. These all open onto a central courtyard beneath which are cisterns. Tunnels and stairways connect different parts of the fort, and a museum is located in one of the bombproof vaults.

The El Morro lighthouse, which took a direct hit during the Spanish-American War, stands on the fort's fifth level. First constructed in 1846, it has been replaced three times since then. A working lighthouse, it helps guide ships entering one of the Caribbean's busiest ports.

Returning to the city streets, the next historic site is **11** **Ballaja Barracks** where Spanish troops and their families once lived. The Museum of the Americas is on its second floor. On the eastern side of the barracks is **12** **Plaza del Quinto Centenario,** constructed for the 1992-93 celebration of the 500th Anniversary of the discovery of the New World. This multi-level square affords a sweeping vista of El Morro and, from its upper western level, a view of the **13** **San Juan Cemetery**.

The steps of the square lead to **14** **Plaza de San Jose** where a statue of Ponce de Leon stands outside San Jose Church – the second oldest church in the Western Hemisphere, built in 1532, and the family church of Ponce de Leon's descendants. A beautiful example of Gothic architecture, the church was originally built as a chapel. Next to the church is the Convento de los Dominicos, containing the Institute of Puerto Rican Culture book and music store. Tucked in a corner townhouse of the plaza is the Museo de Pablo Casals, a small museum containing memorabilia of the famous cellist who spent his final years in San Juan. On the plaza's eastern side is Casa de las Contrafuertes (House of Buttresses), which contains the Museum of Latin American Prints and a Pharmacy Museum.

Cristo Street leads from Plaza de San Jose down the hill to **15** **San Juan Cathedral**. Built in 1540 with early 19th-century modifications, the cathedral contains the marble tomb of Juan

(Above) Visitors inspect one of Old San Juan's sentry boxes.
(Below) Outdoor dining on Cristo Street, near Christ Chapel.

Ponce de Leon. Two blocks south of the Cathedral, at the foot of Cristo Street, you will see **16** **Capilla de Cristo (Christ Chapel)** dedicated to the Christ of Miracles. It was built following a 1753 incident in which a youth was racing his horse down the hill at such a speed that rider and horse could not possibly stop before hurtling over the city wall. One legend is that both miraculously came to a halt just in time, another says the horse stopped but the boy flew over the wall, and a third version claims they both met their maker at this spot. Beside Capilla de Cristo is the

(Above) Quincentennial Square.
(Below) San Juan Cathedral.

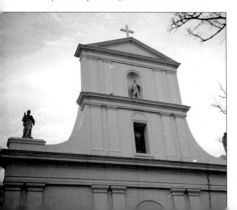

small Parque de las Palomas (Pigeon Park) with a fine view of the harbor. Lying opposite is Casa del Libro (House of Books), a small museum and library with a collection of rare, pre-16th century books.

17 **Plaza de Armas (Army Plaza)** lies a block east of Cristo Street on San Francisco. Several government buildings surround the square, which was originally used for military drills, when built in the 16th century, and is now a social gathering place. City Hall, completed in 1789, stands on the plaza's north side and was designed to resemble its counterpart in Madrid; it contains a visitor information center. An administration building, at the west end of the plaza, and the provincial delegation building at its northwest corner, are fine examples of 19th-century neoclassical architecture. The century-old statues gracing the plaza represent the four seasons.

At the eastern end of Fortaleza Street, where it intersects with O'Donnel, you'll find **18** **Plaza de Colon (Columbus Plaza)** and

Teatro Tapia, a 19th-century theatre. A few blocks north is the entrance to **19** **San Cristobal Fort**, open daily from 9:00 a.m. to 5:00 p.m. East of the historic quarter is the dome-roofed **20** **Capitol Building**.

Area Highlights

El Yunque National Forest – A 45-minute drive from San Juan, this 28,000-acre tropical forest is one of Puerto Rico's natural wonders. Set in the Luquillo Mountains and named for anvil-shaped El Yunque peak, the park contains 240 species of tropical trees, flowers and wildlife, including ferns, orchids, parrots and tiny tree frogs called coqui. Cool and often rainy, the park's verdant forest contains a dozen hiking trails and a lookout tower. Its highest peak is 3,532-foot-high El Toro. A popular restaurant at the entrance to the park is Las Vegas where both Puerto Rican and American cuisine is served.

Las Cabezas de San Juan Nature Reserve – This peninsula at the northeastern tip of the island is often referred to as **El Faro**, which is the name of the 1882 lighthouse located here. Beautifully restored, El Faro now houses a scientific research center with an observation deck added to the building's exterior. The reserve, situated on land acquired by the island's Conservation Trust, encompasses a dry forest, mangroves, lagoons, beaches, reefs and offshore cays. Guided tours, by reservation only, are conducted in safari buses and include informative walks along trails and boardwalks to observe the various species supported by this diverse habitat.

(Below) El Yunque National Forest. (Bottom) El Faro.

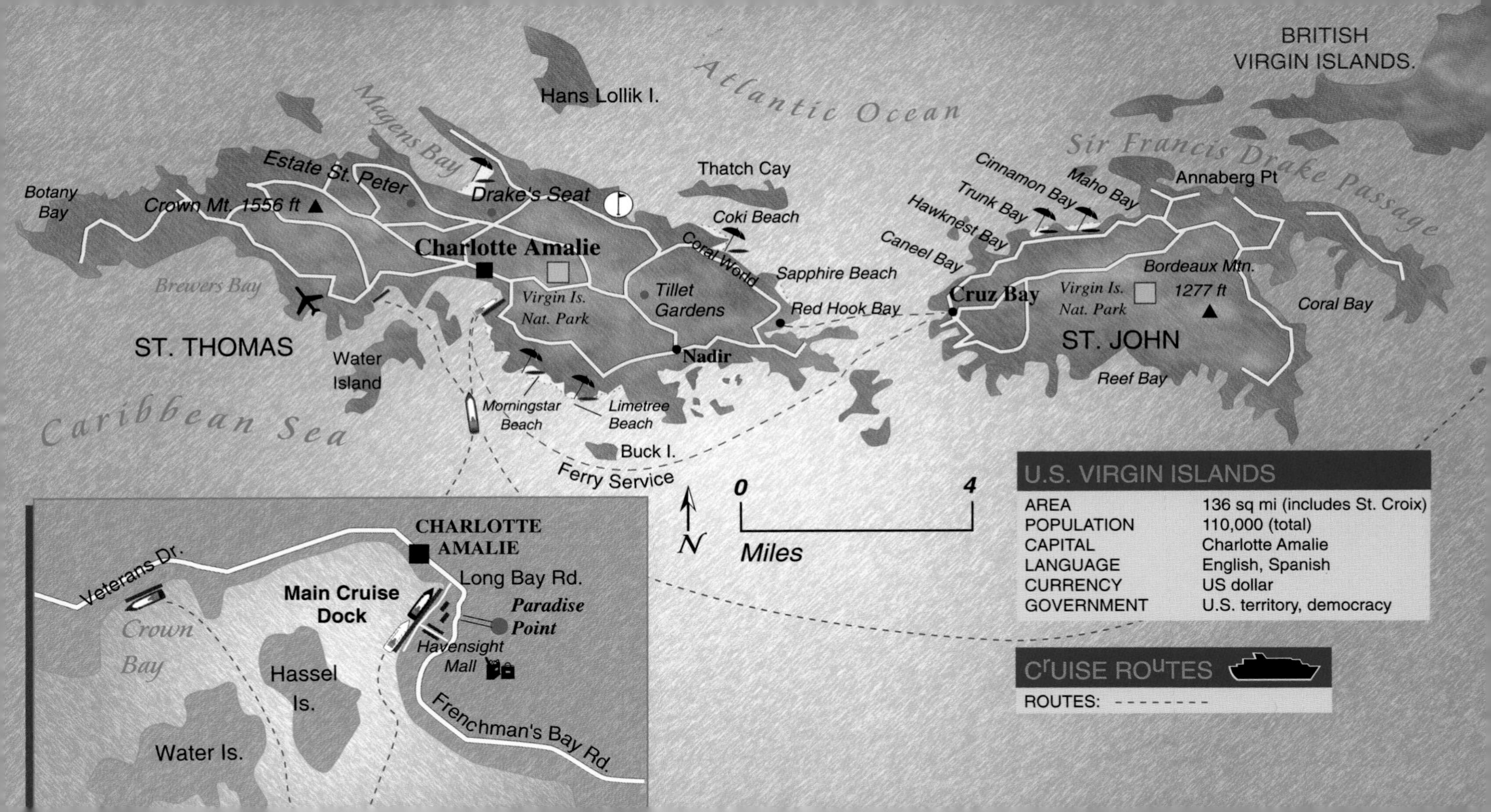

BRITISH
VIRGIN ISLANDS.

Sir Francis Drake Passage

Atlantic Ocean

Annaberg Pt.
Coral Bay

Maho Bay
Cinnamon Bay
Trunk Bay
Hawknest Bay

Bordeaux Mtn.
1277 ft
Virgin Is.
Nat. Park
ST. JOHN
Reef Bay

Cruz Bay

Caneel Bay

Thatch Cay

Coki Beach
Sapphire Beach

Red Hook Bay

Coral World

Tillet
Gardens
Nadir

Hans Lollik I.

Limetree
Beach

Buck I.
Ferry Service

Morningstar
Beach

N
Miles
0   4

Drake's Seat

Virgin Is.
Nat. Park
Charlotte Amalie

Magens Bay

Estate St. Peter
St. Peter
Crown Mt. 1556 ft

Botany
Bay

Brewers Bay

Water
Island

ST. THOMAS

Caribbean Sea

U.S. VIRGIN ISLANDS

AREA	136 sq mi (includes St. Croix)
POPULATION	110,000 (total)
CAPITAL	Charlotte Amalie
LANGUAGE	English, Spanish
CURRENCY	US dollar
GOVERNMENT	U.S. territory, democracy

CRUISE ROUTES

ROUTES: - - - - -

CHARLOTTE
AMALIE

Long Bay Rd.
Paradise
Point

Havensight
Mall

Frenchman's Bay Rd.

Main Cruise
Dock

Hassel
Is.

Water Is.

Veterans Dr.

Crown
Bay

CHAPTER NINE

U.S. VIRGIN ISLANDS

The natural allure of the Virgin Islands prompted Christopher Columbus to name them, in 1493, for the legend of Saint Ursula and her 11,000 virgin martyrs. But not even Columbus could have predicted their potential as a tourist mecca. As recently as 1917, when the United States bought these tropical treasures from Denmark for $25 million, the Danish West Indies were valued mainly for their strategic proximity to the recently opened Panama Canal.

A 100-island chain, the Virgin Islands are divided into the U.S. Virgin Islands and the British Virgin Islands. The U.S. Virgin Islands consist of three principal islands – St. Thomas, St. John and St. Croix – and dozens of smaller islands. They contain many sheltered harbors and lie directly in the path of easterly trade winds, which made them an ideal stop-over point for trading vessels in the days of sail.

The capital of the U.S. Virgin Islands, Charlotte Amalie (pronounced *ah-mahl-ya*), is located on the south coast of St. Thomas and overlooks one of the finest harbors in the Caribbean. The downtown's narrow streets and colonial buildings look much as they did in the mid-1800s when Charlotte Amalie was one of the most important trading centers of the West Indies, bustling with the comings and goings of naval ships, whalers, merchant traders and fishing boats. Import firms flourished here, their warehouses lining the waterfront, and wealthy merchants lived on the surrounding hillsides where they enjoyed

A view of the main cruise dock on the island of St. Thomas.

the sea breezes and magnificent harbor views.

Their gleaming white houses, set among terraced gardens and coconut palms, were rectangular in shape with hipped roofs designed to collect rainwater along the gutters. Inside these homes were polished mahogany floors and comfortable furnishings which included rocking chairs and a large sideboard for holding carafes of chilled drinks. Block ice was imported from Boston and stored in wooden ice houses, the spaces of their triple-layered walls filled with sawdust as insulation from the hot sun. The bedrooms contained huge four-poster beds from which hung mosquito netting. As a fire-safety precaution, the kitchen was contained in a separate building, as were the servants' quarters. Mode of travel around the island, up steep winding roads, was by horseback. Life on St. Thomas,

however, centered around the town. As the 19th-century Danish naturalist A. S. Orsted wrote, "If you know the town, you know the whole island."

The town began in 1672 when the Danish West India Company established the first permanent settlement here. Fort Christian was completed in 1680 and the port quickly became a leading slave-trading center of the West Indies. Denmark allowed the Brandenburg American Company to operate here for a while and the town's four busy taverns soon earned it the name 'Tap Hus' (Beer Hall). In 1691 the settlement was officially declared a town and named Charlotte Amalie, in honor of the Danish Queen who was consort to King Christian V.

In 1717 the neighboring island of St. John was claimed by Denmark, which in 1733 purchased St. Croix from France. St. Thomas, a free port, became a thriving trade center and exporter of contraband trade from the strictly regulated Spanish colonies. It also became a refuge for pirates who sold their cargo here and often hid in the hills overlooking the harbor. The legendary Blackbeard is said to have holed up in a watch tower with a spyglass and supply of rum.

The islands became a Danish royal colony in 1754, and the St. Croix port of Christiansted became the colonial capital. In contrast to the orderly development of Christiansted – with its

Fort Christian, St. Thomas.

well-planned streets and large fort built on the harbor – was the haphazard growth of Charlotte Amalie. Between 1804 and 1832, six fires swept through the town's narrow streets. Building codes were eventually enforced that banned frame construction in the commercial area along the waterfront. These masonry warehouses were fitted with fire-proof roofs of tile or brick which were eventually replaced with corrugated metal due to hurricanes. Following emancipation in 1848, many freed slaves moved into town where existing residential lots were re-subdivided into smaller ones.

By the mid-1800s, the Danish West Indies had reached their zenith as colonial holdings. The price of sugar cane had dropped and, with steamships replacing sailing ships, St. Thomas was losing its importance as a stop-over point. However, the protected harbors of St. Thomas and St. John were still of military value, prompting the purchase of the Danish West Indies by the United States in 1917, to prevent their being used as a German submarine base. The U.S. Navy handled initial administration of the islands, and residents were granted U.S. citizenship in 1927. Local government was established in 1954, with a governor and senate locally elected.

During World War II, the U.S. military constructed a submarine base, airfield, roads and housing on St. Thomas. Tourism began to flourish following the war, especially after the closing of Cuba to American tourists. A total of

Fort Christiansvaern, St. Croix.

26,650 visitors arrived at St. Thomas by ship or by airplane in 1950. Today that annual number is approaching two million. In recent years St. Croix has fallen out of favor as a cruise port, but St. Thomas is one of the busiest in the Caribbean.

St. Thomas

Charlotte Amalie is serviced by two cruise ship terminals, the main one being the West Indian Company Dock which is located on the east side of the harbor, about a mile and a half by road from downtown. The other cruise terminal at Crown Bay is about two miles west of downtown. When ships anchor in the harbor, their passengers are tendered

St. Thomas Harbor, viewed from atop Paradise Point.

ashore to Kings Wharf on the downtown waterfront. The passenger ferry dock, with regular departures to St. John, is at the west end of the harbor, across from Hassel Island which is a national park. St. Thomas is fully geared for visitors with many of the island's 50,000 residents employed in tourism-related industries. English is the official language and the U.S. dollar is the legal tender. Long-distance calls can be direct dialed to the U.S. mainland, and overseas service to Europe is excellent. A post office is located on Main Street, west of the Grand Hotel.

Getting Around

St. Thomas is only 13 miles long and four miles wide, so the island's beautiful beaches are easily reached by taxi. A number of car rental firms operate on the island. Keep in mind that the roads are narrow and winding, and traffic keeps to the left. The port itself is usually busy with car traffic, and is best explored on foot. Open-air shuttle buses run regularly between the cruise dock and downtown ($3 per person).

Taxis – Officially licensed taxis carry a dome light and the letters TP on their license plates. Their rates have been set by the Taxi Commission and approved by the Virgin Islands' Legislature. Some

Complimentary shopping shuttles run between the main cruise pier and nearby Havensight Mall.

sample fares per passenger: main cruise dock to downtown – $3.00; Crown Bay Dock to downtown – $4.00; Charlotte Amalie to: Magens Bay – $6.00, Morningstar Beach – $5.50, Red Hook ferry terminal (for ferry to St. John) – $8.00. Paradise Point Gondola, located across the street from Havensight Mall, whisks visitors up the mountainside for a sweeping view of the harbor. The complex contains a spacious sun deck, a restaurant/bar with umbrella tables, and a handful of gift shops.

Shopping – The Caribbean is famous for its duty-free shopping, and most famous of all is St. Thomas, where American visitors to the U.S. Virgin Islands can take advantage of a $1,200-per-person duty-free allowance. The prices in St. Thomas are generally 20% to 50% less than stateside and there's no sales tax. Imported liquor, jewelry, china, crystal,

(Above) Main Street post office.
(Below) Magens Bay Beach.

designer leather goods, watches and other items are all offered at substantial savings. Dozens of duty-free stores are housed in restored warehouses of the town's historic section, the shopping area concentrated along Main Street, the waterfront and the narrow, palm-shaded alleyways and pedestrian malls that connect these two busy streets. Additional duty-free shops, including branches of downtown retailers, are located at Havensight Mall beside the main cruise dock. The gift shop at Fort Christian sells locally made crafts including hand-carved mahogany rocking chairs, made to order.

Dining – For a taste of authentic Caribbean fare in a casual setting, try The Jamaican Ackee Tree & Bar, popular with local business people at lunch time and conveniently located in Al Cohen's Mall, across the street from Havensight Mall. Downtown's Back Street (one block up from Main Street)

is a good place to escape the shopping crowds with a lunch stop at a number of good restaurants, including Cuzzin's at the corner of Back Street and Raadets Gade.

Beaches – Magens Bay, on the north coast, has been rated by National Geographic as one of the ten most beautiful beaches in the world. Admission is $3.00 and change facilities are available.

Other recommended beaches include Morningstar Beach and Limetree Beach southeast of Charlotte Amalie. On the northeast side of the island are Sapphire Beach and Coki Beach – good for snorkeling and adjacent to Coral World where change facilities are available.

Dive & Snorkel Sites – Off the island's south coast lie Cow and Calf Rocks, named for two humpback whales once seen at this dive site, which contains dramatic caves, archways and cliff overhangs from 25 feet. The Pinnacle (French Cap), about a mile offshore, consists of two stone pillars atop a seamount at 45 feet. Two miles out, at Buck Island, a World War I freighter is resting in 40 feet. Atlantis Submarine has a dive site at Buck Island, taxiing passengers by boat to the submarine which submerges to depths of 90 feet, providing views of the corals and fishes. On the north coast, the calm waters off Coki Beach are excellent for snorkeling and beach dives, with a dive shop right on the beach. Lying opposite is Thatch Cay, another popular diving area.

Shore Excursions

U.S. Virgin Islands

Shore excursions include snorkel expeditions to Buck Island and certified beach dives at Coki Point. Beginner scuba is also offered, as is snuba, parasailing, kayaking and ocean racing aboard a high-tech sailing yacht. Land-based excursions include biking, jeep safaris, and visits to Coral World and Paradise Point, along with shopping. The neighboring island of St. John can be visited by catamaran, or on a snorkel excursion to Trunk Bay.

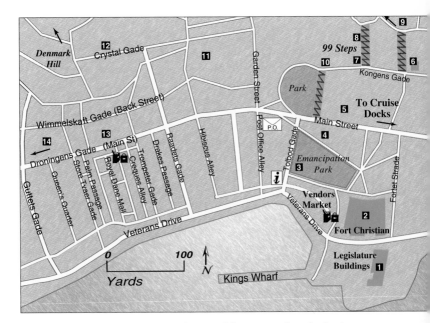

Golf – Mahogany Run on the north coast is an 18-hole, par-70, Fazio-designed championship course. Its famous Devil's Triangle consists of three dramatic holes overlooking the Atlantic.

Downtown Charlotte Amalie

The **1 Legislative Building**, a two-storey green building of Italian Renaissance design, is the seat of the U.S. Virgin Islands Senate. Built in 1874 as barracks for the Danish police, it was later used as housing for U.S. Marines Corps. It's open to visitors Monday through Friday.

2 Fort Christian, built of red brick and rubble, is the oldest standing structure on St. Thomas. It was begun about 1666, completed in 1680 and altered in 1874 when the watch tower was removed and its north facade, with a crenelated clock tower, was added. The fort was later used as a jail, and is now a museum and National Historic Landmark. **3 Emancipation Garden**, the site of many official ceremonies, commemorates the freeing of slaves in 1848 and contains a bust of Danish King Christian and a small replica Liberty Bell. A **tourist information office** is located nearby at the corner of Tolbod Gade and Veterans Drive, opposite which is the open-air Vendors Market. The **4 Grand Hotel**, originally called the Commercial Hotel & Coffee House, is a Greek Revival structure which occupied an entire block when built in 1840. Formerly three storeys tall, the top floor was presumably damaged by a hurricane sometime after 1896. The former hotel now houses a jewelry studio featuring designs by local artisans.

the U.S. Virgin Islands

(Top) Government House.
(Above) A shopping street in
downtown Charlotte Amalie.
(Left) Hawksnest Beach on
St. John.

(Right) Legislative Building. (Below) Frederick Lutheran Church. (Bottom) Haagensen House, a restored 1820s townhouse.

The **5** **Frederick Lutheran Church**, the official church of the Danish West Indies, was established in 1666 with worship services held in the homes of planters and soldiers, and then at Christensfort. The present building was built in 1793, gutted by fire in 1826 and damaged by a hurricane in 1870, after which the tower was added.

6 **Government House**, completed in 1865, is a three-storey masonry building built in the neoclassical design. Its brick walls are painted white, as are the cast-iron verandahs that run the length of the first two storeys. Government offices are located here, including the Governor's Executive Offices. The Governor's official residence is the former Danish Consulate, an imposing two-storey mansion atop Denmark Hill. Two sets of stairs, the westerly one called **7** **The 99 Steps**, lead up the hillside behind Government House, past **8** **Haagensen House**, a restored 1820s townhouse which is now a museum. Standing atop Government Hill is **9** **Skytsborg (Blackbeard's Castle)**, a five-storey conical tower constructed of rubble masonry by the Danish in 1678, with later changes. Now part of a hotel, the stone watch tower is said to have been used by the infamous pirate Blackbeard. **10** **Hotel 1829 (formerly Lavalette House)** was built as a residence for a French sea captain and now houses one of Charlotte Amalie's finest restaurants. **11** **St. Thomas Reformed Church**, constructed in 1846, is a good example of Greek Revival building. **12** **Beracha Veshalom U'gemilut Hasidim**, built of cut stone and brick in 1833, is the second-oldest synagogue in the Western Hemisphere.

The **13** **Camille Pissaro Building** is where the famous impressionist painter lived above the family store in the 1840s. Born in a small Jewish community of Charlotte Amalie in 1830, Pissaro left St. Thomas in 1855 to study art in Paris. He became a teacher and friend of Gauguin and Cezanne, and died near Paris at the age of 73. The Pissaro building now houses the Tropicana Perfume shop and upstairs, above an inner courtyard entered off Main Street, is an art gallery.

14 **Market Square** was, in 1946, officially named Rothschild Francis Square to honor the public service of this champion of civil rights and liberties. The square has long been a central meeting place where fresh produce, fish and spices are sold, with French farmers from the north side of the island bringing their fruits and vegetables to town by donkey. In the early 1900s, an open-air iron shed called the Bungalow was erected and the regular female vendors, called 'Market Women', each had their own spot under the shade of the bungalow – to the exclusion of any male vendors. The annual Carnival Food Fair is held here each April.

Area Attractions

West of Downtown – Frenchtown, founded as a fishing village by French Huguenots from St. Barts, lies west of Charlotte

Amalie on the way to the Crown Bay cruise pier. Its restaurants and bars now create a lively night scene. The **University of the Virgin Islands** was founded in 1963 and the campus contains the Reichhold Center for the Arts where concerts and other events are held in its open-air amphitheater.

East End – Coral World at Coki Point is a popular attraction with its underwater observatory, natural reef exhibit, aquarium and semi-submarine rides along a coral reef. Sharks, moray eels, stingrays and pink flamingos are some of the exotic creatures that can be seen here. **Tillet Gardens**, on the way to Coral World, is the site of an historic Danish cattle farm and a gallery featuring local arts and crafts.

North of Town – Drake's Seat, said to be used by Francis Drake as a lookout for Spanish ships while his fleet lay concealed in Magens Bay, offers breathtaking views of Magens Bay and the British Virgin Islands. **Estate St. Peter Great House & Botanical Gardens**, a former plantation estate, has been developed into a beautiful botanical garden with breathtaking ocean views from its mountainside location. The elegant, open-plan house is wrapped with white latticework and broad decks from which visitors can gaze at more than twenty offshore islands. Local art is on display and outside, on the lushly landscaped grounds, are more than 500 varieties of plants and trees.

A drive to **Mountain Top**, highest viewing point on the island, provides stunning views of St. John, the British Virgin Islands and Charlotte Amalie Harbor. Refreshments served here include the original banana daiquiri. The attractive complex includes Caribbean shops, an aviary and aquarium.

St. John

In contrast to bustling Charlotte Amalie, a shopper's paradise, is the peaceful island of St. John, a nature lover's paradise. Lush and mountainous, St. John is indented by numerous bays at the head of which lie some of the world's most beautiful beaches. The island is also a botanist's delight with its proliferation of tropical plants and flowers.

When A. S. Orsted, discoverer of plankton, travelled by barkentine to the Danish West Indies in 1845, he was so captivated by the plant life he found that he changed his field of study from zoology to botany. Born of an illustrious Danish family, Orsted was especially besotted with St. John where uncultivated slopes presented him with an array of indigenous plant species, including bamboo, guava berry, century plant and coconut palms. A century later, in the early '50s, Laurance Rockefeller paid St. John a visit. A member of the wealthy American family famous for its philanthropy, he too arrived by sailboat and was so impressed with the serene and natural beauty of the island that he purchased about two thirds of it, which he donated to the United States federal government for the establishment of the Virgin Islands National Park in 1956.

The park has expanded since its inception and now covers about three-quarters of the island.

Residents of St. John, who number about 3,000, call their island 'Love City' and most visitors do fall in love with this protected paradise. Its highest point is Bordeaux Mountain at 1,277 feet, and the island's steep slopes provide dramatic views of distant islands and nearby cays where the deep blue sea fades to pale aquamarine at the head of beach-lined bays.

Getting Around

Cruise ships stopping at St. Thomas usually offer shore excursions to nearby St. John. Independent travellers can take one of the passenger ferries that connect St. John with St. Thomas, and these depart regularly from both Charlotte Amalie and Red Hook on St. Thomas for Cruz Bay on St. John. The Red Hook/Cruz Bay ferry leaves every hour on the hour both ways, is a 20-minute ride and costs $3.00 one way. The Charlotte Amalie/Cruz Bay ferry ride takes 45 minutes, costs $7.00 one way, and leaves Charlotte Amalie at one- to two-hour intervals throughout the day.

Cruz Bay is the main town on the island and open-air safari buses await here to transport visitors around the island. A Visitors Center at Cruz Bay provides

(Left) The ruins of Annaberg Sugar Mill.
(Below) Cruz Bay is the main port on St. John.

information on the Park – its beaches, trails and activities, including organized hikes and historic bus tours.

Beaches – Inviting beaches line St. John's northwest coast, including the sugary white sands and clear turquoise waters of Trunk Bay – considered one the most beautiful beaches in the world. Excellent for swimming, Trunk Bay also has an underwater snorkel trail. On shore are shaded picnic areas and a snack bar. Cinnamon Bay has open-air dining and a watersports center that rents snorkel gear and beach chairs. Sailing and windsurfing can also be enjoyed here, as well as National Park interpretive programs. Other lovely beaches include those at Hawksnest Bay and Caneel Bay, where a resort owned by Laurance Rockefeller is located.

Dive & Snorkel Sites – Cinnamon Bay has good snorkeling and a watersports center that rents snorkel gear. Trunk Bay has an underwater snorkeling trail with red, white and blue markers to guide snorkelers and identify the coral and marine life. Caneel Bay is recommended for the chance to view stingrays, green turtles, cushion sea stars, pipes-of-pan sponges and sargent majors. Popular dive sites are Steven's Cay, Carval Rock and Congo Cay.

Shopping – Cruz Bay is where most of the island shops are located, offering both duty-free goods and local arts and crafts. Mongoose Junction, across from the National Park Dock, is a pleasant shopping complex built of Caribbean stone. Its multi-level design of shaded terraces and tropical foliage contains fine shops, galleries and open-air restaurants.

Island Attractions – Points of interest on the island include the Annaberg Sugar Mill ruins, beautifully situated on the north side of the island overlooking Sir Francis Drake Passage. Also of note are the prehistoric petroglyphs at Reef Bay.

St. John's Trunk Bay, one of the world's most beautiful beaches, is ideal for swimming and snorkeling.

BRITISH VIRGIN ISLANDS

AREA	59 sq mi
POPULATION	21,000
CAPITAL	Road Town
LANGUAGE	English
CURRENCY	US dollar
GOVERNMENT	UK overseas territory

"Avast!"

Miles
0   4

Atlantic Ocean

Great Tobago
Little Tobago

Jost Van Dyke

Green Cay

Great Thatch

St John
(US Virgin Islands)

TORTOLA

Mt. Sage
1708 ft ▲

Cane Garden Bay

Mt. Healthy
Nat. Park

Road Town

East End

Beef Island

Sir Francis Drake Passage

Deadchest →

Norman Island

Peter Island

Rhone National Marine Park

Salt Island

Ferry

St. Thomas Bay

The Baths

VIRGIN GORDA

Gorda Peak
1359 ft ▲

North Sound

Anegada Is.

Ginger Island

Cooper Island

Caribbean Sea

CHAPTER TEN

BRITISH VIRGIN ISLANDS

Christopher Columbus named the Virgin Islands in 1493, but Francis Drake set the tone a century later when he sailed along the channel now bearing his name. Sir Francis Drake Channel runs through the middle of the British Virgin Islands, commonly called the B.V.I., which are a labyrinth of islands and channels rich in pirate lore and legend. The island of Jost Van Dyke, popular with yachtsmen who frequent famous Foxy's Tamarind Bar, was named for a Dutch pirate. Norman Island was possibly the inspired setting for Robert Louis Stevenson's Treasure Island, an adventure story published in 1883 about a search for Captain Kidd's buried treasure. And Peter Island is associated with the pirate Blackbeard who is said to have anchored in Deadman's Bay after a successful raid. While splitting the booty, an argument ensued and Blackbeard marooned 15 of his men on the nearby island of Dead Chest with a bottle of rum and their sea chests. The iconic pirate lyric "Fifteen men on dead men's chest, Yo ho ho and a bottle of rum!" comes from this incident.

The B.V.I., with their steady breezes and pristine anchorages, have long been a mariner's mecca. They were ideal for buccaneers who hid in secluded coves while fleeing enemy ships, and today they attract island-hopping yachtsmen from around the world. Large charter fleets are moored at marinas on the main islands of Tortola and Virgin Gorda, and boat bunks account for nearly half the total tourist beds in the B.V.I. There are no high-rise hotels in this chain of 30-plus islands, just plenty of white beaches and blue bays dotted with sailboats.

Road Town Bay

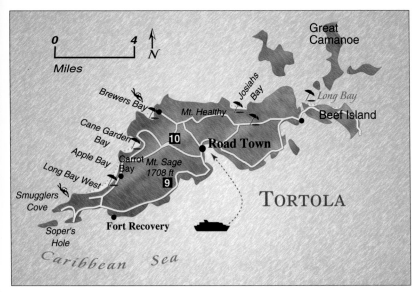

Inhabited by Taino Indians when discovered by Columbus, the B.V.I. were first colonized by the Dutch in 1648, then annexed by Britain in 1672. Plantations were established during the 18th century's sugar boom and fortifications were erected at strategic points to protect the islands from seaborne attacks. In the hills surrounding Road Town are the ruins of forts built by the Royal Engineers in 1794 – Fort George on Fort Hill and Fort Charlotte on Harrigan's Hill. Another fort west of Road Town at Pockwood Pond, called the Dungeon, contains a set of stairs leading to an underground cell.

Other vestiges from colonial times include the remains of a stone windmill in **Mount Healthy National Park**, and a round tower at Fort Recovery on Tortola's West End – believed to be built by Tortola's earliest Dutch settlers. Salt Island contains evaporation ponds that are still panned for salt

just as they were two centuries ago, and at the south end of Virgin Gorda is an abandoned copper mine worked by Cornish miners between 1838 and 1867 – the year in which the *HMS Rhone* sank off Salt Island during a hurricane. This wreck is now one of the Caribbean's most popular dive sites and the centerpiece of **Rhone National Marine Park**.

The first national parks were established in the 1960s, when the Rockefellers gave three sites to the B.V.I. government: **Devil's Bay** and **Spring Bay** on **Virgin Gorda**, and **Sage Mountain** on Tortola. Re-forestation and the re-introduction of original vegetation in Sage Mountain National Park have returned this 92-acre parcel of land to its original habitat. At 1,780 feet, Sage Mountain is the highest point in all of the Virgin Islands. Views from its hiking trails are dramatic and, although the mountaintop receives only 100 inches of rain a year, its vegetation is similar to a rainforest with tree ferns and bromeliads thriving in the ocean mist that's carried upwards by the wind.

Other natural attractions include **The Baths** – beached granite boulders forming a series of pools and grottoes on Virgin Gorda. Green Cay, ringed with white sand beaches, is your classic 'desert isle' and has been featured in various commercials. The islands' marine life includes tropical fish, eagle rays and nurse sharks. In winter, humpback whales arrive in local waters to breed.

The B.V.I. are volcanic in origin, except for the low-lying coral and limestone atoll of **Anegada** which lies about 15 miles to the northwest. Its highest point is 28 feet above sea level, and the island is ringed with extensive beaches and reefs that have claimed more than 300 ships. Animals outnumber people on this island of about 200 residents. Wild goats, donkeys and iguanas all live here, as does a colony of flamingos for which a bird sanctuary has been established at one of the island's salt ponds. This protected nesting ground is also used by herons, ospreys and terns.

Piracy and plantations have been replaced with tourism and offshore banking as the major industries in the B.V.I. A politically stable British crown colony, the territory is ruled by a governor who is appointed by the Crown and by an elected chief minister and government. Tourism was introduced to the islands in the mid-1960s when Laurance Rockefeller built a resort at Little Dix Bay on Virgin Gorda. This was followed by the opening of The Moorings in 1969, which marked the beginning of the local charter yacht business. The future development of tourism is being planned carefully to preserve the islands' natural beauty, although

Cane Garden Bay is one of many beautiful beaches on Tortola.

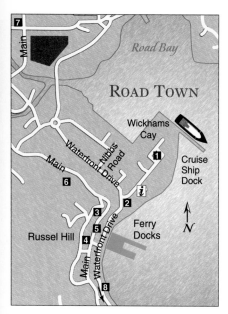

the approved construction of a high-end resort and golf course on Beef Island has aroused opposition from biologists concerned about the potential impact on the island's reefs and mangrove forests.

Road Town, Tortola

Tortola, named for the turtle dove, is the largest island of the B.V.I. chain. Most of the island's 17,000 inhabitants live in Road Town, the colony's capital, administrative center and main harbor. The cruise pier is located at the north end of town on Wickhams Cay. Nearby is the **Tourist Information Office** and the Cable & Wireless Public Office, on Waterfront Drive near Nibbs Road, which sells phone cards and other long-distance services. Road Town is a charming port of shuttered wooden houses, brightly painted and trimmed with fretwork.

Getting Around

Taxis – The B.V.I. Taxi Assn is located at Wickhams Cay and its fleet includes open-air safari buses and air-conditioned vans. Rates are unmetered and some sample fares are: Road Town to Cane Garden Bay, $15 for 1-3 passengers, $20 for 4 passengers; Two-Hour Island Tour, $45 for 1-3 passengers, $60 for 4 passengers. A Budget Rent-A-Car office is located in the **1 Mill Mall** near the pier.

Passenger ferries connect Tortola with Virgin Gorda, Peter Island and Jost Van Dyke. The ferry dock is opposite the town center and ferries depart two or three times daily. The 1/2 hour ride from Road Town to Virgin Gorda is about $10 one way. For an up-to-date schedule, visit the Tourist Information Office.

Shopping & Dining – The **2 open-air market** on Wickhams Cay includes the B.V.I. House of Crafts where locally made tropical clothing and souvenirs can be bought. Main and Waterfront are the primary shopping streets, where quaint shops sell Caribbean arts and crafts, cotton clothing, spices and preserves, and wines and spirits.

Pusser's Co. Store is located on Waterfront Drive and its famous Royal Navy Rum is sold here along with unique nautical gifts and sports clothing. Adjoining the store is Pusser's Pub where an English-style pub lunch can be enjoyed. Excellent West Indian curries are served at The Roti Palace, located above Samarkand Jewelers on Main Street.

Beaches – Tortola's best beaches are concentrated on the northwest coastline. Cane Garden Bay is a beautiful, crescent-shaped beach with watersports, restaurants and bars. To the south is Long Bay, a mile-long stretch of white sand. Apple Bay is the 'surfing beach' and location of Bomba's Shack, a popular beach bar. Brewers Bay has two beach bars and good snorkeling, as does Smugglers Cove, a small sandy beach at the northwest end of the island. Josiahs Bay is a dramatic beach on the north shore, and Long Bay on Beef Island offers seclusion and sheltered waters.

Dive & Snorkel Sites – There are two dozen established **dive sites** in the B.V.I.'s sheltered waters, a number of which can be enjoyed by snorkelers. Rhone National Marine Park was established to preserve the wreck of the Rhone, a 310-foot mail ship that went down in a hurricane off Salt Island in 1867 (see map on page 224). Its broken hull, encrusted in coral, lies 20 to 80 feet beneath the water's surface and is frequented by schools of tropical fish such as the queen angelfish and the parrotfish. Underwater footage in the movie *The Deep* was filmed at this famous wreck, which can also be viewed by snorkelers. Blonde Rock – a pinnacle between Salt Island and Dead Chest – has ledges that descend from 15 to 60 feet, the top one crowned with fire coral. Dead Chest Island is also part of the park and Painted Walls, off the island's southern point, con-

Pusser's Co. Store & Pub is a good place to shop and dine.

Shore Excursions

BVI's

Shore excursions include a dolphin encounter (swim or just observe) at the Dolphin Discovery facility at Prospect Reef. Certified scuba divers can partake in a dive at Wreck of the Rhone, and snorkelers can visit Norman Island. Kayaking, sailing and an excursion to Virgin Gorda's the Baths are also offered, as are several beach breaks. Tortola can be explored by 4X4 jeep or on a hiking excursion to Sage Mountain.

Sailboats lie at anchor in idyllic Cane Garden Bay.

sists of four long gullies covered with corals and sponges in depths of 20 to 30 feet.

Good **snorkeling** on Tortola can be had at Smugglers Cove on the island's western tip and at Brewers Bay on its north coast. On Virgin Gorda, The Baths and Spring Bay are excellent snorkeling sites. The Caves on Norman Island are ideal for snorkeling, as is nearby Angelfish Reef where divers will find excellent visibility at 90 feet. Santa Monica Rock, a pinnacle about a mile south of the island, is a good spot to see eagle rays and other open-ocean fish in depths of 10 to 100 feet.

Local Attractions

Most of Road Town's historic sites are on Main Street. The **3 Virgin Islands Folk Museum**, housed in a traditional West Indian building, contains artifacts from the islands' Taino and plantation eras, as well as items from the wreck of the Rhone. A few doors down from the museum is the **4 Post Office**, built in 1866 with stone walls and Gothic arches. Across the street is **5 Sir Olva George's Plaza**, a shady spot that once served as a busy market place.

Farther north on Main is **6 Britannic Hall**, an interesting structure perched atop a massive boulder, which houses a private business. Also on Main are St. George's Anglican Church, rebuilt following the hurricane of 1819, and the Methodist Church, built after the hurricane of 1924. In between the two churches is HM Prison where the infamous William Arthur Hodge was executed for murdering a slave. The Sunday Morning Well on Upper Main Street is marked with a plaque commemorating it as the site where the Proclamation of Emancipation was read in 1834.

The **7 J.R. O'Neal Botanic Gardens,** created by the B.V.I. National Parks Trust, are located northwest of the town center and contain nearly three acres of indigenous and exotic tropical plants. Landscaped paths lead past flowering hibiscus and bougainvillea, a lily pond and a waterfall.

8 Government House, overlooking Road Harbor, is south of

the ferry docks on Waterfront Drive. A bit further along is **Queen Elizabeth Park**. Part of the B.V.I. national park system, this small waterfront park contains shrubs, flowers and rows of white cedars.

Island Attractions (shown on map on page 228):

The architect William Thornton, who designed the Capitol in Washington, was born

(Above) A 17th-century round-tower at Fort Recovery. (Below) The quaint shops in Road Town.

on Tortola in 1759. He trained as a physician in London and practised medicine on Tortola before emigrating to the United States in 1787. The ruins of his family plantation estate can be seen at **9** **Pleasant Valley**.

Country roads lead to mountaintop views on the pastoral island of Tortola.

The **🔟 Briercliffe-Davis Observatory**, established in 1984 atop Tortola's mountain ridge, provides panoramic views of the B.V.I. and U.S. Virgin Islands. Located along Ridge Road, a half-mile north of the Cane Garden Bay turn-off, it is part of a complex containing the Skyworld restaurant and bar, and a gift shop selling local artwork.

Callwood Rum Distillery at Cane Garden Bay is housed in a stone building from the plantation era. Copper boiling vats, an old still and a cane crusher remain in use, and bottles of Arundel Rum line the shelves.

Sopers Hole at the West End is where Dutch settlers first landed in 1648. A sheltered harbor with several restaurants and shops, it is today a major anchorage and location of Tortola's main ferry terminal.

Beef Island, at the eastern end of Tortola, used to be a buccaneer hang-out and is now the location of the B.V.I.'s international airport. Beef Island is connected to Tortola by the Territory's only toll bridge – a one-lane structure dedicated by Queen Elizabeth in 1966.

Virgin Gorda

Virgin Gorda (the fat virgin), was named by Columbus who may have anchored off the island in 1493. Today about 2,500 people live on the island, which consists of three distinct sections.

The northern third rings North Sound, a beautiful blue lagoon of protected coral reefs and white beaches. Yachts anchor here and the shore facilities include a number of resorts, dive operators and the famous Bitter End Yacht Club. The island's middle section is mountainous and crowned by Gorda Peak which, at 1,370 feet, rises in the middle of Gorda Peak National Park.

The southern third of the island is flat, its western shore lined with lovely beaches. The ferry from Road Town pulls into St. Thomas Bay, just north of the Yacht Harbor which is home to luxury yachts and charter fleets, as well as a shopping center which includes a dive shop, bar and restaurant. South of here is Little Fort National Park where a wildlife sanctuary and ruins of a Spanish fortress are located.

Further south is Virgin Gorda's famous landmark – **The Baths**. The beach here is dominated by unique rock formations containing sea caves and shallow pools of seawater connected by passageways. Geologists remain puzzled by the origin of these enormous granite boulders which could be the result of glacial action.

Virgin Gorda's most popular beaches, for both swimming and snorkeling, are The Baths and neighboring Spring Bay. Trunk Bay, a wide sandy beach, can be reached by a rough path from Spring Bay.

Giant boulders dot the sands of The Baths on Virgin Gorda.

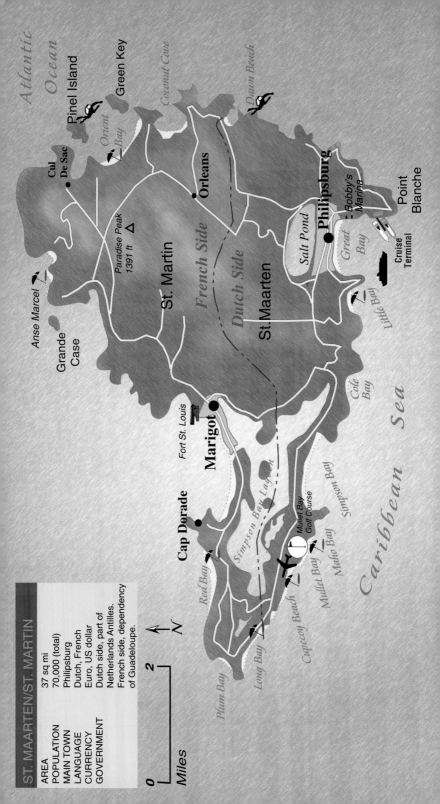

CHAPTER ELEVEN

ST. MAARTEN / ST. MARTIN

It's been called the island with a split personality, but both sides are friendly. The Netherlands and France have peacefully shared this semi- arid island since 1648 when a border was established dividing it in two. Variations of a popular legend explain why the French ended up with 20 square miles versus the Dutch share of 17 square miles. A foot race, so the story goes, was held between a Frenchman and a Dutchman, who walked in opposite directions around the shoreline until they met again and a line was drawn across the island between these two points. The Frenchman was drinking either wine or brandy, while the Dutchman was indulging in gin or perhaps beer. One version of the legend has the Frenchman abstaining, but this seems unlikely. Whatever their respective choices of beverage, the Frenchman walked faster than the Dutchman. Some say the critical factor was not the drink but the fetching French maiden deployed to delay the Dutchman.

Foot races aside, the Dutch were no doubt happy with their share of the island because the Great Salt Pond, with its high-quality salt, was what they wanted and what they got. The island

was called Sualouiga (Salt Land) by the island's original inhabitants, the Arawaks. A seafaring people from South America, their ancient artifacts are still being discovered by local archaeologists. Columbus was the first European to sight and name the island in 1493, although some historians believe it was another island he saw.

The Spanish were seeking gold and they paid St. Maarten little attention. The Dutch and French, however, saw great worth in the island's salt flats. The Dutch West India Company needed a secure source of salt for preserving fish and in the mid-1620s some Dutch traders landed on St.

St. Maarten's Great Bay viewed from Fort Amsterdam.

Maarten's south shore. About the same time, a handful of French families settled on the island's north side and a peaceful co-existence prevailed until a Spanish fleet landed 1,300 soldiers on the island in 1633. The Dutch company's 80-man garrison was quickly overcome and a force of Spanish soldiers held the island for the next 15 years, fending off a Dutch attack in 1644 led by Curacao governor Peter Stuyvesant, who lost a leg in the battle and soon afterwards was appointed governor of New Amsterdam (later New York City).

In 1648, Spain withdrew and the remaining Dutch and French inhabitants returned to their peaceful co-existence, dividing the island along a customary boundary (or perhaps one determined by that legendary foot race). A hilly island, St. Maarten was cultivated with sugar plantations during the 18th century,

Pointe Blanche in Great Bay is the cruise port for St. Maarten.

along with cattle ranches. Britain seized it and other Dutch colonies after Napoleon invaded Holland in 1795, then returned the island in 1815.

When France ended slavery on St. Martin in 1848, slaves on the Dutch side simply took their freedom. Official emancipation came in 1863 and the plantation system disappeared, with planters unable to pay wages and still make a profit. The freed slaves and white settlers grew subsistence crops in the arid climate and sought seasonal work on other islands. The island lacks an adequate water supply and a desalination plant now provides fresh water for today's influx of tourists and an exploding population which now exceeds 60,000 residents.

St. Maarten was one of the first Caribbean islands to open up to tourism, which has boomed since the early 1970s. An extensively developed island with an infrastructure to accommodate the thousands of tourists who come here each year, St. Maarten calls

itself the Friendly Island. There are no border checks, just a monument commemorating the 300th anniversary (1648-1948) of the two nations' peaceful sharing of the island. Both sides have retained their colonial ties – St. Martin is an overseas region of France and a prefecture of Guadeloupe, while St. Maarten is part of the Netherlands Antilles, an autonomous part of the Kingdom of the Netherlands. Capitalizing on its strong links to Europe, the island has forged its own identity in which French and Dutch influences have combined with West Indian heritage to create a vibrant Creole culture. It's a high-energy island offering cosmopolitan flair with a calypso beat.

Today it's a toss-up which country got the better half of the island. Philipsburg, the Dutch capital, is where most of the cruise ships moor. Marigot, the French capital, is where cruise passengers go to sample French boutiques and bistros. The Dutch side has gambling casinos and a golf course; the French side has Fort Louis and topless sunbathing. Both capitals are free ports and the entire island contains beach-lined bays which attract tourists in such numbers that the road leading from Philipsburg to Marigot is often clogged with bumper-to-bumper traffic. The Princess Juliana International Airport is one of the busiest in the West Indies and the island is one of the Caribbean's most popular ports of call, offering great shopping, dozens of beaches, and an impressive array

Marigot, on the island's French side, offers elegant shops and inviting sidewalk cafes.

of shore excursions. Yet, in spite of the island's high level of development, it's still possible to find a quiet stretch of sand on which to enjoy the island's ever-present sunshine.

Getting Around

The cruise pier, which opened in 2001, is located at Pointe Blanche, about a mile from Philipsburg. It's possible to walk into town, take a taxi ($4 per person each way) or use Bobby's Marina tender service, which runs between the terminal and the town pier at a cost of $5 for the entire day. On busy port days, some cruise ships anchor in Great Bay and tender their passengers ashore to the town pier which is adjacent to **1** **Cyrus Wathney Square** where a Tourist Information Bureau **i** and taxi stand are located.

Philipsburg is easy to explore on foot with its two main streets – Front and Back (Vorstraat and Achterstraat) – running parallel with the waterfront. Front Street, lined with duty-free shops, features West Indian-style buildings trimmed with gingerbread fretwork. Back Street, the former site of salt warehouses, is connected with Front Street by a series of interesting alleyways called *steegjes*.

The cheapest way to travel directly between Philipsburg and Marigot is by **public bus**. These vans pick up passengers on Back Street and drop off in downtown Marigot. The fare is about $2 each way and the buses run regu-larly throughout the day.

Taxis are unmetered and a few sample one-way fares from Philipsburg (1-4 passengers per taxi) are: to Marigot $14, to Maho Beach $12, to Dawn Beach $15, to Orient Beach $18.

There are numerous car rental agencies in both St. Maarten and St. Martin, however the main roads are often congested and there have been reports of rental car break-ins by thieves looking for valuables (especially vulnerable are vehicles parked by beaches).

Dutch and French are the offi-cial languages but English is widely spoken – especially in the shops.

Shopping – The official curren-cies are the Netherlands Antilles florin and the euro, but U.S. dollars are accepted throughout the island. With about 500 duty-free shops and savings of up to 50%, the island is a great place to shop for such goods as French perfume, Irish linen and designer fashions. Good buys are available in cameras, electronics, watches, jewelry, china, crystal, leather shoes and handbags, and Finnish stoneware. Bargains in liquor include fine cognac and St. Maarten's own guavaberry liqueur which can be purchased at the Guavaberry Emporium – housed in a townhouse (formerly the gov-ernor's home) on Front Street.

Beaches – On St. Maarten/St. Martin, there's a beach (37 in total) to suit everyone's taste, whether it's resort

The Guavaberry Emporium is on Front Street in Philipsburg.

facilities, coral reefs or sandy solitude that you're seeking. All beaches have public access and those designated 'topless' and 'clothing optional' are on the French side.

Fine beaches on the Dutch side include **Great Bay**, just a few steps from Front Street. Nearby is **Little Bay**, a small but lovely beach backed by a number of resorts. **Maho Bay** has sparkling white sand and a surf that is sometimes rough. Facilities are available at the Maho Beach Hotel. The mile-long beach at **Mullet Bay** also has resort facilities. The island's only golf course is located beside this beach.

Cupecoy Bay's beach of powdery white sand is backed by sandstone cliffs and caves. A dramatic setting, there are no change facilities or watersports here, and there is topless bathing at the far end.

More beautiful beaches await on the French side. Those near Marigot include **Red Bay**, with snack facilities and good snorkeling at its eastern end. **Long Bay** is one of the island's largest

Long Bay, on the French side, is one the longest and quietest beaches on the island.

beaches and is fairly quiet with little resort development. Topless bathers frequent this beach, and the neighboring beach at **Plum Bay** can be reached by walking west around Canonnier Point. Plum Point is a good snorkeling spot.

At the north end of the island is **Orient Bay** – one of St. Martin's busiest beaches, offering restaurants, snack bars, watersports and a non-stop water taxi to Green Key Island. Beach chairs, umbrellas, catamarans and windsurfers can all be rented here and those who like sunbathing in the buff can do so in front of the Club Orient Hotel.

For visitors with children, the beaches at **Anse Marcel** (north end) and **Coconut Grove** (east side) are quiet and shady. The one at Coconut Grove has change facilities, refreshments, chairs and sailboard rentals.

Pasanggrahan Royal Guest House has hosted Dutch royalty.

Dive & Snorkel Sites – At the island's north end, Flat Island, Pinel Island (reached by boat from Cul de Sac) and Orient Bay/Green Key are part of a Regional Underwater Reserve and offer excellent snorkeling. Also within the reserve is Grand Cayes, a unique diving site on the coral reef barrier. On the east side, Dawn Beach has some of the island's best snorkeling along its offshore reefs, and refreshments are available here.

Dive shops are located at various hotels, including Mullet Bay Resort. Some fascinating wrecks are within easy reach, such as the British ship *HMS Proselyte* which sank in 1801 about one mile off the eastern entrance to Great Bay. Near the western entrance point, off Fort Amsterdam, a 17th-century warship is resting on Man-O-War Reef, its scattered cannons still visible.

Golf – An 18-hole course, with a great view of the Caribbean Sea, is located at Mullet Bay Resort on the Dutch side of the island.

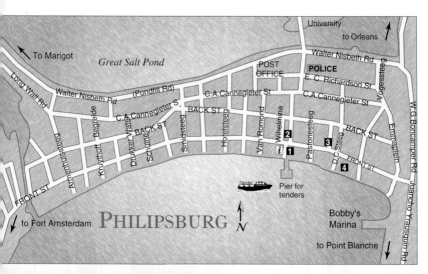

Shore Excursions

St. Maarten

Shore Excursions – St. Maarten offers a good selection of boating excursions, including lively sight-seeing cruises with unlimited rum punch and private-island beach stops for a chance to swim, snorkel and sunbathe.

A highly popular boating attraction is the 'America's Cup' Sailing Regatta out of Philipsburg. No sailing experience is necessary to sign on as 'deckhand' in this friendly regatta that takes place outside Great Bay onboard original 12-meter yachts that were raced in the 1987 America's Cup in Fremantle, Australia. The boats, about 70 feet in length, are manned with an experienced skipper and crew who assign each deckhand a task and explain its execution. A few practice tacks and jibes are made on the way to the race course, and then it's time to leap into action and experience the exhilaration of world-class yacht racing.

Other shore excursions include a driving tour to Marigot, a butterfly farm and other highlights, or island sightseeing on a Harley motorcycle. Hiking, horseback riding and jeep safaris are also offered, as is scuba diving and deep sea fishing.

Local Sights

2 The **Courthouse** overlooks the square on Front Street. Built in the 1790s, it has at various times housed a barracks, prison cells, secretariat and post office, in addition to its courtroom. The original wood-and-stone building was repaired following hurricane damage in 1819. Its most recent restoration was completed in 1969, and the building is now occupied by the Court of First Instance.

Entered off Front and Back Streets, **3** **Old Street Mall** is a colorful shopping alley featuring several dozen shops, boutiques and restaurants. Nearby, at the east end of Front Street, is **4** **Pasanggrahan Royal Guest House**. The oldest and most authentic colonial style inn on St. Maarten, it used to be the Governor's home and was a royal residence for Dutch Queen Juliana during World War II when, as a princess fleeing the Nazi invasion of her homeland, she stayed there while en route to Canada.

The Courthouse overlooks the main square on Front Street.

Fort St. Louis stands atop a hill overlooking Marigot Bay.

Island Attractions

The ruins of Fort Amsterdam stand on Great Bay's western point, and directly north atop Fort Hill are the remains of Fort William. The St. Maarten Zoological and Botanical Garden, which focuses on education and contains baboons and St. Kitts monkeys, is located just north of Great Salt Pond.

The winding road from Philipsburg to Marigot provides scenic views of yacht-filled Simpson Bay Lagoon as it ascends the hilly terrain. An observation platform on top of Cole Bay Hill offers sweeping views of neighboring islands, including Anguilla and St. Barts. The Cole Bay Hill Cemetery contains the grave of Scottish adventurer John Philips, for whom Philipsburg is named.

Paradise Peak is the island's highest point at 1,500 feet above sea level and a number of hiking trails lead in all directions from this point. It can be reached by a secondary road from Rambaud, which is located on the main road

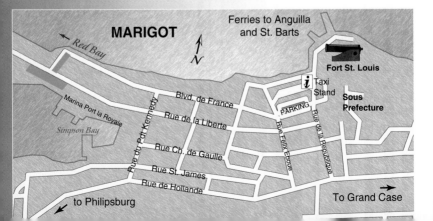

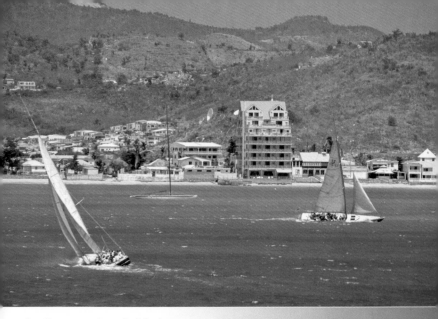

leading north of Marigot to **Grande Case** – a fishing village renowned for its gourmet restaurants and restored creole houses. This waterfront village is also the location of the Seaworld Explorer, a semi-submersible glass-bottom boat that provides narrated tours of the coral reefs around Creole Rock. The northern tip of the island, around Anse Marcel, consists of secluded coves and scenic hiking trails. The island's oldest French settlement of Orleans is located on the island's east side.

Marigot is a pretty port of French colonial buildings and elegant shops. The harborfront is a pleasant place to stroll and gaze at anchored sailboats or relax at an outdoor cafe beneath the shade of colorful awnings. Marigot's Tourist Information Center **i** is located near the waterfront, at the north end of Rue De La Republique. Beside it is a taxi stand and opposite is an open-air market where vendors sell their wares beneath multi-colored

Two 12-meter yachts tack toward Philipsburg, their deckhands enjoying one of the Caribbean's most popular shore excursions.

canopies. Perched above this festive scene is Fort St. Louis, its hilltop ruins reached by stairs leading from the Sous-Prefecture parking lot. With its sweeping view over Marigot Bay and the lagoon, this spot is a wonderful place to indulge in a picnic after wandering about the site. Built in 1767 during the reign of Louis XVI, the fort was armed with 15 cannons.

Anguilla

Anguilla is a short ferry ride from St. Martin but is worlds apart in terms of atmosphere. The northernmost of the Leeward Islands, this British territory of 10,000 residents is a true island hideaway, favored by celebrities, with miles of white powdery beaches and luxury resort accommodations. There is no poverty on the

island, which has a nearly-nonexistent crime rate.

While Anguilla's main attractions are the beaches and coral gardens, a unique feature on the island is the Fountain – a cavern containing several fresh-water pools, a fountain, a dozen or so petroglyphs, and a 16-foot stalagmite carved by Taino Indians. Archaeologists believe this dome-shaped cavern was a major Amerindian center for worship.

St. Barts

Named St-Barthelemy by Christopher Columbus and once governed by Sweden, the island everyone calls St. Barts is unabashedly French and very chic. It lies 15 miles southeast of St. Maarten and is part of the French overseas *departement* of Guadeloupe. The island's capital is **Gustavia**, its sheltered natural harbor often filled with sailing craft and luxury yachts, its streets of northern-European style homes overlooked by the ruins of forts

that once defended this tiny island.

During colonial times, in the mid-1600s, the island was settled by Huguenots from Brittany and Normandy. In 1784, France's Louis XVI ceded the island to King Gustav III of Sweden in return for duty-free trading rights in Gothenburg. Gustavia was soon declared a free port and the island, benefiting from Sweden's neutrality, prospered until struck by hurricanes and a great fire in Gustavia in 1852.

In 1877, France bought the island back for 320,000 francs and to this day the island's French culture remains strong. Residents, about 5,000 in number, speak a French patois sprinkled with English and Swedish words, and women can still be seen wearing starched white caps like those of their Norman ancestors. The population is predominantly white, for the semi-arid island never supported a plantation economy, and in the past, local commerce was based on trade and fishing.

That all changed when the jet set discovered this island hideaway, and tourism is now its major industry.

The Rockefeller, Ford and Rothschild families all have vacation homes on St. Barts, and this 8-1/2-square mile island is dotted with luxury resorts. Its varied shoreline of pristine coves and idyllic beaches includes Anse du Gouverneur, accessible only on foot and considered one of the finest in the West Indies, and Saint-Jean, the island's most photographed beach with its two crescents of pale sand separated by a rocky promontory. The remote beach at Columbier on the island's north shore is where David Rockefeller built a vacation home, and Grand Cul-de-Sac Bay, a favorite with windsurfers, has two beaches – one embracing the tranquil waters of a sheltered bay, the other facing the ocean.

Beach hopping can be done by rented mini-moke and beach buggy, or by taxi. A taxi stand is located in Gustavia where local attractions include duty-free shops and the town's two historic churches – the Roman Catholic French church and the Anglican Swedish church. Fort Oscar, built in the 17th century, stands at the tip of a peninsula and is occupied by the Ministry of Armed Forces. The ruins of Fort Carl stand in the heights of Gustavia and provide a spectacular view of the harbor. Fort Gustave also provides panoramic views of Gustavia and neighboring islands.

Other island attractions include the Wall House Museum & Library, housed in a Swedish colonial building, and the Inter Oceans shell museum which is located in Corossol, one of the island's oldest villages.

French is the official language on St. Barts and the euro its official currency, but English is widely spoken and prices are often quoted in U.S. dollars.

Gustavia, on the tiny French island of St. Barts, is a popular port of call for sailing yachts and small luxury cruise ships.

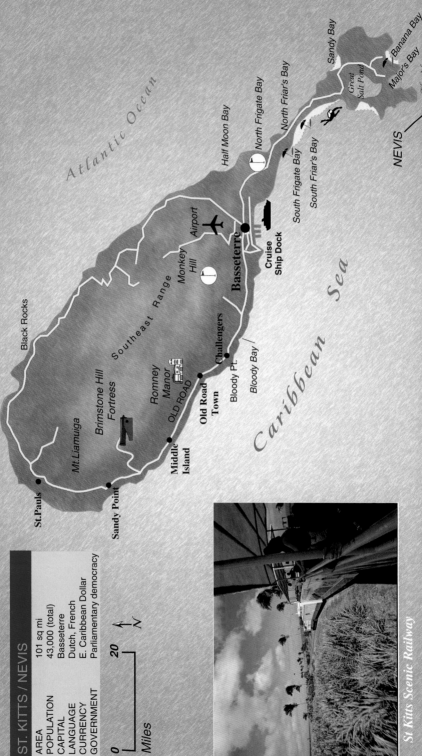

ST. KITTS / NEVIS

AREA	101 sq mi
POPULATION	43,000 (total)
CAPITAL	Basseterre
LANGUAGE	Dutch, French
CURRENCY	E. Caribbean Dollar
GOVERNMENT	Parliamentary democracy

N

Miles

0   20

Atlantic Ocean

Black Rocks

Mt. Liamuiga

Brimstone Hill Fortress

Southeast Range

St.Pauls

Sandy Point

Middle Island

Romney Manor

OLD ROAD

Monkey Hill

Airport

Challengers

Old Road Town

Bloody Pt.

Bloody Bay

Half Moon Bay

North Frigate Bay

North Friar's Bay

South Frigate Bay

South Friar's Bay

Basseterre

Cruise Ship Dock

Caribbean Sea

Sandy Bay

Great Salt Pond

Banana Bay

Major's Bay

NEVIS

St Kitts Scenic Railway

CHAPTER TWELVE

ST. KITTS

The verdant mountains of St. Kitts are a beautiful sight as your ship draws close to this island of patchwork fields and sandy beaches. Its pastoral charm belies the bloody battles that took place on this island, called Liamuiga ('fertile land') by its early Carib inhabitants. So valued was St. Kitts for its sugarcane, the British eventually built a massive fortress on Brimstone Hill, which became known as the 'Gibraltar of the West Indies'.

A massive fortification of volcanic rock and limestone mortar, the fortress took more than a century to build using slave labor. When completed in 1794, its walls encompassed a citadel, bastions, barracks, officers quarters, storehouses, cookhouses and a hospital. Both impregnable and impressive, the Brimstone Hill Fortress looms nearly a thousand feet above the surrounding countryside with sweeping views of the coastline and other islands. Its name refers to the odor of sulphur that seeps from nearby volcanic vents. The fortress itself stands atop an upthrust of solidified lava covered by limestone.

St. Kitts and its neighboring island of Nevis are the upper slopes and cones of volcanoes resting on a submarine rock base. Mount Liamuiga, the highest peak on St. Kitts at 3,793 feet, was last active in 1692. Nevis Peak, a single volcano in the center of Nevis Island, rises to 3,232 feet. The two islands are separated by a two-mile-wide channel called the Narrows, its shallow sea floor covered with coral reefs.

The lower slopes of St. Kitts are cultivated right down to the coast, except on the island's south end where the vegetation is thorny scrub and dry forest. This relatively undeveloped area is inhabited with Green Vervet monkeys, often seen scampering across the road. They were brought to St. Kitts by the French who, along with the British, drew supplies of salt and timber from the island in the late 1600s. A hundred years earlier, the island had been named St. Christopher by Columbus, in honor of his patron saint, but it became known as St. Kitts and the name was officially changed in 1988.

In 1605 England took possession of St. Kitts and in 1623 the island's first white settlers arrived, led by Sir Thomas Warner, a Suffolk gentleman who planned to grow tobacco here with the financial support of a syndicate of British merchants. He drove off a small group of hostile Carib natives, cleared the land and established the first permanent British settlement in the West Indies, only to have a hurricane destroy his first crop of tobacco. But Warner and his followers persevered and a new crop was planted the next year. They soon had company in the form of French pirates, their damaged ship putting in to what is now Basseterre for repairs. The French, led by Belain d'Esnambuc, decided to stay and plant tobacco too.

The British and French joined forces to massacre some avenging Caribs and wipe them from the island. They then divided the island, which is 23 miles long and up to seven miles across. The central mountainous region went to the English; the north and south ends went to the French. But the living was far from easy, and frequent quarrels flared between the British and French farmers, many of whom died of diseases such as yellow fever and malaria. In 1628, a wealthy British planter led a group of settlers to Nevis, and by 1632 others had left St. Kitts to settle on Montserrat and Antigua. The French also used St. Kitts as a staging area for the settlement of their other islands, such as Guadeloupe, Martinique and St. Martin.

Mother colony of the West Indies for both the British and the French, St. Kitts was battled over for the next century and a half until the 1783 Treaty of Versailles recognized it as a British posses-sion. In 1871, St. Kitts and Nevis were incorporated in the colony of Leeward Islands, and in 1983 they became, along with a small coral island called Sombrero (which lies about 35 miles northwest of Anguilla), an independent state within the British Commonwealth.

The fertile soil on St. Kitts supported three centuries of sugar-cane crops and showed no signs of exhaustion until the 20th century, when modern methods of cultivation initially doubled the yield per acre, followed by a marked decrease. Agriculture is still the island's major export with the entire sugarcane crop of St. Kitts and Nevis processed at a refinery in Basseterre. Nearly 40 miles of narrow-gauge railway encircles St. Kitts, built between 1912 and 1925 to transport wagon loads of cane from the plantations to the refinery.

Basseterre

About 36,000 people live on St. Kitts and the chief town is Basseterre (pronounced *bass-terr*), originally founded by the French but developed by the English from 1706 onwards. The town suffered widespread destruction from an earthquake in 1843 and was rebuilt in 1867 following a great fire that

Brimstone Hill Fortress, built of volcanic rock and limestone mortar, took over a century to complete.

destroyed most of the town. The town's main cruise pier – Port Zante – is located on the Basseterre harbor and can accommodate the world's largest ocean liners (such as Queen Mary 2). The other pier – Birdrock Deepwater Port – is located 2.5 miles south of the town center and is used mainly for freight but does accommodate cruise ships when the main pier is full.

A tourist office is located on the ground floor of the Pelican Mall overlooking the cruise pier. Continuing west along the harborfront you will pass a post office and National Museum on our way to the Treasury Building, its archway leading to Fort Street and the Circus.

American money is widely accepted on St. Kitts, although the official currency is the East Caribbean dollar, worth approximately $2.70 EC per $1 US (or approximately $1 EC per 40¢ US).

Getting Around

St. Kitts has good roads and beautiful scenery, so touring the island by taxi, rental car or organized shore excursion is a pleasurable way to spend your time in

A cruise ship pulls into Basseterre on the island of St. Kitts.

port. English is the official language and residents also speak a local patois.

Taxi cabs are widely available in Basseterre, both at the cruise pier and the Circus. A taxi dispatcher at the cruise pier will quote you a fare and direct you to a driver. The set fare is per car, one to four persons. Approximate fares from Basseterre: Romney Manor (return) $30.00; Brimstone Hill (return) $35; Frigate Bay (one-way) $13; Friars Beach (one-way) $15; Tour of South East Peninsula $45; Island Tour $65. On round-trip fares, a 15-minute wait at each destination is included. After that, a small waiting fee is charged.

There are several car rental agencies in Basseterre, including Avis and Thrifty/TDC in Independence Square. A local driving license (obtained by presenting your current license and $24 at the Police Station) is required. Driving is on the left-hand side of the road. The highway circling the island is well maintained with good signage, making it easy to get around.

A Victorian clock-tower stands in the center of the Circus, Basseterre's main traffic circle.

Shopping – St. Kitts is famous for its locally produced clothing made of beautiful batik and tie-dyed cotton. Other local crafts include hand-embroidered items, straw goods and ceramics. Duty-free items sold here include perfumes, jewelry, crystal and porcelain. Port Zante offers duty-free jewelry, liquor and souvenirs.

Shopping areas in Basseterre are found along Bay Road, Liverpool Row and Fort Street. The Circus is where Island Hopper sells Caribelle Batik's famous dresses, caftans, wraps and wall murals. The Caribelle Batik studio, where these exquisite fashions are designed and made, is located at Romney Manor (northwest of Basseterre). Duty-free shopping can be found on Liverpool Row and at the Pelican Shopping Mall on the downtown waterfront. A philatelic bureau selling colorful collectors issues of postage stamps is also located in this mall.

Local art, including the renowned Carnival Clown series by Rose Cameron Smith, can be bought in The Spencer Cameron Gallery on North Independence Square. The Plantation Picture House, home to Kate Spencer's studio and gallery, is at the northwest end of the island near Rawlins Plantation.

A colorful **public market** is located on Bay Road, a few blocks west of the Treasury Pier.

Beaches – Several attractive beaches are situated at the island's southern end. South Frigate Bay has resort facilities and watersports equipment rental, including snorkeling gear. Considered the island's best beach by locals, South Friars Bay provides good snorkeling and a family atmosphere. At the southern tip lies Turtle Beach, with an excellent beach bar and restaurant. Other fine beaches in the area are found at at Cockleshell Bay and Banana Bay, with an excellent view across the Narrows to Nevis. Dramatic beaches with surf on the Atlantic side include Conaree Beach and North Frigate Bay – where the St. Kitts Marriott Resort and Sugar Bay Club are located.

Diving & Snorkeling – The Caribbean side of the island has protected waters and extensive reefs that begin in shallow water and drop off to depths of 100 feet or more. Dive sites on St. Kitts include Bloody Bay Reef, laced with small caves filled with purple anemones and yellow sea fans, and the Grid Iron, an undersea shelf in the Narrows which is covered with shallow-water corals, sea fans and sponges. Snorkeling can be enjoyed at many of the island's beaches, especially those on the Caribbean side, such as South Frigate Bay and South Friars Bay.

Golf – Courses on St. Kitts include the Golden Rock Golf Club (near the airport north of Basseterre), and the Royal St. Kitts Golf Course at Frigate Bay. The latter is an 18-hole championship course bordered by the Atlantic Ocean and the Caribbean Sea. Designed by the Golf Course Architectural Group, this par-72 course is both challenging and scenic, its fairways and greens adorned with ponds, palm trees and tropical flowers.

Shore Excursions
St. Kitts

Shore Excursions on St. Kitts include a scenic ride on the island's historic, narrow-gauge railroad (see photo, page 248), or various driving tours to visit island highlights such as Brimstone Hill Fortress and Romney Manor. Mountain biking, 4WD safaris, kayaking and guided volcano hikes are also offered, as are walking tours of Basseterre and golfing at Royal St. Kitts Golf Course. On-the-water excursions include a catamaran ride to Nevis for snorkeling in a sheltered cove and lounging at Pinney's Beach, or taking the ferry to Nevis for a tour of Charlestown and other island attractions.

Fine beaches near Basseterre include North Frigate Bay.

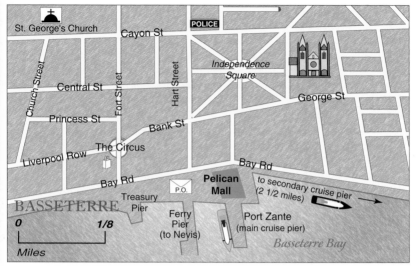

Local Attractions

The Circus, in the heart of Basseterre, is a traffic circle modeled after London's famous Piccadilly Circus. In the center of this busy hub stands Berkeley Memorial, a Victorian clocktower monument commemorating a former president of the General Legislative Council.

Bank Street leads off The Circus to Independence Square (originally

Independence Square and Church of the Immaculate Conception.

called Pall Mall Square) which was built in 1790 for slave auctions and council meetings. This open square, lined with colonial buildings, consists of eight paths converging on a central fountain, its pattern resembling the Union Jack when seen from the air. Facing the square on its east side is the Roman Catholic Church of the Immaculate Conception, and at its southeast corner is the Court House with a public library upstairs.

St. George's Anglican Church, an impressive brownstone structure surrounded by lawns and

flowering shrubs on Cayon Street, was originally called Notre Dame when built by the French in 1670. Burned to the ground by the British in 1706, it was rebuilt four years later and named for England's patron saint. Two fires and an earthquake between 1763 and 1843 resulted in the church being rebuilt three more times, followed by its most recent restoration in 1869.

Island Attractions

Bloody Point at the mouth of Stone Fort River is the former site of a Carib village. Within the walls of the river's narrow canyon, 2,000 Carib Indians were massacred by the British and French in 1626. The Caribs, unhappy with the increasing number of Europeans settling their island, had been planning their own attack when they were trapped here and slaughtered. The river is said to have run red with their blood. Local taxi drivers will stop at Bloody Point if asked and young children with pet monkeys often wait here for camera-toting tourists. Carib carvings (petroglyphs) can be seen on the canyon walls, which are about a half hour hike from Bloody Point.

Old Road Town is where **Thomas Warner** landed on St. Kitts in 1623 and established the first permanent British settlement in the West Indies. It was the island's capital until 1727. Nearby, at what is now Wingfield Estate, are Carib petroglyphs and pictographs sketched on boulders.

Romney Manor, site of a 17th-century plantation with sugar mill

(Above) Treasury Building.
(Below) St. George's Anglican Church.

The Brimstone Hill citadel known as 'Gibraltar of the West Indies'.

and great house ruins, is now home to Caribelle Batik, where local artisans practice the Indonesian art of batik to produce high-quality fabrics and fashions of striking designs and colors. The lovely grounds feature an enormous 350-year-old saman (rain) tree and five acres of flowers, shrubbery and terraced lawns.

Thomas Warner's tomb is located in the churchyard of St. Thomas Church in Middle Island.

The second-largest fortress in the Caribbean, **Brimstone Hill** was inaugurated as a national park by Queen Elizabeth in 1985 and declared a UNESCO World Heritage Site in 2000. The impressive fortifications contain a visitor center at the base of the restored citadel, atop which 24-pounder cannons overlook the sea and surrounding countryside. The sweeping view includes the island of St. Eustatius to the northwest.

Beyond Brimstone Hill, at the northwest end of St. Kitts, are scenic sugarcane plantations and estates. At Black Rocks, on the north coast, you can view black cliffs and boulders formed by lava flowing from Mount Liamuiga and eroded by a pounding sea.

The island's Southeast Peninsula is easily accessible by modern highway from Basseterre. The Frigate Bay area contains several luxury resorts, sandy beaches and a golf course. At the far end of the peninsula, nestled among the cone-shaped hills, is the Great Salt Pond. This undeveloped area of breathtaking vistas and pristine beaches is also the place to spot wild monkeys in the low scrub that lines the quiet roads.

Nevis

Dominated by a single central mountain peak, the small island of Nevis (pronounced Nee-vis), is steeped in Old World charm. It was called Nieves (Spanish for snow) by Columbus because cloud-covered Nevis Peak reminded him of a snow-capped mountain. The main port of

Charlestown is where most of the island's 9,000 residents live and is connected to Basseterre by passenger ferry (a 45-minute crossing).

Charlestown was once a fashionable health spa destination for the wealthy who stayed at the grand Bath Hotel and Spring House, built in 1778. The resort's bath houses were positioned on a fault over a hot spring, and a soak in the thermal mineral water brought relief from rheumatism and gout. Today's visitors can still take a mineral bath and tour the reconstructed hotel, much of its original structure destroyed by a 1950 earthquake.

Other historic attractions in Charlestown include a cotton ginney (still used during the March/April picking season) and the Alexander Hamilton House, birthplace of the American statesman and aide to Washington. The Hamilton Museum, housed in a Georgian-style building, contains papers by Hamilton and other archival documents. Nevis's other famous figure is Horatio Nelson, the British naval hero

Nevis Peak dominates the verdant island of Nevis.

who, as a young captain stationed in the West Indies, met and married in 1787 a local woman named Francis Nesbitt. A record of their marriage (and Alexander Hamilton's birth) is registered at St. John's Church in Fig Tree Village. There's also a Nelson Museum in Morning Star, and Nelson's Spring is where he took on water for his ships before sailing to North America during the American War of Independence. Other attractions on Nevis include its restored plantation estates, the golden sands of Pinney's Beach, and an 18-hole championship golf course at the Four Seasons Resort Nevis, one of the Caribbean's top-rated resorts.

St. Eustatius

The small Dutch island of St. Eustatius, commonly called Statia, was known as the 'Golden Rock' during colonial times when, as the headquarters of the

Netherlands West Indies Company, its population grew to almost 20,000 and trade in rum, sugar and tobacco was brisk. The island also served as a transhipment port for supplies to the American colonies during the American War of Independence. A salute fired by an American warship on November 16, 1776, was replied to by Fort Oranjestad, thus making the Netherlands the first foreign power to recognize America's new flag, the Stars and Stripes. The fort, perched on a crag above the sea, was built in 1636 and restored in 1976. The town of Oranjestad contains one of the oldest synagogues in the Western Hemisphere and a number of restored 18th-century houses. The island's scenic beauty can be enjoyed on nature trails that crisscross the island, including one that leads through tropical rainforest to the crater of an extinct volcanic peak called The Quill. For snorkelers and scuba divers, the island's surrounding waters are dotted with ship wrecks, coral reefs and rare fish.

Saba

The tiny volcanic island of Saba (pronounced *say-ba*) is part of the Netherlands Antilles and is a unique piece of Caribbean geography. There are no beaches on Saba, which is the top of a dormant volcano, and its steep coastline consists of cliffs that plunge into the sea. Only five square miles in size, Saba's single road – called The Road – winds across the island and connects a handful of villages of red-roofed houses nestled at the base of green slopes.

The waters surrounding Saba contain a microcosm of sea life due to the continual currents flowing past the island's shores. A marine park completely encircles the island and features groove channels filled with juvenile tropical fish, underwater tunnels, barrel sponges and soft corals. Nearby is a range of underwater sea mounts, their peaks 80 feet beneath the surface. Thirty permanent moorings have been installed in Saba Marine Park to accommodate dive boats while protecting the coral. The island's decompression chamber at the Fort Bay Pier was donated by the royal Dutch Navy, and local dive operators help with many of the park's projects, which include the ongoing collection of data and sharing of marine information.

0   16
Miles

St. Barts

Saba

St. Eustatius

Oranjestad

Atlantic Ocean

St. Kitts

Basseterre

Caribbean Sea

The Narrows

N

Charlestown

Nevis

(Above) Southeast Peninsula on St. Kitts. (Left) The Narrows.

(Right) South Friar's Bay. (Below) St. Eustatius viewed from Brimstone Hill.

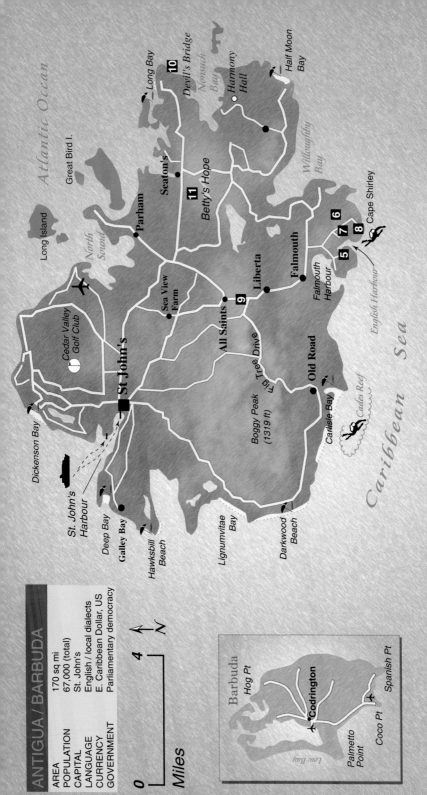

ANTIGUA / BARBUDA

AREA	170 sq mi
POPULATION	67,000 (total)
CAPITAL	St. John's
LANGUAGE	English / local dialects
CURRENCY	E. Caribbean Dollar, US
GOVERNMENT	Parliamentary democracy

Miles

0   4

N

Atlantic Ocean

Long Island

Great Bird I.

Long Bay

Devil's Bridge

Nonsuch Bay

Harmony Hall

Half Moon Bay

North Sound

Seaton's

Parham

Betty's Hope

Willoughby Bay

Cape Shirley

English Harbour

Falmouth

Falmouth Harbour

Liberta

All Saints

Sea View Farm

Cedar Valley Golf Club

St. John's

St. John's Harbour

Dickenson Bay

Deep Bay

Galley Bay

Hawksbill Beach

Lignumvitae Bay

Darkwood Beach

Fig Tree Drive

Boggy Peak (1319 ft)

Old Road

Carlisle Bay

Cades Reef

Caribbean Sea

10

11

9

5

6

7

8

Barbuda

Hog Pt

Codrington

Spanish Pt

Coco Pt

Palmetto Point

Low Bay

CHAPTER THIRTEEN

ANTIGUA

Antigua's beautiful bays and harbors have been providing shelter to seagoing vessels since the days of Columbus. In fact, English Harbour was already a popular hurricane haven when the Royal Navy began using it in 1725 as a dockyard. One of the finest natural harbors in the world with its narrow entrance and surrounding hillsides, English Harbour soon became Britain's major naval port in the West Indies. Fortifications were built on hilltops overlooking this and other harbors on the island, and ships would regularly pull in for repairs and provisions, or to ride out a storm during the hurricane season. This busy dockyard reached its zenith in the late 18th century when 26-year-old Horatio Nelson was headquartered here as commander of the Northern Division of the Leeward Island Station.

The sailing tradition continues today with Antigua's annual Sailing Week in April. One of the world's largest ocean racing events, attracting over 200 yachts from nearly 40 countries, this regatta has been called a 'sailor's Woodstock' for the fun-loving spirit of its competitors. The racing is serious but away from the course the rum punch flows and the dockside events are pure frivolity. A certain decorum does prevail, however, when the winning prizes are presented from the Old Officer's Quarters Balcony in Nelson's Dockyard, after which the Royal Antiguan Police Band 'Beats the Retreat'. The festivities conclude with the Lord Nelson Ball, a formal-dress affair complete with fireworks display.

Such is Antigua, an island conducive to languid lazing on beautiful beaches, but with a hint of British crispness in the accents of its people whose friendliness is tempered with a touch of reserve. The local school children wear uniforms, and cricket is a popular here with international matches played at the Recreation Ground in St. John's. The bat used by Antigua-born Viv Richards, famous captain of the West Indies cricket team, is on display at the local museum.

Antigua is also a recluse for British royalty and rock stars, with the Queen herself once taking a dip in the sea at one of many secluded beaches. Princess Margaret and Lord Snowden honeymooned on Antigua and Princess Diana twice vacationed at the exclusive K Club on Antigua's sister island of Barbuda. Eric Clapton has a home near English Harbour, and Michael Jordan, Whitney Houston and Elton John have all vacationed on Antigua, its powdery white beaches stretching past some of the Caribbean's most elegant resorts.

Antigua (pronounced *An-tee-ga*) was named in 1493 by Columbus for Santa Maria de la

Darkwood Beach, on the west coast, is just one of the many beautiful beaches on Antigua.

Antigua, a miracle-working saint of the Seville Cathedral in Spain. The island's earliest signs of habitation date back to 1775 BC, and settlement by the Arawaks, who migrated here from South America, began in about 35 AD. The island's lack of natural springs discouraged European settlement until, in 1632, some hardy English farmers arrived from St. Kitts, claimed the island for the British crown, and planted crops of tobacco, indigo and ginger. The island remained under British rule for the next three and a half centuries, apart from a brief occupation by the French in 1666.

In 1674, Sir Christopher Codrington arrived from Barbados and, with an army of slaves, established the island's first large sugar plantation, naming it Betty's Hope for his daughter. The plantation's success encouraged others and within 25 years the island's landscape was transformed. Its natural vegetation was cleared to grow sugarcane, and more than 150 sugar mills dotted the countryside. The slave laborers plotted an insurrection in 1736 but the slave trade didn't end until 1808, followed by the abolition of slavery in 1834. The boom market in sugar collapsed but, despite the demise of plantation estates on Antigua, the production of sugar remained the island's major industry well into the 20th century, until surpassed by tourism.

Antigua, its neighboring island of Barbuda and the tiny uninhabited island of Redonda, 20 miles to the west, gained their partial independence from Great Britain in 1967 and have been independent since 1981. The islands' population of 70,000 is mostly of African origin with a small community of Europeans, Americans and Canadians living here. English is the official language.

St. John's is the capital and although this historic trading port has been ravaged by earthquakes, hurricanes and fires over the centuries, its colonial past endures in the British street names and restored harborfront warehouses. Rising above the narrow streets and hip-roofed buildings are the twin spires of St. John's Cathedral – easily visible as your ship pulls into port and docks at the town's doorstep.

Getting Around

Cruise passengers step ashore at **Heritage Quay**, a duty-free shopping complex where a tourist information booth 🛈 and public telephones are located. The quay is just a few minutes walk to the main part of St. John's. The post office is beside Heritage Quay on High Street. On busy port days some ships moor at St. John's Docks, located on the harbor's north side, about one mile from town.

Taxi fares are regulated but you should agree on the price in advance. Sample fares (for the whole taxi, one-way) from Heritage Quay to: Dickenson Bay $8; Deep Bay/Ramada Renaissance $10; Hawksbill Beach Resort $14; English Harbour $20.

Local **car rental** agencies include Avis, Budget and Hertz, and the daily rental rate is about $50. Driving is on the left side of the road and a temporary license ($20) is required. Many of the roads are unmarked, unpaved and in need of repairs.

The **shore excursions** organized by the cruise lines usually include an island drive to Shirley Heights and Nelson's Dockyard, a Jolly Roger Pirate Cruise along the northwest coast, and a catamaran cruise featuring a stop at a secluded beach for snorkeling, swimming and sunbathing.

Official **currency** is the Eastern Caribbean (EC) dollar which is tied to the U.S. dollar at approximately $2.70 EC to $1 US (or $1 EC to 40¢ US), but American currency is accepted everywhere.

Heritage Quay (above) and St. Mary's Street (below) lead up the hillside from the cruise pier.

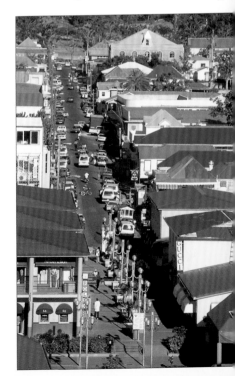

Shopping – Batik island cotton, hand-painted clothing and tropical jewelry are among the Caribbean keepsakes sold in Antigua. Duty-free shopping is available at Heritage Quay, with dozens of international and local stores, and at adjacent Redcliffe Quay, where 19th-century warehouses have been carefully restored and transformed into a shopping district of inviting boutiques and courtyard cafes. More shops are located on St. Mary's Street, including Caribelle Batik, and on High and Long Streets. A colorful produce market is located at the junction of Valley and All Saints Roads and is a good place to buy some local pineapple – highly touted for its delicious sweetness.

Out-of-town shopping opportunities include The Art Center at Nelson's Dockyard, which features the island's largest collection of local art. Local handicrafts are also sold at Dow's Hill Interpretation Center and Shirley Heights Lookout. Harmony Hall, on the east side of the island, is a complex built around an old sugar mill which houses an art gallery featuring works by local artists. At Sea View Farm, a traditional pottery-making village in the middle of the island, residents still make and sell pinched pots from the local clay.

Beaches – Antiguans claim their island has 365 beaches – one for every day of the year. Watersports equipment and lounge chairs can be rented at most of the beach-front resorts, many of which are located along the island's west side. **Dickenson**

Shore Excursions

Antigua

Shore Excursions – Scenic island drives to historic highlights, such as Nelson's Dockyard, are offered. Also available are 4X4 safaris and ATV off-road touring. A round of golf can be enjoyed at Cedar Valley Golf Club. Beach breaks include a catamaran ride to a secluded island. Also featured is the opportunity to swim and snorkel with southern stingrays on a boating expedition out of Seaton's fishing village. Another excursion offers a combination of kayaking, boating and reef snorkeling.

Bay, at the northwest end, is the island's most popular beach with its resort facilities, dive shop and glass-bottom boat tours. **Deep Bay**, due west of St. John's and the location of a Ramada Renaissance resort, is also popular with cruise visitors. Directly south of Deep Bay the beaches become progressively quieter. **Galley Bay** is good for windsurfing and **Hawksbill Beach** Resort is located adjacent to four beach-lined coves, the southernmost one used by nude sunbathers.

Secluded and beautiful beaches lie south of St. John's, such as **Darkwood Beach**, popular with locals on the weekend but usually quiet during the week, and **Carlisle Bay** where an exclusive resort hotel stands atop Curtain Bluff at one end of this inviting stretch of sand.

On the Atlantic side, **Half Moon Bay** is considered by many

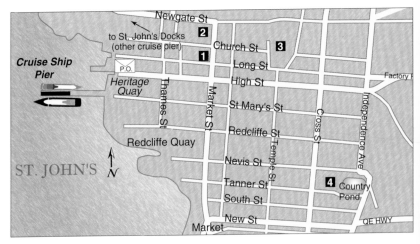

ST. JOHN'S

Cruise Ship Pier

Heritage Quay

Redcliffe Quay

to St. John's Docks (other cruise pier)

Newgate St

Church St

Long St

High St

St Mary's St

Redcliffe St

Nevis St

Tanner St

South St

New St

Market

Thames St

Market St

Cross St

Temple St

Independence Ave

Factory

Country Pond

QE HWY

P.O.

2 **1** **3** **4**

Antiguans to be their most beautiful beach with its circular shape and ocean surf that can range from crashing waves to gentle swells. A reef protects the north side of the beach, where the snorkeling is good, while the body surfing is good in the exposed part of the bay. **Long Bay Beach**, also on the Atlantic side, is just around the point from Devil's Bridge, an eroded arch of limestone.

Dive & Snorkel Sites – Barrier reefs surround much of the island and wrecks are plentiful, including three in Deep Bay, with the Andes lying just off the beach in less than 30 feet. Cape Shirley is a premier dive site, with coral reefs, ledges and overhangs. Cades Reef, off the southwest coast, is a popular dive site and an underwater park. For advanced divers, the ledge of Sunken Rock is a popular site on the south coast. Dive shops are located around the island and include those at Dickenson Bay, Nelson's Dockyard and Club Antigua on Lignumvitae Bay.

Golf – The 18-hole course at The Cedar Valley Golf Club, a few minutes from St. John's, is a 6100-yard, par-70 course and home to the Antigua Open each March.

St. John's Anglican Cathedral

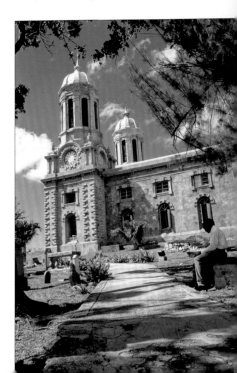

Another 18-hole course is located at Jolly Harbour Marina Club, and the 9-hole course at Half Moon Bay has lovely sea views.

Local Attractions

The **1 Museum of Antigua and Barbuda** is housed in the Old Court House, Antigua's oldest building, which was built in 1747 from stone quarried on some of

(Left) Antigua and Barbuda Museum. (Below) English Harbour, location of Nelson's Dockyard, is one of the most sheltered anchorages in the Caribbean.

Antigua's satellite islands. The museum is located at the corner of Long and Market Streets, and contains hands-on exhibits designed with children in mind, including a life-sized Arawak house. Nearby is the **2 Police Station**, built in 1772 with a fence railing made from musket barrels, some with bayonets still attached.

The twin baroque spires of the **3 Anglican Cathedral of St. John the Divine** stand 70 feet high and are a town landmark. The third church built on this site, it is made of freestone with an interior encased in pitch pine to protect the structure from ruin

(Above) Nelson's Dockyard is a showcase of 18th-century Georgian architecture. (Right) A guide shows one of the capstans that was used to careen ships when repairing their hulls.

during an earthquake or hurricane. The first church was built here in 1681 and the second one was destroyed by an earthquake in 1843. Five years later the present structure was completed and locals refer to it as 'big church'. The pillars of the south gate are topped with white-painted figures representing St. John the Divine and St. John the Baptist, and are said to have been taken from a French ship.

The **4** **Country Pond**, at the top of Tanner Street, was constructed in the mid-1700s by early settlers. Its name is likely a corruption of 'Congo Pond' because this and other ponds on the island were built by contract workers from the Congo. Its purpose was to collect water during heavy rainfalls, with the overflow running into a drainage ditch that divides Tanner Street and runs down to the waterfront. During prolonged droughts, as the Pond's

water level dropped, it could be accessed by steps built along its western wall.

Island Attractions

5 **Nelson's Dockyard** at English Harbour is the premier attraction on Antigua. The island's first national park, this 18th-century naval dockyard maintained a continuous squadron of British ships in the Caribbean and contains beautiful examples of Georgian architecture now housing a museum, two inns, boutiques, restaurants, several businesses and a major marina. Established at its present site in 1743, the dockyard came under the command of Horatio Nelson from 1784 to 1787. Its historic buildings include the Admiral's House, which now houses a museum; The Copper and Lumber Store (now a hotel and restaurant); the Engineer's Office (now the Admiral's Inn Hotel & Restaurant); the Officer's Quarters Building where officers lived during the hurricane season (now housing an art gallery, craft shop and other businesses); and the site of the Capstan House, where the walls no longer remain but the capstans used to careen the ships have been restored. Also intact are the Boat House Pillars that once supported a sail loft and the 200-year-old Sandbox Tree which stands beside the Admiral's House. The dockyard, closed by the Royal Navy in

LORD NELSON

Horatio Nelson, Britain's celebrated naval hero, was a man of great leadership abilities who inspired devotion and exceptional service in his men. Yet, while serving his only peacetime commission in the West Indies from 1784 to 1787, the young captain was anything but popular with the merchants of Antigua. As leader of the Leeward Islands Squadron, Nelson strictly enforced the Navigation Act, which prevented trade with American ships. This enraged the local merchants who threatened legal action over lost business. Nelson, to avoid arrest, confined himself to his ship for eight weeks. This was no great sacrifice for he regarded the island as 'barbarous' and the dockyard that today bears his name as 'vile'. In fact, he always slept aboard his ship while in English Harbour – a common practice among naval officers of the day who wished to avoid the mosquito-carried diseases of yellow fever and malaria.

A plantation owner on the nearby island of Nevis posted Nelson's bail, and when he went ashore at Nevis to thank his benefactor, Nelson met his future wife, a young widow named Fanny Nesbit. At their wedding in 1787, the bride was given away by Nelson's friend and fellow naval captain, Prince William Henry, who eventually became England's King William IV. As for Nelson, he returned to England with his wife and stepson, and pursued a brilliant naval career that ended with his famous victory at the Battle of Trafalgar in 1805. His marriage to Fanny came undone when he fell in love with Lady Emma Hamilton in 1798, but the notoriety of this liaison did not tarnish his reputation with the British public and his legendary status endures to this day.

1889, was reconstructed in the 1950s and officially reopened in 1961. Many of the businesses operating here now serve the local sailing community, a reflection of the dockyard's original function.

6 Dow's Hill Interpretation Center, situated on a ridge overlooking English Harbour, is an educational complex in which visitors can watch a 15-minute light and sound show, imaginatively presented, that depicts six different periods of Antigua's history. Lookout Trail, a nature walk

The Dow's Hill Interpretation Center includes a viewing platform overlooking English Harbour.

connecting English Harbour with Shirley Heights, runs past the Center.

7 Clarence House, the official country residence of the island's Governor General, was built in 1787 as a residence for Prince William Henry while stationed in Antigua as a captain of the Royal Navy. This Georgian country

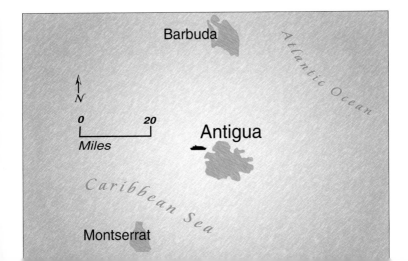

(Above) Shirley Heights Lookout. (Bottom) Tyrells Catholic Church.

house overlooks Nelson's Dockyard and, following the Prince's departure, was used as a residence for senior naval officers.

8 Shirley Heights, a fortified ridge of hills above the town of English Harbour, is one of the most famous views in the Caribbean. With its panoramic perspective, it was the principal lookout for enemy ships approaching English Harbour and is today a popular photo opportunity for visitors. Its restaurant facilities and refreshing breezes make it an ideal spot for the island's regular Sunday barbecue, popular with both locals and tourists, and featuring plenty of rum punch and steel band music. The heights are named after one of the island's early governors, Sir Thomas Shirley.

Natural attractions on Antigua include Boggy Peak, the island's highest point at 1,360 feet, and Fig Tree Drive – four miles of hilly road that winds from Carlisle Bay to Liberta past groves of fruit trees. These include the mango, coconut and fig, which is the Antiguan name for banana. At the east end of Fig Tree Drive is eye-catching **9 Tyrells Catholic Church**, made of pink coral, and south of here, on the way to English Harbour, is the town of Liberta which was one of the first to be settled by freed slaves.

At the northeast end of Antigua at Indian Town Point stands a nat-

ural limestone arch called  **10 Devil's Bridge**. Carved by the sea, this rock formation is a dramatic sight when a surf is running.

11 Betty's Hope, located southwest of Devil's Bridge, is a recently restored historical site. The original sugar plantation was founded here in the mid-1600s and its cotton house storeroom has been converted into a small museum. One of its twin windmills has been restored to a fully operational wind-powered sugar mill.

Barbuda

Sparsely populated Barbuda is a flat coral island lying 30 miles north of Antigua. Dominated by a large lagoon on its western side, the island's handful of upscale resorts are located on the south coast where beautiful pink coral beaches lie between Palmetto Point and Coco Point. The Martello Tower, a stone fort near Palmetto Point, is 56 feet tall with a view of almost the entire island.

The Frigate Bird Sanctuary, in the northwest area of the island, is a breeding ground for various indigenous species, including thousands of frigate birds that nest here in the tops of mangrove bushes.

Montserrat

The green and mountainous island of Montserrat, named by Columbus and claimed by the British, was known as the Caribbean's 'Emerald Isle' until part of it was devastated by a series of volcanic eruptions that began in 1995 and climaxed in June 1997 when the abandoned capital of Plymouth was destroyed. About half of the island's 11,000 residents had already evacuated the island's southern off-limits zone, its ash-covered ruins now deemed safe from any further eruptions. Peaceful, friendly and uncommercial, Montserrat is struggling to rebuild both its infrastructure and its tourism industry. Hidden, beach-lined coves lie at the base of steep mountains, and a hike up Garibaldi Hill provides panoramic views of the volcano's destruction. The island also has a bird sanctuary at Fox's Bay and a 9-hole golf course. Most of its beaches are of dark volcanic sand while the island's most beautiful white sand beach is found at secluded Rendezvous Bay.

Chances Peak on Montserrat.

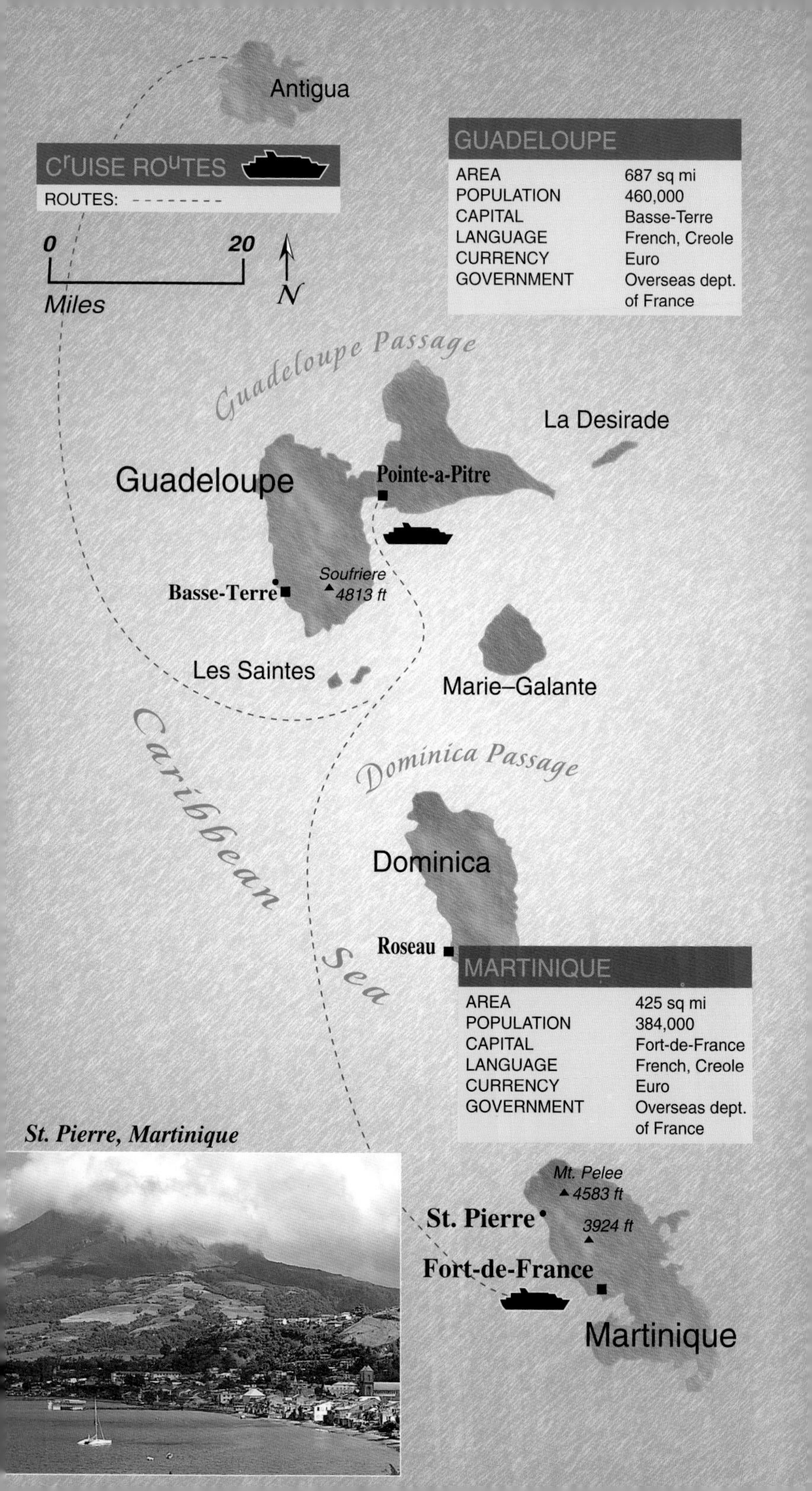

Antigua
CRUISE ROUTES
ROUTES:
0
20
Miles
N
Guadeloupe Passage
La Desirade
Guadeloupe
Pointe-a-Pitre
Soufriere
4813 ft
Basse-Terre
Les Saintes
Marie–Galante
Caribbean Sea
Dominica Passage
Dominica
Roseau
Mt. Pelee
4583 ft
St. Pierre
3924 ft
Fort-de-France
Martinique

GUADELOUPE	
AREA	687 sq mi
POPULATION	460,000
CAPITAL	Basse-Terre
LANGUAGE	French, Creole
CURRENCY	Euro
GOVERNMENT	Overseas dept. of France

MARTINIQUE	
AREA	425 sq mi
POPULATION	384,000
CAPITAL	Fort-de-France
LANGUAGE	French, Creole
CURRENCY	Euro
GOVERNMENT	Overseas dept. of France

St. Pierre, Martinique

CHAPTER FOURTEEN

GUADELOUPE &

MARTINIQUE

Guadeloupe and Martinique, the major islands of the French West Indies, are former colonies of France. They both became *departements* in 1946 and and are now full-fledged regions with representation in the French government. These islanders, as citizens of France, can enjoy a bit of French culture while retaining customs of their African and East Indian ancestors. The result is a vibrant Creole culture, and one that visitors can experience first-hand on the crowded streets of Fort-de-France and Pointe-a-Pitre.

Parisian-style shops stand next to public markets selling piles of papayas and breadfruit, the aroma of freshly baked baguettes mixing with the pungent spices used in Creole cooking, while boutiques featuring imported porcelain and crystal compete with street vendors selling hand-painted wood carvings. Busy as the port towns are with their traffic-clogged streets and narrow sidewalks, the main squares are an oasis from the heat and bustle, with lawns that sweep past historic monuments and palm-shaded benches.

English-speaking visitors are encouraged to try a few words of French with the locals who, when conversing with each other, speak a Creole dialect based on West

African grammatical structures and French vocabulary. A smile and a gesture are often all that's needed to communicate, especially if you're interested in purchasing something, and most shopkeepers can speak at least a smattering of English. The islands' official currency is the euro, but American dollars are widely accepted.

The economies of Guadeloupe and Martinique are based on food exports – bananas, pineapple, sugar and rum – and tourism is steadily increasing, but unemployment is widespread and there is a heavy reliance on subsidies from France. Funds used to flow the other way when these islands were major sugar producers and prized colonies of France.

The French connection began in 1635, when settlers from France landed on the two islands. Those arriving at Guadeloupe spent the next five years repelling attacks by the resident Caribs, while those on Martinique built Fort Saint-Pierre on its west coast, sharing the island for 20 years with the local Caribs before driving them away. Within a century both islands were covered with sugar plantations employing tens of thousands of African slaves. Meanwhile, the French repelled attacks by the British who eventually conquered

Street scenes in Pointe-a-Pitre on Guadeloupe include traditional West Indian markets and upscale shops featuring fine porcelain.

Guadeloupe during the Seven Years War and held it for four years. This change of ownership did not, however, slow sugar production, and about 25,000 more slaves were imported and additional windmills were built under British occupation. In 1763, a bargain was struck with the Treaty of Paris in which Britain returned Guadeloupe to the French in exchange for Canada.

This allocation of New World colonies was short lived, for the American War of Independence began in 1776. Continued fighting ensued between the British and the pro-revolutionary French, including a famous naval battle

off Les Saintes in 1782 in which a fleet of French warships was defeated by the British under Admiral Rodney. Turmoil continued with the outbreak of the French Revolution and the subsequent abolishment of slavery by the new Convention.

A mini-French Revolution was staged on Guadeloupe when Victor Hugues, commissaire of the Convention, arrived from France in 1794 and, after defeating the British, proceeded to guillotine the local plantation owners. This action made their counterparts on Martinique understandably nervous and they welcomed British occupation of their island until 1802, when it was returned to France under the Treaty of Amiens. At this point, slavery was reinstated in the French West Indies by Napoleon Bonaparte whose Creole wife, Josephine, was born on Martinique.

Nelson's annihilation of Napoleon's fleet at the Battle of Trafalgar in 1805 all but eliminated the French West Indian planters' lifeline to France. There was also, in keeping with the romantic spirit of the French, a hero by the name of Victor Schoelcher – son of a Parisian porcelain merchant – who campaigned for 15 years to free the slaves of the French West Indies. When the French Republic was proclaimed in Paris in 1848,

Schoelcher drafted a decree that freed the 160,000 slaves of Guadeloupe and Martinique. Following the emancipation of slavery, contract workers from India took up the slack, but the era of plantation prosperity had ended. France's sugar islands, for two centuries a prolific source of 'white gold', were now bastions of black freedom.

Guadeloupe

Named by Columbus in 1493 for a monastery in Spain, Guadeloupe consists of two main islands – Basse-Terre and Grande-Terre – which are separated by a narrow saltwater channel. Basse-Terre, the western island, is mountainous and volcanic in origin, while the eastern island is chalky and flat. The nearby smaller islands of Marie-Galante, Les Saintes and La Desirade are part of Guadeloupe, which, as an overseas department of France, also administers the distant dependencies of St. Barthelemy and St. Martin. Basse-Terre, situated on the island of the same name, is the capital of Guadeloupe.

Pointe-a-Pitre on Grande-Terre is Guadeloupe's major port and commercial hub, its modern cruise facility located right downtown. Adjacent to the cruise pier is the **1** **Centre St. John Perse**, an air-conditioned complex designed in the French West Indies style. Here you will find a number of shops and restaurants as well as a currency exchange, car rental agency and public telephones.

Getting Around

Most taxi drivers can speak English and are eager for business. The approximate one-way fares from Pointe-a-Pitre to the beaches east of town are, per vehicle (holding one to four persons): $20 to Gossier; $30 to Caravelle Beach; and $50 to St. Francois. A two-hour tour to Ste. Rose or Vernou is $20 per person, and a 3-hour tour to the Carbet Falls, based on four to six persons per vehicle, is $30 each. Guadeloupe has a network of modern highways and its car rental companies include Avis, Budget, Hertz and Thrifty. Ship-organized shore excursions include a tour of Basse-Terre to view its lush rainforest and mountain waterfalls, a highlight being Soufriere Volcano. Also offered is a glass-bottom boat ride to Pigeon Island.

Shopping – 'Made in France' luxury items are good buys, sold at French domestic prices, and these include scarves, perfume, porcelain, crystal and liquor. Foreigners are entitled to a 20% discount on purchases made with traveller's checks or a major credit card. In Pointe-a-Pitre, the shops are concentrated at Centre St. John Perse, and on the main shopping streets of Rue Frebault, Rue Schoelcher and Rue de Nozieres. For local wares, the **2** **public market** on Rue Frebault features hand-painted wood carvings, jewelry and spices. In Basse-Terre, the principal shopping streets are rue Maurice Marie-Claire, rue du Cours Nolivos and rue du

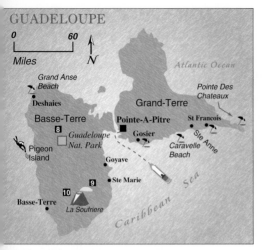

Watersports equipment, change facilities and beach chairs are available to non-guests for a small fee. Caravelle Beach, outside Sainte-Anne, is the island's longest stretch of powdery white sand and, protected by reefs, is ideal for snorkeling. Watersports equipment can be rented at the Club Med. The Raisins-Clairs Beach at Saint-Francois is another lovely beach where sail boards and other watersports equipment can be rented at the Meridien Hotel. Pointe Des Chateaux, at the island's eastern tip, is a rugged section of coastline with wave-pounded boulders and beaches, including Beach of Tarare which attracts skinny dippers. On Basse-Terre, many of the beaches have dark sand. One of its best beaches is La Plage de Grande-Anse – a stretch of golden sand near Deshaies on the northwest coast.

Snorkel & Dive Sites – Pigeon Island, off the west coast of Basse-Terre, was described by Jacques Cousteau as "one of the world's 10 best diving spots." Glass-bottom boats and snorkeling trips can be taken to the underwater reserve at Pigeon Island from Malendure Beach. The snorkeling is also good at Caravelle Beach on Grande-Terre's south coast.

Golf – An 18-hole golf course, designed by Robert Trent-Jones, is located at the Meridien St. Francois. At 6,755 yards with a par-71, the course is fairly challenging.

Docteur Cabre. An outdoor market is located on Boulevard du General de Gaulle opposite the Conseil General.

Beaches – The most accessible of Guadeloupe's beaches lie east of Pointe-a-Pitre. Closest is Gosier, where many of the island's resorts are situated along a white sand beach.

Local Attractions

Pointe-a-Pitre was named for a Dutch fisherman and was first developed by the British in 1759, when they held Guadeloupe during the Seven Years War. The town was damaged by an earthquake in 1843, followed by a fire in 1899. Hurricanes have also wreaked devastation, including David and Frederick in 1979.

A number of attractions are in the vicinity of the cruise port, and a walk along the waterfront will take you past a bustling produce market to the **3** **Tourism Office** which is housed in a colonnaded colonial building overlooking **4** **Place de la Victoire (Victory Square)** – an expansive square lined on three sides with French colonial architecture and shaded with flamboyant trees. Commemorating Victor Hugues's 1794 defeat of the British, this square is where he guillotined the island's aristocracy. Today the square is an inviting place to linger, with sidewalk cafes tucked beneath the brightly colored awnings on Rue Bebian.

A block west of Rue Bebian is the **5** **Cathedral of St. Pierre and St. Paul**, built in 1847. Fresh flowers are sold at a stand in front of the church.

The **6** **Schoelcher Museum** on rue Peynier is housed in a beautiful colonial building, its rose-colored facade decorated with relief stonework and ornate ironwork. Inside are exhibits dedicated to Victor Schoelcher, a key figure in the movement to abolish slavery.

The **7** **St. John Perse**

Museum, a colonial-style house on Rue de Nozieres, is dedicated to the great poet and diplomat who was born Alexis Saint-Leger Leger in Guadeloupe in 1887. He served in France's foreign office and, as an opponent of Nazi

(Above) Cathedral of St. Pierre and St. Paul. (Below) Pointe-a-Pitre's Tourism Office overlooks Victory Square.

appeasement, he became one of Europe's foremost diplomats. His reputation grew as a poet following his self-imposed exile to the U.S. in 1940. Using the pseudonym St. John Perse, he was awarded the Nobel Prize for Literature in 1960.

(Below) Caravelle Beach, outside Saint-Anne.
(Bottom) Isles des Saintes.

Island Attractions: Some of Guadeloupe's most scenic attractions are on the island of Basse-Terre. These include the **8** **National Park** which covers 74,000 acres of rainforest and includes 186 miles of trails. To the south is **9** **Carbet Waterfalls,** its three separate cascades spilling 400 feet. The **10** **Soufriere volcano**, surrounded by rainforest and banana plantations, is still active, with puffs of steam rising from its summit.

Basse-Terre is Guadeloupe's secondary cruise port, its historic architecture including the Cathedral of our Lady of Guadeloupe, the Conseil General, Palais de Justice and the Prefecture. Nearby is Fort Louis Delgres, dating back to 1650 and the site of numerous battles between the French and British.

Iles des Saintes, a cluster of islands off Guadeloupe's south coast, is a port of call for the smaller cruise ships. They often anchor in the spectacular harbor of Terre-de-Haute where a village of the same name is nestled at the base of a mountain, its streets of gingerbread houses easily explored on foot. A bus or taxi ride away is Fort Napoleon, with its barracks, drawbridge, art gallery and exotic garden. Nearby are underwater grottoes, coral beds and numerous beach-lined coves.

Martinique

Martinique – beautiful, sophisticated and slightly snobbish – has long been a flower in the lapel of France. The Caribs originally called her Madinina – 'Island of

(Above) A cruise ship docks at Fort-de-France's downtown pier. (Right) The port's yacht-filled harbor.

Flowers' – and Columbus, who first laid eyes on Martinique in 1493, was so moved by her beauty when he came ashore in 1502, he described the island as "the most fertile, most delightful and most charming land in the world." But it was the French who eventually conquered Martinique and established the island's first capital of St-Pierre on the west coast.

Called the 'Paris of the West Indies', the town's 30,000 residents were so enamored by their surroundings they ignored warning signs that the nearby volcano – **Mount Pelee** – was about to erupt. The local wildlife evacuated the area before the town was smothered in ash and stones on the morning of May 8, 1902. Only one person survived – he was inside a prison cell at the time, the walls of which protected him from the hail of ash and burning gases. As the sole survivor of this catastrophic explosion, he became a sideshow with Barnum's Circus, complete with a replica of his prison cell.

Following the destruction of St-Pierre, the island's new capital became Fort-de-France, where about a third of Martinique's 360,000 residents now live. Often compared to the French Quarter of New Orleans with its narrow streets and iron grille balconies, Fort-de-France is a fascinating port to explore on foot.

Getting Around

For passengers disembarking at the pier east of downtown, it's a 15- to 20-minute walk or an $8 cab ride into town. Passengers disembarking at the western pier are a 5-minute walk from the main shopping streets and attractions. The round-trip ferry ride from the Fort-de-France waterfront to the beaches at Pointe du Bout is about $6.

Unless you're fluent in French, you may want to tour the island with one of the ship-organized shore excursions; these include a panoramic tour by land and sea, a historic walking tour of Fort-de-France, and a 4X4 jeep tour. The roads here are good, although steep and winding, and driving is on the right, so renting a car is an option if you're not intimidated by the French road signs and speedy drivers. Local rental agencies include Avis, Budget and Hertz, and the average daily cost is $60.

Taxis can be hired beside the cruise piers, along the downtown waterfront and beside Savannah Park. Many of the drivers speak basic English but they tend to strike a hard bargain, so indicate on a map exactly where you want to go, the stops you would like to make along the way, and write down the price agreed upon so there is no misunderstanding and renewed bargaining at the end of the tour. A round trip from Fort-de-France to St. Pierre with a half-dozen stops, including Morne-Rouge and Balata, costs about $100 (based on one to four persons sharing a taxi).

The **cruise line shore excursions** usually feature tours to St. Pierre, Balata and a butterfly farm, with opportunities to see the abundant flora of a tropical rainforest. Boat excursions include a catamaran cruise to a beach-lined cove and an opportunity to view a coral reef along the way.

Tourist Information is provided at various locations, including the cruise piers. A post office is at Rue de la Liberte and Rue Blenac.

Shopping – Best buys are in French-made luxury items, including perfume, jewelry, designer fashions, cosmetics, leather goods, watches, crystal, china and porcelain, with savings as high as 40% thanks in part to the 20% tax refund available to foreigners who pay by credit card or traveller's check. Local items of note include rum, fruit-flavored liqueurs and jams, wickerwork and handicrafts of bamboo, shell and madras cotton. Rue Victor Hugo is a major shopping street, with more shops located in the blocks between it and Rue Victor Severe. A handicraft market is located in Savannah Park.

Beaches – A 20-minute ferry ride from Fort-de-France provides access to some excellent beaches. The blue ferry goes to Plage Pointe du Bout where a there's a marina and luxury resorts. The red ferry goes to Plage Anse Mitan, a public beach of white sand with superb snorkeling, and to quieter Plage Anse a l'Ane, with picnic tables and a hotel/bar nearby. Either ferry costs about $6, return trip. More beautiful beaches lie along the island's south coast at Diamant and near St. Anne (about 30 miles

from Fort-de-France), but reaching these beaches entails an expensive cab ride.

Dive & Snorkel Sites – There are good reefs for snorkeling around Pointe du Bout and off Anse Mitan. Two dive operations are located at Pointe du Bout.

Golf – The Golf Country Club is located one mile south of Pointe du Bout near the birthplace of Empress Josephine. A par-71 course designed by Robert Trent-Jones, its rolling hills offer scenic sea views.

Local Attractions

Originally a parade ground, **Place de La Savane (Savannah Park)** is 12 acres of lawns, stately palms and statues. A bronze statue of Pierre Belain D'Esnambuc (who led the first party of settlers to Martinique) faces the ferry pier, and a white marble statue of Empress Josephine, a gift from Napoleon III in 1859, stands near the park's northwest corner. The statue was beheaded in 1991 as a rather gruesome reminder that native-born Josephine, of Creole ancestry, was the Emperor's consort when he restored slavery in the French West Indies a decade after the Republic had abolished it.

The construction of **2 Fort Saint-Louis** took three centuries

(Above) Beaches south of Fort-de-France can be reached by a 20-minute ferry ride. (Below) An eaterie in Fort-de-France. (Bottom) Schoelcher Library.

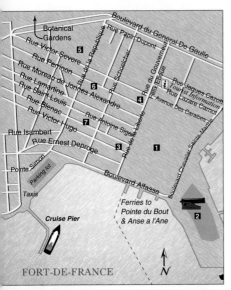

FORT-DE-FRANCE

to complete, starting in the 1600s. Standing on a point of land overlooking the harbor, it is surrounded on three sides by water.

The **3** **Museum of Archaeology** is located beside Savannah Park and its exhibits of pre-Columbian art include pottery and ceramic pieces that date back 1,700 years. The **4** **Schoelcher Library**, designed by the 19th-century architect Henri Pick (a contemporary of Gustave Eiffel), was shipped in pieces from France and completed in 1893. Restored between 1980 and 1982, this magnificent multi-colored chrome structure, with a Byzantine glasswork dome, is registered as a historical monument of France. It's named for Victor Schoelcher – humanitarian, writer and book collector – who believed that freedom for slaves would be in vain without their receiving an education, and so donated his own library of 9,000 volumes to Martinique in 1883 to provide free access to knowledge. These books were destroyed in the huge fire of 1890, but Schoelcher's good intentions survive in the library now bearing his name.

The Prefecture (police station) on Rue Victor Severe (facing the library) is the former Government House and beside it is a colonial-style villa now housing an exhibition gallery. A few blocks down the street is the **5** **Old City Hall**, now a theatre, built in 1912. French

(Above left) Court of Justice.
(Left) Old City Hall.

President Charles De Gaulle gave a speech from its balcony in 1964.

Nearby is the **Court of Justice**, built between 1906 and 1907, when iron and glass were widely used as building materials. A statue of Victor Schoelcher stands out front in a garden setting of greenery and benches. Three blocks over is the **7 Saint-Louis Cathedral**, inaugurated in 1895 and designed by Henri Pick to resist fire, hurricanes and earthquakes (see photo on page 85).

Island Attractions

A few miles north of Fort-de-France, at **Balata**, is the Sacred Heart Basilica, an exact but smaller replica of Montmartre Basilica in Paris (see photo, page 85). It was built in 1915 to accommodate the influx of worshippers to the Fort-de-France area following the eruption of Mount Pelee in 1902. The Balata Tropical & Botanical Park features plants and flowers from around the world and offers splendid views of Fort-de-France and the peaks of Carbet.

The inland route between Fort-de-France and St. Pierre winds past volcanic peaks and verdant rainforests. Le Morne Rouge, a pleasant resort town at the north end of this scenic drive, provides good views of Mount Pelee, as does **St. Pierre**, where a museum recalls that fateful day in 1902 when the mountain looming to the north brought death and destruction to this coastal community. South of St. Pierre along the coast is **Anse Turin**, where

the French painter Paul Gauguin lived in 1887, and **Le Carbet**, where Columbus is believed to have landed.

South of Fort-de-France, near **Les Trois Ilets**, is the Pagerie Museum, a stone house commemorating the birthplace of the Empress Josephine, born in 1763 as Marie Josephe Rose Tascher de La Pageriein. Her first husband was guillotined during the French Revolution, in 1794, but she escaped with a brief imprisonment, and in 1796 she married Napoleon. In 1804, as his consort, she became Empress of France and her two children by her first marriage became titled heads of Europe. However, her union with Napoleon produced no heir and he had the marriage annulled in 1809 so he could marry the daughter of the Austrian emperor. Josephine, who had played a prominent role in the French court's social life, lived in retirement until her death in 1814.

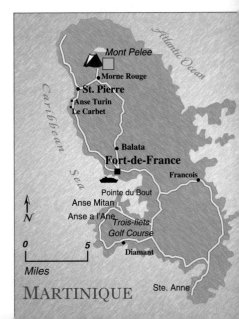

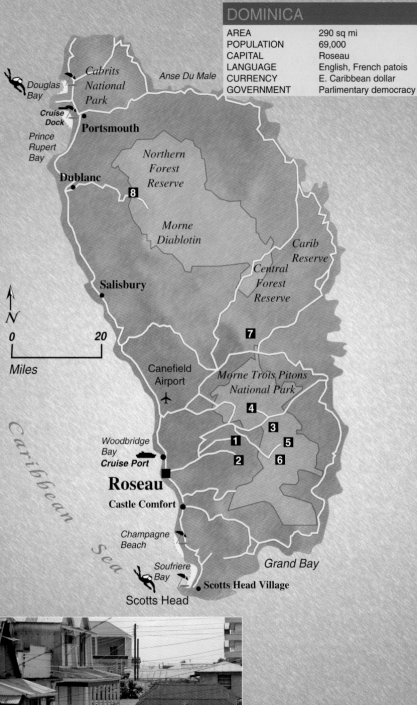

DOMINICA

AREA	290 sq mi
POPULATION	69,000
CAPITAL	Roseau
LANGUAGE	English, French patois
CURRENCY	E. Caribbean dollar
GOVERNMENT	Parlimentary democracy

Cabrits National Park

Anse Du Male

Douglas Bay

Cruise Dock

Portsmouth

Prince Rupert Bay

Dublanc

Northern Forest Reserve

8

Morne Diablotin

Carib Reserve

Central Forest Reserve

Salisbury

N

0   20

Miles

7

Canefield Airport

Morne Trois Pitons National Park

4

3

Woodbridge Bay
Cruise Port

1

5

2

6

Roseau

Castle Comfort

Champagne Beach

Caribbean

Sea

Soufriere Bay

Scotts Head

Scotts Head Village

Grand Bay

Roseau, Dominica

CHAPTER FIFTEEN

DOMINICA & ST. LUCIA

When comparing Dominica and St. Lucia, it's a toss up which is more ruggedly beautiful. Both consist of volcanic peaks, dense tropical forests and fertile valleys filled with banana plantations. Each was coveted by the British and French who battled one another and the local Caribs for ownership. Neither nation fully succeeded, for the mountainous interiors of these islands discouraged colonization and provided cover for resisting Caribs and runaway slaves.

About 3,000 descendants of the early Caribs now live on a 3,700-acre territory of Dominica, their final enclave in a region they once dominated. The inhabitants of both islands are today mostly of African descent and, although both islands entered the 20th century as British colonies with English the official language, the unofficial culture is French. The common language is a Creole dialect like that used on Martinique and Guadeloupe, the dominant religion is Roman Catholic and the place names are frequently French. Still, the surname of many an islander reflects a British past, as does their love of cricket.

It's the natural beauty of these two islands, however, that most encourages comparison, their similar vegetation including plants and animals that are South or Central American in origin. Each island is a naturalist's dream with towering mountains, verdant valleys, rushing rivers and cascading waterfalls.

Dominica

Pronounced *Dom-in-eek-a*, this island of 78,000 inhabitants was named by Columbus when he sailed past on a Sunday in 1493. One of the least developed of the West Indies, Dominica rightly calls itself the Nature Island of the Caribbean, its large areas of virgin forest protected within parks and reserves. Dominica has 20 major rivers and two freshwater lakes, both located in the National Park, and the government is committed to protecting this precious watershed. Water is currently shipped to St. Maarten, and bulk water could become a chief export. Meanwhile, bananas are a major export, as well as citrus fruits and coconut oil.

The island was badly hit by Hurricanes David and Frederick in 1979, with David causing 37 deaths and leaving 80% of the population homeless. The island's social history has also been stormy. The Caribs refused to give up their island without a fight and, in 1748, the British and French, both thwarted in their attempts at conquest, agreed to leave the island to its warlike inhabitants. But neither power could resist trying to conquer this fertile island, and France finally ceded it to Britain, but not before burning the capital of Roseau. The Commonwealth of Dominica gained independence from Britain in 1978, and its first election was held in 1980.

Getting Around

Roseau, located at the mouth of the Roseau River on Dominica's southwest coast, is the island's capital and chief port, with a population of about 20,000. A cruise pier is located on the town center's waterfront and another pier, the Woodbridge Bay Deep Water Harbor, is about a mile north of

(Above) A view of Rouseau and its downtown cruise pier.
(Below) Prince Rupert Bay.

the town center. A shuttle runs between the two locations and to nearby beaches. A Tourist Information Office at both cruise piers provides general information and prices for visitors looking to hire a taxi/tour operator. Dominica's third cruise ship pier at Prince Rupert Bay, near Portsmouth, was inaugurated in 1992 and is unique in that passengers disembark directly into a national park. The terminal building has displays and presentations to introduce passengers to the area's attractions.

Local **taxi drivers** are friendly, informed guides and their hourly sightseeing rate is about $20 an hour per car (1-4 passengers). Some sample fares from the Woodbridge pier to: Botanical Gardens – $2; Trafalgar Falls – $15 per person round trip; and Morne Trois Piton National Park – $20 per person round trip. Several car rental firms operate on Dominica, including Avis and Budget. Driving is on the left side of the road and a local driver's permit is required at a cost of EC $50 (approx $20 US).

Local currency is the East Caribbean dollar (approximately EC$2.70 per US$1) but American currency is accepted. An entrance fee ($2) is charged by Dominica National Parks at its nature sites.

Shopping – Local handicrafts are sold at the cruise piers. Items to look for include straw crafts, pottery, hand-painted candles, wood carvings, handmade cigars and coconut-oil-based soaps, as well as unique Carib crafts such as tri-color baskets woven of larouma reeds. Authentic Carib weave baskets and hats are sold throughout the Carib Reserve and at various shops in Roseau, including Tropicrafts at the corner of Queen Mary Street and Turkey Lane. Cotton House Batiks at 8 Kings Lane sells original hand-painted clothing, as does the Artwear Gallery at 54 King George Street. The NDF Small Business Complex at 9 Great Marlborough Street houses a collection of craft shops selling batiks, jewelry and other hand-crafted items.

Shore Excursions

Dominica

Ship-organized shore excursions feature island drives to the Botanical Gardens, Morne Bruce, Trafalgar Falls and the Emerald Pool. Longer tours take in the Northern Forest Reserve and the Carib Territory, terminating at Cabrits National Park where passengers are picked up by the ship. Also available is a rainforest aerial tram ride, ATV or 4WD off-road touring, river tubing, mountain biking, ocean kayaking and river boat safaris. Wacky Rollers is a local eco-adventure tour operator, located at #8 Fort Street in Roseau, which supplies several of the cruise line shore excursion and also operates an adventure park where you can explore acres of rainforest by walking on elevated bridges from tree to tree or sliding down a cable across a river. Guided snorkeling of Champagne Reef and Cabrits Marine Park are also offered by some of the cruise lines, as are certified and beginner scuba diving.

Scotts Head Beach

Beaches – Most of Dominica's beaches consist of dark to silver-gray volcanic sand, although a few are honey-colored. Two of the best, both golden brown in color, are found north of Portsmouth, at Prince Rupert Bay and nearby Douglas Bay. Good beaches near Roseau include the one at Scotts Head.

Dive & Snorkel Sites – Dominica is a premier dive destination, its west coast lined with numerous underwater sites. Some of the best lie near or within the Scotts Head/Soufriere Bay Marine Reserve, at the south end of the island. A submerged volcanic crater forms this bay, which contains vertical drops from 800 to 1,500 feet within a half mile of shore. Snorkeling can be enjoyed at Champagne Reef, where walls of tiny bubbles rise continually from geo-thermal vents that are releasing hot gases. Coral reefs and drop-offs also lie within

(Left) Roseau's waterfront.

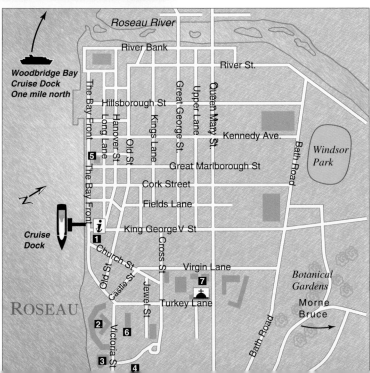

Cabrits National Park. A half-dozen dive operators are located on Dominica, including two in Castle Comfort (just south of Roseau) and one at Soufriere.

Local Attractions

The **1** **Dominica Museum** is a good introduction to Roseau's historic buildings, which are clustered near the harborfront on Victoria Street, including the 18th-century **2** **Fort Young** (now a hotel) and a number of Georgian-style buildings, namely the **3** **Public Library**, **4** **Government House** and the **5** **Court House** (located a few blocks away on Bay Front). Also in the vicinity is **6** **St. George's Church**, a 19th-century Anglican church, and the impressive **7** **Cathedral of Our Lady of Fair Haven**, the island's principal Roman Catholic church. The town's main attraction is the **Botanical Gardens**, 40 acres of landscaped gardens nestled at the base of Morne Bruce hill on land once cultivated with sugarcane. The planning and planting of the Gardens began in 1890, and the many exotic and indigenous trees and shrubs that grow here are identified with a number or letter referenced on a written guide. Also located here is the Aviary – a breeding facility for Dominica's endangered parrots, the Jaco and the Sisserou (Dominica's national bird). The Gardens were once a popular cricket ground and have been visited twice by Queen Elizabeth. Sometimes seen parked at the Botanical Gardens is the Sisserou Express, a bus

painted with tropical flora and fauna that travels the roads of Dominica to raise local awareness of conservation issues. Equipped with video recorder, monitor and other visual aids, its exhibits are used to further environmental education among the island's pre-school children. A look-out at the top of **Morne Bruce** provides panoramic views of Roseau and the coastline.

Island Attractions

1 **Trafalgar Falls**, not far from Roseau, can be reached by a steep winding road that terminates within a 15-minute walk to the base of the falls. A path, lined with ferns and mosses, leads from the parking lot to Trafalgar Falls, which consists of two major falls where visitors can bathe in rocky pools. Plants in the area include nutmeg, coffee, cocoa and banana, and the songbirds that can be heard include the Mountain Whistler. The **2** **Wotten Waven Sulphur Springs** are located across the valley from Trafalgar Falls.

Morne Trois Pitons National Park, named for a three-peaked mountain within the park, was established in 1975 and declared a world heritage site in 1998. Its 16,000 acres of steep volcanic landscape are filled with natural wonders. Water from **3** **Freshwater Lake** feeds the Trafalgar Falls which flow into the Roseau River. A trail, which takes about three-quarters of an hour to hike, leads from Freshwater Lake to **4** **Boeri Lake** – a crater 3,000 feet above sea level which is filled with fresh water. In the other direction is **5 Boiling Lake**, the largest of its kind in the world. It's cupped in a volcanic crater, the heat of which keeps the water bubbling. Nearby, on the flanks of Morne Watt, is the **6 Valley of Desolation** – a barren landscape where smoking fumaroles and boiling sulphur springs indicate there are heated rocks lying just below the surface. The sights include pools of gray, bubbling mud and multi-colored streams, their water containing minerals from old volcanic activity. The **7 Emerald Pool**, at the north end of the park, is a grotto filled with water that is brilliant

One of two spectacular cascades at Trafalgar Falls.

green in color and fed by a waterfall. This Garden of Eden setting, with its profusion of plants, flowers and ferns, is an easy 10-minute walk through woodlands from the main road.

The 22,000-acre Northern Forest Reserve contains Dominica's highest peak – Morne Diablotin – which rises to 4,747 feet. The reserve's vegetation runs the gamut of a mountain ecosystem, with secondary and rain forests at lower levels, a montane (mist) forest at higher altitudes, and an elfin woodland near the summit.

A tract of land bordering the northwest side of the reserve, often referred to as the **8 'Parrot Preserve'**, is a habitat for the indigenous and endangered Sisserou and Jaco Parrots. The Syndicate Nature Trail, less than a mile long and easy to walk, loops through the Parrot Preserve's stand of mature rain forest, where orchids and bromeliads grow. The bird life here, in addition to parrots, includes blue-headed hummingbirds and broad-winged hawks.

At the Carib Reserve, on the northeast side of the island, about 3,000 descendants of the Caribbean's original inhabitants engage in farming, fishing and their traditional basket making and canoe building.

Portsmouth's Attractions

Dominica's second town, Portsmouth is situated on a natural harbor backed by mountains. It contains sheltered Prince Rupert Bay, once home to the Caribs and a former port of call for Spanish conquistadors heading to the South American mainland. Cabrits National Park is situated on a forested peninsula at the north end of Portsmouth Harbor. The park contains two peaks which can reached by hiking trails, and the restored ruins of historic Fort Shirley stand on the hillsides. The park's extensive marine area offers good snorkeling among corals and tropical fish, and rowboat rides are available on the Indian River which winds past mangroves south of Portsmouth.

St. Lucia

Saint Lucia (pronounced *Loosha*) is the Caribbean's poster island. Gracing many a brochure (and the cover of this book) is its famous landmark, the Pitons – twin volcanic peaks rising from the water's edge. Conical in shape and lushly vegetated, they are evocative of the South Pacific. St. Lucia also has a 'drive-in volcano', and its National Rain Forest, home to the jacquot (St. Lucia's parrot), is a tropical paradise of wild orchids and giant ferns.

It's believed Columbus's navigator, Juan de la Cosa, was the first European to discover St. Lucia in 1499. When the British first attempted to colonize the island, it was inhabited by Caribs with whom the British signed a treaty in 1660. This situation was short lived, for the French West India Company took control of the island in 1667. This too was short lived, and from 1674 to 1814 the French and the British fought over possession of St. Lucia, the island changing hands no less than 14 times.

Since 1979 St. Lucia has been an independent country within the British Commonwealth, and its population of 154,000 enjoys a stable parliamentary democracy. This tiny country is the birthplace of two Nobel Laureates – the late Sir W. Arthur Lewis (Nobel Prize in Economics in 1979) and the poet Derek Walcott who won the

(Below) The town of Soufriere.

(Bottom) The spectacular Pitons rise above Soufriere Bay.

Shore Excursions

St. Lucia

Ship-organized shore excursions often include a scenic drive to Marigot Bay. A longer tour to the Sulphur Springs and Diamond Falls usually terminates at Soufriere where passengers are returned to their ship which pulls into Soufriere Bay to retrieve them. Other excursions include a catamaran cruise to the Pitons, sea kayaking to Pigeon Island, whale and dolphin watching, and sailing aboard a tall ship. Aerial tram rides, canopy adventures and horseback riding are also offered, as are snorkel tours and certified scuba diving.

ST. LUCIA	
AREA	238 sq mi
POPULATION	166,000
CAPITAL	Castries
LANGUAGE	English, patois
CURRENCY	E. Carib dollar
GOVERNMENT	Parl democracy

Pigeon Island National Park

Gros Islet

Rodney Bay

Vigie Beach

Union

LaToc Bay

CASTRIES

Marigot Bay

Anse La Raye

Anse Cochon

National Rain Forest

Dennery

Anse Chastanet

Morne Gimie (3117 ft)

Sulphur Springs

Soufriere Bay

Petit Piton

Forest Reserve

Anse des Pitons

Gros Piton

Choiseul

Caribbean Sea

0   5

Miles   N

Vieux Fort

1992 Nobel Prize in Literature.

Growing and exporting bananas and other tropical produce is a major industry in St. Lucia. An oil refinery and trans-shipment facilities are also located here, near the capital of Castries on the northwest coast.

Getting Around

Castries, named for a French colonial minister, is the island's main cruise port. The Elizabeth II dock is downtown at the commercial docks, and another pier is located at Pointe Seraphine, where the St. Lucia Tourist Board office is located. AT&T telephones are also located here and on Jeremie Street in downtown Castries.

The roads on St. Lucia are steep and winding, with many a hairpin turn, so booking a ship-organized shore excursion or hiring a taxi are the best ways to see the island. The Courtesy Taxi Co-Operative Society operates at the waterfront and its drivers are capable, courteous guides. They charge government-set rates for standard trips, and island tours (1-4 persons) are $20 (US) per hour. Some sample fares are:

From Elizabeth II Dock to: Bagshaw Studio – $6; Pigeon Island – $16; Marigot Bay – $16. From Pointe Seraphine to: Bagshaw Studio – $10; Caribelle Batik – $12; Pigeon Island (return) – $34; Marigot Bay – $20; Vigie Beach Hotel – $5. A water taxi ($1 each way) travels between the Castries cruise pier and Pointe

Seraphine. The cab fare between these two points is $4.00.

Shopping – For duty-free shopping, visit the modern harbor-front shopping complex at Pointe Seraphine, where the selection of shops includes an outlet of Bagshaw's famous tropical clothing, made of high-quality, hand-printed cotton. Bagshaw Studios is located at La Toc Bay, just north of the Sandals resort. Caribelle Batik, another famous name in Caribbean clothing, has a workshop and store at Howelton House, a Victorian Caribbean house located on Old Victoria Road, The Morne. Local crafts, such as baskets, wood carvings and pottery, are sold at the craft market at the head of the harbor on Jeremie Street. Official currency is the East Caribbean dollar (EC$2.70 to US$1.00) but American dollars are widely accepted.

Beaches – North of Castries is the main resort area where excellent beaches include Vigie Beach (1 1/2 miles from Castries) and Reduit Beach on Rodney Bay, where watersports equipment and bar facilities are available. South of Castries, a fine beach lies on La Toc Bay, where a Sandals resort is located, and at lovely Marigot Bay (see photo, page 23), where there are several bars and restaurants.

Dive & Snorkel Sites – Diving off the island's west side is excellent, with dive operations located at Marigot Bay and Anse Chastanet. A Marine National Park is located off Anse Chastanet near Soufriere Bay where a beach-entry dive or snorkeling excursion can be made

to an underwater shelf that drops from 10 to 60 feet. Another good dive site is off Anse Des Pitons (below the Petit Piton) where a wall of coral drops to 200 feet, and at Anse Cochan, where a sunken freighter lies in 60 feet. Snorkeling and wall dives can be enjoyed at Anse La Raye.

Golf – There are two nine-hole courses on St. Lucia – one at Sandals St. Lucia on La Toc Bay, the other at Cap Estate Golf Club the island's northern tip.

Local Attractions

There is limited colonial architecture in Castries due to a 1948 fire that destroyed most of the town's wooden buildings. **1 Derek Walcott Square** (formerly Columbus Square) is where a 400-year-old samaan tree stands in front of the **2 Cathedral of the Immaculate Conception**, built in 1897. On the other side of

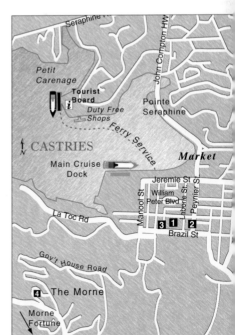

*(Above) Brazil Street,
Derek Walcott Square.*
(Left) A friendly St. Lucian.
(Bottom) Vigie Beach.

the square, on Bourbon Street, is the colonial-style **3** **Central Library**. The wooden buildings lining Brazil Street on the square's south side were among the few to survive the last fire. They were built in the 19th century in the French fashion with gabled roofs and second-floor fretwork balconies overhanging the sidewalk. **4** **Government House** is situated west of the downtown, along Government House Road, which snakes up a hillside called **The Morne**.

Island Attractions

Overlooking Castries is **Morne Fortune** (Hill of Good Luck), a key battleground during skirmishes between the English and the French. North of Castries, a short distance inland from Choc Bay, is the **Union** nature trail, interpretive center and small zoo with a pair of St. Lucian parrots. Near the island's northern tip is **Pigeon Island National Park**, the spectacular open-air setting for St. Lucia's annual Jazz Festival held in May. Visitors can wander among the ruins of Fort Rodney, or enjoy the beaches. Owned by the National Trust, the park's museum is housed in the former Officers Mess. Local history includes stories of the French pirate Francois Leclerc (call Jamb de Bois because of his wooden leg) who used a large cave on the north shore as a hideout. Britain's Admiral Rodney set sail from here in 1782 to defeat the French fleet off Guadeloupe in the famous Battle of Les Saintes.

South of Castries lies the lush,

mountainous scenery so often associated with St. Lucia, including valleys filled with banana plantations and Morne Gimie, the island's highest peak at 3,117 feet. Beautiful Marigot Bay is where a British fleet once ambushed the French by camouflaging its ships with palm fronds. Today a fleet of pleasure yachts uses this sheltered bay as a base. Some scenes from the film *Dr. Doolittle*, starring Rex Harrison, were filmed at this idyllic location. South of here is the quiet fishing village of Anse la Raye.

Soufriere is St. Lucia's oldest town, established by the French in 1746. It lies at the base of the spectacular Pitons on the shores of Soufriere Bay. The town, with its old wooden buildings, colorful

(Above and below) Marigot Bay.

murals and a marketplace, is an authentic West Indian community. Nearby is La Soufriere, a dormant volcano that was about eight miles in diameter until it collapsed about 40,000 years ago. Entry is made on foot along the crater's west rim and guides take visitors on a steamy tour of the active Sulphur Springs, with its bubbling pools of ash. Also in this area are the Diamond Falls and Mineral Baths, originally developed by France's King Louis XVI when he had bathhouses built here for his troops. Today visitors can shower in the natural falls and soak in the mineral-rich baths.

CRUISE ROUTES 🚢

ROUTES: - - - - - - - -

Caribbean Sea

Atlantic Ocean

Georgetown ▪

St. Vincent

Kingstown ●

Bequia

Mustique

The Grenadines

Canouan

Mayreau

Union I.

Tobago Cays

Petit Martinique

Carriacou

0   20

Miles

↑ N

To Barbados

Grenada

▪ **St. George's**

St. George's, Grenada

CHAPTER SIXTEEN

GRENADA

Should you step on deck one evening while your ship plies the waters of the Southern Caribbean, you may detect the sweet scent of nutmeg being carried by the warm breezes. The aroma of this and other spices, such as cloves, cinnamon and ginger, is often detected when passing Grenada, the Caribbean's Spice Island. A third of the world's supply of nutmeg is grown and processed here, the ripened pericarps picked from sweet-smelling evergreen trees that were introduced to the island more than 200 years ago by a French sea captain.

Many exotic plants were brought to the West Indies during the era of European colonization, including the breadfruit tree that Captain Bligh went to great lengths to collect in Tahiti and transport to St. Vincent. The plants and trees that thrive on St. Vincent and Grenada (pronounced *gra-nay-da*) come in all varieties, from flowering to medicinal. Residents grow most of their own fruits and vegetables, and it has been said that even a nail would grow in the rich soil of St. Vincent. Rugged and fertile, St. Vincent and Grenada lie at either end of the Grenadines, a string of beach-ringed isles frequented by yachts and small sailing ships. Most of this island chain belongs to St. Vincent, while the southern islands of Carriacou (*carry-coo*) and Petit

Martinique come under Grenada's jurisdiction.

European settlement of Grenada began in 1650 when the French purchased some land from the resident Caribs in return for knives and baubles. The Caribs soon had a change of heart however, but their rebellion was swiftly put down. When defeat was all but certain, the remaining Caribs – men, women and children – threw themselves over a cliff now called Le Morne de Sauteur (Leaper's Hill). With that enemy exterminated, the French then had to fend off the British who seized control of the island in 1762. The French regained Grenada in 1779, but a few years later – under the terms of the Treaty of Versailles – the island was once again Britain's.

The next violent clash was caused by mounting tensions between British settlers and the French planters who remained on Grenada. A free colored Grenadian named Fedon, who owned a large coffee and cocoa estate in the mountains north of St. George's, plotted an uprising inspired by the French Revolution's principles of liberty and equality. His estate became Camp Belvedere as the insurrection swept across the island and rebelling slaves set fire to crops and buildings. The British governor was taken prisoner and executed. For a time, the entire island was under a siege of terror during

(Above) St. George's inner harbor, called The Carenage.

which British settlers found safety in fortified St. George's, the island's only stronghold until reinforcements arrived and eventually quashed the rebellion. As British troops closed in on Camp Belvedere, mountain warfare ensued with specially trained troops silently climbing under cover of darkness to the insurgents' armed camp, which they attacked at dawn. Fedon and his men fled but all were eventually captured, except for Fedon who, it's believed, escaped by small boat only to drown at sea.

Following emancipation in the mid-1800s, the island became a British Crown Colony and in 1974 it gained independence as a full member of the Commonwealth of Nations. This was followed by a bloodless coup in 1979 and the establishment of the People's Revolutionary Government under radical leftist Prime Minister Maurice Bishop. His close ties to Cuba and the U.S.S.R. strained relations with the U.S. and other Caribbean nations, and Grenada was once again gripped by turmoil when, during an internal coup in 1983, the army seized control. Prime Minister Bishop, ten of his cabinet colleagues and an undetermined number of civilians were executed.

Within weeks the U.S., at the request of other Caribbean nations, invaded the island and quickly restored law and order. The U.S. military, which received the overwhelming support of the Grenadian population, also rescued some American medical students who had been stranded on the island during the coup. A general election in late 1984 re-established democratic government.

Grenada was hard hit by Hurricane Ivan in September 2004, and while the local hotels were able to rebuild, many residents were left homeless.

The island capital is **St. George's** and its inner harbor, called The Carenage, is considered one of the prettiest in the Caribbean. Its historic harbor-front warehouses are brightly painted, casting mirror images on the water where fishing boats and schooners moor alongside the seawall, their lines tied to bollards made from cannons. The town's cobblestone streets and walkways are lined with old churches and brick-and-stone warehouses, some roofed with red tiles brought as ballast by trading ships.

Getting Around

Most cruise ships anchor in St. George's Bay and tender passengers ashore to the water taxi dock in the Carenage where a Tourist Information Center is conveniently located for disembarking passengers. A small cruise ship pier is located just south of the water taxi dock.

English is the official language of Grenada, but a French-African patois is still used around the island, and many of the place names are in French.

The official currency is the East Caribbean (EC) dollar (approximately $2.70 EC to $1.00 US) but American currency is accepted.

Card-operated phones are located at Grenada Telecommunications on the Carenage, and the card and coin phone booths located throughout the city are on the international direct dial system. A Board of Tourism office is located at the pier on the Carenage, and a post

Shore Excursions

Grenada

Ship-organized excursions often include the 'Royal Drive' which traces the tour once given to Queen Elizabeth on an official visit. This tour takes in Fort Frederick, the Morne Jaloux Ridge, the south coast and Grand Anse Beach. Another popular drive is the one to Grand Etang National Park and Annandale Falls. 4WD adventures, hiking tours, nature walks and river tubing are also offered. Boat excursions include a catamaran cruise with guided snorkeling and a beach stop. Clear-bottom kayaking and scuba diving are also offered.

office is located just to the east.

Rental car firms operating on Grenada include Avis (Spice Isle Rentals) on Lagoon Road. Driving is on the left and a local driving permit ($12 US) can be obtained through most rental companies or at the Fire Station on the Carenage. Some of the roads on Grenada are in need of repair and are quite rough and bumpy in places.

Local buses depart from Market Square and the Esplanade, the traditional ones painted bright colors with wooden seats. They cost between $1 EC and $5 EC, depending on the distance travelled.

Taxis holding one to four persons can be hired for about $20 US per hour. Sample fares from the cruise pier to: downtown St. George's – $3; from St. George's to: Grand Anse Beach – $10; Point Salines $15. Water taxi fares are: Carenage to Grand Anse Beach – $4 (round-trip); across the harbor – $2.

Shopping – The Spice Market 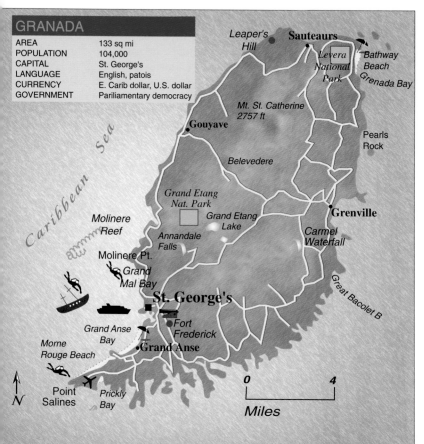 is located near the pier on the Carenage and is a good place to buy gift baskets filled with spices. Other local items to look for on Grenada include batik, wood carvings, pottery and rum, as well as jams and jellies made from nutmeg and guava. The Carenage is where a number of stores are located, selling Caribbean crafts and duty-free perfumes, china and crystal. (The Nutmeg, on the Carenage, is a recommended restaurant, popular with locals and visitors, serving homemade West Indian dishes.) Another good place to shop for duty-free goods and Caribbean handicrafts, including dolls, clothing and jewelry, is in Grand Anse.

Beaches – Just south of St. George's is **Grand Anse Bay** with two miles of beautiful white sand. The island's resort and watersports center, Grand Anse Beach is one of the best in the Caribbean and can be reached by water taxi from the Carenage. A quiet beach lies below **Point Salines**, where a reef near shore offers good snorkeling. At the island's north end, in Levera National Park, is beautiful

GRANADA

AREA	133 sq mi
POPULATION	104,000
CAPITAL	St. George's
LANGUAGE	English, patois
CURRENCY	E. Carib dollar, U.S. dollar
GOVERNMENT	Pariliamentary democracy

Leaper's Hill
Sauteurs
Levera National Park
Bathway Beach
Grenada Bay

Mt. St. Catherine 2757 ft

Gouyave

Pearls Rock

Belevedere

Caribbean Sea

Grand Etang Nat. Park
Grand Etang Lake
Grenville

Molinere Reef
Annandale Falls
Carmel Waterfall

Molinere Pt.
Grand Mal Bay

St. George's

Great Bacolet B

Grand Anse Bay
Fort Frederick

Morne Rouge Beach
Grand Anse

N

Point Salines
Prickly Bay

0   4
Miles

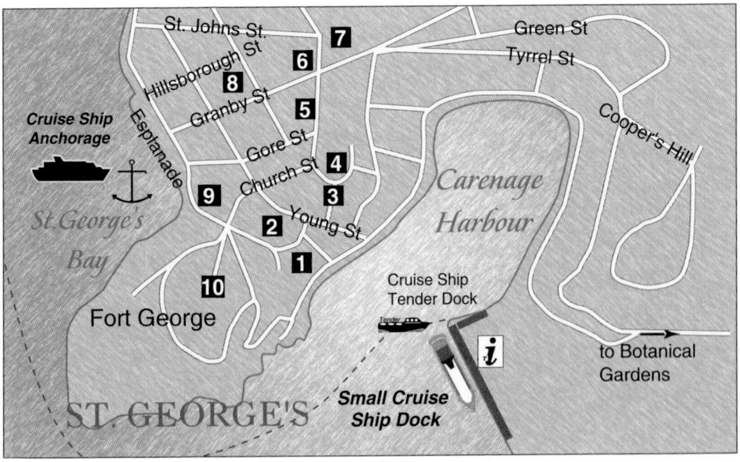
St. Johns St.
Hillsborough St
Green St
Tyrrel St
Cruise Ship Anchorage
Esplanade
Granby St
Gore St
Church St
Cooper's Hill
Carenage Harbour
St. George's Bay
Young St
Cruise Ship Tender Dock
Fort George
to Botanical Gardens
Small Cruise Ship Dock
ST. GEORGE'S
1
2
3
4
5
6
7
8
9
10

Bathway Beach, protected from the Atlantic surf by a reef barrier.

Dive & Snorkel Sites – Grenada has plenty of reefs and wrecks to satisfy snorkelers, novice divers and advanced divers. A number of dive and snorkel operations are located at Grand Anse Beach. Morne Rouge Beach, beside Grand Anse Beach, is popular with snorkelers. An extensive reef lies south of Morne Rouge off Point Salines, its three main dive sites being The Hole, which starts in sand bars and descends 50 feet; the Valley of Whales, which contains hills of coral and canyon floors of sand; and Forests of Dean, where rays and octopus are often sighted. Snorkelers can explore the reef close to shore. North of St. George's the sites include Molinere Reef, which starts at 20 feet and is a good spot for

Grand Anse Beach

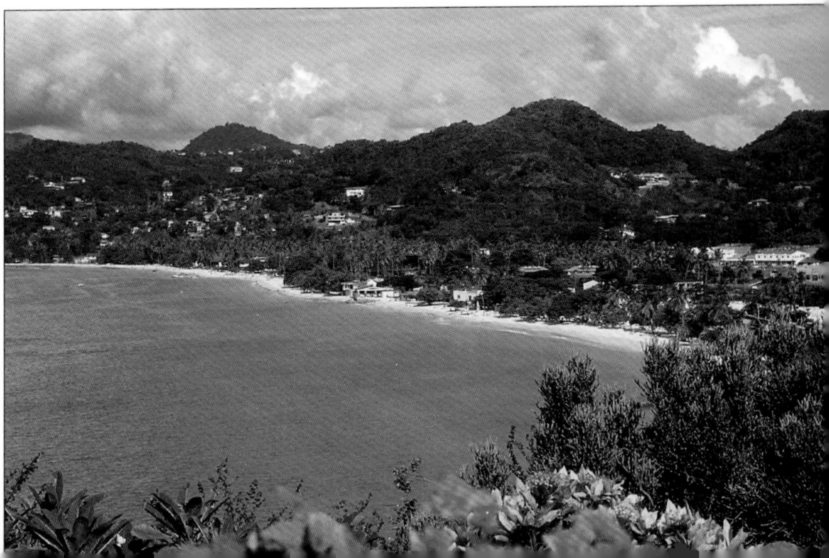

snorkelers and novice divers. Other dive sites include the wall dive at Grand Mal Point; Channel Reef at the entrance to St. George's Harbor; and numerous wrecks, including the Bianca C – a cruise ship that caught fire in 1961 and which, after all the passengers were evacuated, sank in 100 feet of water.

Golf – The nine-hole course at the Grenada Golf & Country Club, near Grand Anse, is open to visitors and has scenic ocean views of both the Caribbean and Atlantic.

(Above) Grenada's famous Spice Market is located on The Carenage, near the tender dock. (Below) Beach at Pt. Salines.

Local Attractions

A walking tour of St. George's will take you past many historical buildings. **1** The **National Library** has been at its present

waterfront location, housed in a former warehouse, since 1892. The **2** **National Museum**, housed in a brick warehouse built by the French in 1704, contains pre-Columbian exhibits including petroglyphs, and its gift shop carries books on the local history. Beside the museum is the Antilles Hotel, one of the oldest buildings in St. George's which was once a French barracks. **3** **Simmons Alley**, a stepped pedestrian walkway, leads up to **4** **St. George's Anglican Church**, built by the British in 1825 using stone and pink stucco.

The residential **5** **Sedan Porches** were originally built open at each end so that people riding in sedan chairs could disembark without getting wet from the rain. The **6** **Houses of Parliament** and its neighboring Registry, built in 1780, are good examples of early Georgian architecture.

The town's **7** **Roman Catholic Cathedral** stands high on the hillside with an unobstructed view down St. Johns Street to

(Above) Historic buildings overlook St. George's Bay. (Below) Scenic inlets dot the south coast.

the water. Local produce is sold at colorful **8** **Market Square** which is also the site of parades and political rallies.

9 **St. Andrew's Presbyterian Kirk**, often called the Scot's Kirk, stands at the bottom of Church Street and was built in 1831 with help from the Freemasons.

10 **Fort George**, at the entrance to St. George's Harbor,

was built by the French in 1705, with later additions by the British. Its ramparts provide commanding views of the Carenage, and within its walls are tunnels, staircases and narrow passageways. Grenada's former leftist Prime Minister Maurice Bishop was executed inside this fort, which is currently used as headquarters of the Royal Grenada Police.

Island Attractions

The restored remains of Fort Frederick stand on the tallest point of a ridge overlooking St. George's, providing visitors with panoramic views of the coast and surrounding countryside. Built by the British around 1791 to protect the rear flank of St. George's from attack, it is the central fort in a chain of defence along Richmond Hill which included Fort Matthew to the north and two other fortifications to the south, said to be connected by tunnels.

The **Annandale Falls** cascade into a freshwater pool surrounded by tropical gardens and paths. Swimming and refreshments can be enjoyed here.

Grand Etang National Park is located in the central, mountainous part of the island, its centerpiece a crater lake surrounded by 2,000-foot mountain peaks. An Information Center provides audiovisual presentations on the flora and fauna of the park's tropical rainforest.

Carmel Waterfall, the island's highest at 75 feet, was recently developed. A walking trail with hand rails, botanical labels and benches leads to this once-hidden waterfall.

Grenada's spice plantations are concentrated at the north end of the island and a nutmeg processing station is located outside Gouyave on the northwest coast. The 1994 opening of Levera National Park, on the rugged northeast coast, increased the island's protected area to 13% of its total land mass. Levera's pristine beaches and mangrove swamps provide habitat for sea turtles and a variety of birds. The islands of the Grenadines can be seen on the horizon, the two southernmost – Carriacou and Petit Martinique – forming a tri-island nation with Grenada.

St. Vincent & The Grenadines

When the creators of *Pirates of the Caribbean*, starring Johnny Depp as Captain Jack Sparrow, were seeking a locale for filming their blockbuster movies, they had trouble finding an island that was relatively undeveloped. Then they saw **St. Vincent** and their quest for a natural locale was over. Known as the Garden

Ground nutmeg is made from the fruit's inner seed.

Island, St. Vincent was a Carib stronghold when Columbus sighted and named it in 1493 for the feast day of the Spanish patron saint St. Vincent. But the island remained untouched by outsiders until 1675, when a Dutch slave ship foundered off the rugged east coast and the survivors, mostly slaves, were taken in by the local Caribs.

The British claimed the fertile island a few years later, but it was the French who established the first European settlement on the leeward coast in 1719. The island changed hands a dozen times until the Treaty of Paris in 1783 officially ceded it to the British, under whose rule it remained until 1979, when St. Vincent gained its independence.

The island today is a melting pot of Caribs, Africans and immigrants from India, Portugal and the Middle East who came to the island following emancipation in 1838. This racial mix has nurtured the second-largest Carnival celebration in the Caribbean, after Trinidad's renowned gala, and this takes place the first week of July. In the hills outside the island's capital and port of **Kingstown** are the first Botanical Gardens established in the Western Hemisphere. A sucker from one of the original breadfruit trees unloaded here by Captain Bligh in 1793 still grows in the Gardens. At the north end of the island stands La Soufriere, an active volcano that last erupted in 1979.

St. Vincent **shore excursions** include tours of Kingston's historic fort and botanical gardens, a guided hike to the summit of La Soufriere, and sailing to the Grenadine island of Bequia. Kayaking, snorkeling and whale watching are also offered.

Stretching south from St. Vincent, in a 60-mile arc, are the

St. Vincent's Leeward Coast –
where rugged slopes and fertile
valleys run down to a tranquil
Caribbean Sea.

(Above) A Windstar cruise ship shares an anchorage with private yachts at Mustique. (Left) The poolside view at Princess Margaret's former villa. (Below) The grounds of the famous Cotton House hotel.

Grenadines – tiny islands ringed with white-sand beaches and coral reefs. Because of their small size and limited rainfall, the Grenadines remained uninhabited until the early 1800s when a band of French colonists established cotton plantations on two of them.

Bequia (*beck-way*) is the largest of the group (5 miles long by 2 miles wide), with a population of 6,000. Its name is from the Carib word *becouya* – Island in the Clouds. The island became a busy whaling station in the mid-1800s when some seafaring Scots settled here. Port Elizabeth, in Admiralty Bay, is the center of island life, and the nearby beaches can be reached by water taxi.

The small, hilly island of **Mustique** was bought in 1958 by Colin Tennant, a Scottish heir whose title is Lord Glenconner. He paid 45,000 pounds sterling for the neglected island of about 100 inhabitants and spent an additional fortune reviving the local farming and fishing industries. In 1960, Princess Margaret, Queen Elizabeth's younger sister, accepted a plot of land as a wedding gift and built a waterfront villa, thus prompting her wealthy and well-connected friends to buy and build on Mustique. Today the island is run as a private company, its 60-some homeowner-

shareholders including Mick Jagger. The Cotton House, an old plantation house converted by Tennant into a luxury hotel, remains one of the most elegant accommodations available in the Caribbean. The island's private villas are rented out when the owners aren't there.

One of the oldest Catholic churches in the Windward Islands stands on the tiny islet of **Mayreau** (pronounced *my-ro*), atop the island's only hill. Built in the early 1800s by the St. Heliers family from France, the church functions as a Sunday gathering place for most of the island's 100 inhabitants. Sharing the hilltop is the island's school, and on the other side of the hill is Salt Whistle Bay, one of the finest beaches and anchorages in the island chain.

The four, deserted islets of **Tobago Cays**, surrounded by the huge Horseshoe Reef, have been declared a wildlife reserve. The brilliant white beaches and surrounding seas in shades of blue ranging from indigo to aquamarine, make this cluster of islands a tropical paradise for visitors arriving by sailing vessel.

(Above) Mayreau's idyllic Salt Whistle Bay.
(Left) The pristine islands of Tobago Cays.

Near the southern end of the chain is **Union Island**, with a population of 2,000. For decades it has been a port of entry for yachts plying the quiet waters of St. Vincent and the Grenadines, earning it the nickname Gateway to the Grenadines.

PARISH OF
ST. LUCY

Farley Hill
Nat. Park

Charles Duncan ONeal Hwy

Atlantic Ocean

Speightstown

PARISH OF
ST. PETER

Mullins
Bay

Folkstone Marine
Reserve

East Coast Hwy

Bathsheba
Beach

Holetown

Mount
Hillaby 1115 ft

Paynes
Bay

Harrison's
Cave

PARISH OF
ST. JOHN

Spring Garden Hwy

Gun Hill
Signal Stn.

Barrow Hwy

PARISH OF
ST. GEORGE

Sam Lord's
Castle

**Cruise
Port**

Bridgetown

Carlisle
Bay

Crane
Bay

PARISH OF
CHRIST CHURCH

Needhams
Point

Bardados
Golf Club

Cobbler's Reef

Casuarina
Beach

Oistins
Bay

Grantley Adams
Int'l Airport

Caribbean   *Sea*

0   4

Miles

↑
N

BARBADOS

AREA	166 sq mi
POPULATION	169,000
CAPITAL	Bridgetown
LANGUAGE	English
CURRENCY	Barbados dollar, U.S. dollar
GOVERNMENT	Pariliamentary democracy

CHAPTER SEVENTEEN

BARBADOS

Barbados is perhaps the most British of the Caribbean islands. For more than three centuries the island was under continuous British rule, and its parliament, formed in 1639, is the third oldest in the English-speaking world (after Britain and Bermuda). An independent member of the British Commonwealth of Nations since 1966, Barbados is a stable democracy with a thriving economy. Cricket is the national sport, and the capital of Bridgetown has its own Trafalgar Square, complete with Nelson's Column.

The similarities to Olde England continue outside of **Bridgetown**, where a drive along narrow winding roads, past village greens and cricket fields, is a step back in time to the days of the British Empire when wealthy plantation owners lived in Georgian-style great houses built of coral stone, their thick walls a barrier to the tropical heat. The English tradition of discretion is also widely practised, much to the frustration of journalists trying to pry information from locals in the fall of 2004 as golf pro Tiger Woods prepared to marry his Swedish bride in a sunset ceremony at the island's west-coast resort of Sandy Lane.

There were no permanent inhabitants on Barbados back in 1625 when the first English ship visited its shores. Lying 100 miles east of the volcanic arc of Windward Islands, Barbados was at one time inhabited by Arawaks but the island escaped detection by migrating Caribs and, later, by Columbus. A coral island of ridges and hills, Barbados is the only non-volcanic island in the Lesser Antilles and it remained in isolation, visited mostly by birds. The seeds left in their droppings and the coconuts that washed up on beaches were a source of vegetation that slowly took root, including the Bearded Fig Tree for which the island was named Isla de los Barbados (Island of the Bearded) by a passing Portuguese explorer in the early 16th century.

When British settlers arrived in 1627 and established Jamestown near present-day Holetown, they initially planted tobacco, then switched to sugarcane. African slaves were brought in to work the fields when indentured servants began avoiding Barbados, partly because its planters had a reputation as cruel masters who paid meager freedom dues, but mainly because it was a white man's graveyard. Europeans had no immunity to tropical diseases, several of which were brought over by the Africans, and the majority of white settlers perished within their first year on the island. Those who survived, however, became extremely wealthy and for decades Barbados dominated the sugar markets in England. The island's easterly

Morgan Lewis Mill was built in the 1700s to grind sugar cane.

location (i.e. closer to England) and a coastline that was easily accessible from any point on the island, kept transport costs lower than on other islands. The island's location also helped preserve its British status, for the prevailing winds prevented enemy sailing ships from approaching the island's west side without tacking to and fro, making it difficult to stage a surprise attack.

The island's plantation era endures in the many historic mansions that have been preserved through the efforts of Barbados National Trust, founded in 1961 by an expatriate Briton and a group of interested Barbadians. Following the end of the slave trade in 1832, communities began to center around each parish's local church and school. Chattel houses, which were a miniature version of the Georgian-style manor house, appeared after emancipation when freed slaves built themselves moveable wooden homes. Education became

widespread and today 97% of the island's population is literate.

Only 21 by 14 miles in size, Barbados is densely populated with about a third of its quarter-million population living in the Bridgetown area. Yet, once you're away from the busy streets of Bridgetown, the island's natural beauty, healthy climate and sense of gentility exert their appeal. Protected powdery beaches line the west side of the island, in contrast to the rugged east coast where Atlantic swells roll ashore. Inland, the rolling countryside of parks and gardens exudes a pastoral charm, as do the villages where parish churches swell with singing on Sunday mornings.

Barbadian rum is among the finest and oldest in the world, the locally produced Mount Gay brand first distilled here in 1663 by Abel Gay. The island's ideal climate has long attracted visitors, one of its most famous being George Washington when, in 1751, he accompanied his ill half-brother who came for a change of air, as was fashionable at the time. Much has changed since the days of British colonialism but the island's summer festival, called Crop Over, still celebrates the end of the sugar harvest – an annual event in Barbados for the past three and a half centuries. Sugar remains an important export but tourism is well established, with close to a million visitors arriving annually, half of these by cruise ship.

Getting Around

The deepwater harbor, located about a mile north of Bridgetown's center, opened in 1961. It occupies Pelican Island, upon which pelicans once nested before it was joined to the mainland during the harbor's construction. The port's spacious and modern complex contains a tourist information office and an assortment of shops carrying duty-free and locally made items. It takes about 15 minutes to walk into Bridgetown.

Barbados is a very pleasant island to tour, whether by rental car, hired taxi or group excursion. The roads are in good condition, although they are generally narrow and winding, and visibility is sometimes restricted by bordering cane fields. Driving is on the left, roundabout lanes are common, and Bridgetown is best avoided during rush hour. A temporary license (available through local car rental firms) costs $5 US. Rental cars and taxis can be hired just outside the shopping complex at the kiosks, and daily rental car rates are $55-$75. A car and driver can be hired for about $80 per day. Taxi rates (posted in the terminal building in Barbadian dollars) are fixed.

Shore Excursions
Barbados

Ship-organized excursions usually include a countryside tour with popular stops being Gun Hill, St. John's Parish Church and one of the island's great houses. Also organized by most cruise lines is a visit to Harrison's Cave and a ride on the Atlantis Submarine. Ocean Park Aquarium in Christ Church Parish is a new attraction offered as a shore excursion in combination with a beach getaway. A brewery tour includes a visit to Mount Gay Distillery, and golf is available at Sandy Lane Golf Club and Barbados Golf Club. Touring by horseback, mountain bike, mini-buggy, ATV and land rover are all offered. Barbados is home to a healthy population of sea turtles and a variety of sailboat, sea kayaking, snorkeling and diving excursions are offered for up-close viewing of hawksbill and other turtles.

Bridgetown's cruise port.

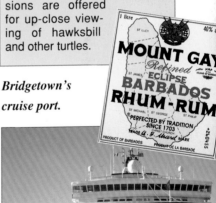

'Red Roof Top' by Barbadian artist Neville Oluyemi Legall, whose paintings are sold at local galleries.

Some sample fares, in US dollars, per cab, from the cruise port to: Bridgetown – $4; Hilton Hotel – $6; Crane Bay – $18; Sam Lord's Castle – $20; and Harrison's Cave – $15.

The official currency is the Barbados dollar (worth approximately 50¢ US) but American and Canadian money is widely accepted.

Shopping – There is a good selection of duty-free shops at the cruise terminal, including branch stores of Cave Shepherd and Harrison's. Local arts and crafts are sold at Pelican Village, on the main highway leading into town. In Bridgetown, the duty-free shops are concen-trated on Broad Street and its side streets, where good buys can be found in crystal, fine bone china, jewelry, perfumes and clothing. Harrisons, established in 1854, is considered the island's premier store. Local handicrafts, batik, ceramics and original paintings and prints can be bought at various galleries, including Verandah Art Gallery, 'Creative Expressions' in The Shops of the Ginger Bread House, Colours of de Caribbean and Mango Jam Gallery.

Mahogany woodcarvings and sculptures can be found at Best of Barbados Shops (with a location at the Cruise Ship Terminal) and Potter's House Gallery in Shop Hill. Contemporary and traditional pottery is sold at various rural potteries, including Chalky Mount and Castle Pottery in St. Peter, Earthworks Pottery at Shop Hill in St. Thomas, and Fairfield Pottery in St. Michael.

Beaches – Because Barbados is a coral island, beautiful beaches line its shores. All beaches are public and accessible by right-of-ways; nude bathing is illegal. The most sheltered beaches lie on the west coast, including Mullins Beach which offers glassy smooth water and good snorkeling, and Paynes Bay which is good for swimming and watersports. Restaurant facilities are available at both beaches.

Just south of Bridgetown's central district is a crescent of white sand on Carlisle Bay which is popular with both locals and visitors, and is serviced by The Boatyard – a high-energy beach club offering day packages to cruise passengers (about $15 per person) which include the use of a lounge chair, showers, change rooms and reduced rental rates on kayaks, snorkel gear and other watersports equipment. A day ticket also includes a free shuttle back to the cruise pier, one complimentary beverage, and access to the club's bar and restaurant.

On the south coast, at Needhams Point, the grounds of the Hilton Hotel overlook a beach of soft white sand which is also the densest hawksbill turtle nesting beach in the Eastern Caribbean. Barbados Blue, located at the Hilton, offers kayaking, snorkeling and diving excursions during which you are likely to see a Hawskbill turtle.

On the southeast coast, a beach of sugary white sand and fairly big waves is located at Crane Bay, often making the short list of 'The World's Best Beaches.' Another beautiful beach washed by surf is Bottom Bay, which lies at the base of a cliff north of Sam Lord's Castle and is reached by some steps, as is the fine beach right below Sam Lord's – a Georgian mansion built in 1820 by a 'gentleman pirate' and now part of a hotel resort. On the island's Atlantic coast, a dramatic sight is the pounding surf and eroded boulders at Bathsheba Beach, where signs warn that swimming is dangerous.

Dive & Snorkel Sites – The Folkestone Underwater Park and Marine Reserve is just north of Holetown. In addition to the park headquarters and interpretation center, the underwater park itself is divided into four zones – scientific, recreational, and a northern and southern watersports zone. The Recreational Zone contains a snorkel trail near shore and dive boats are available for trips to Dottin's Reef – part of a seven-mile stretch of intermittent banking reef about 1/3 mile offshore. South of the recreational zones, a 356-foot freighter has been sunk in 120 feet about a half mile from shore to form an artificial reef. Dive shops are located in Holetown.

A number of wrecks lie on the bottom of Carlisle Bay where ships once anchored before the harbor was constructed; these include the Berwyn (scuttled in 1919), which is ideal for snorkelers.

Barbados Blue is located at the Hilton on Needhams Point, offering snorkel tours, and beach and boat dives for all levels of experience. Drift diving is popular on the south coast along the barrier reef that starts at depths of 60 feet and lies from a half mile to two miles offshore. Hawksbill turtles are commonly sighted there.

Several good beaches are found near Sam Lord's Castle.

(Above and left) Mullins Beach, on the sheltered west coast, is ideal for swimming and snorkeling. (Below) Beaches on the southeast coast are partially protected by Cobbler's Reef.

Non-divers can view the island's underwater world to depths of 150 feet aboard an Atlantis Submarine or enjoy a snorkeler's perspective of the near-shore reefs on board the Atlantis Seatrec observation vessel, both based in Bridgetown.

Golf – The 18-hole course at Sandy Lane Golf Club is set in the upscale area of Sandy Lane Estate north of Bridgetown. A 6,533-yard, par-72 course, its signature hole is a 70-foot drop from tee to green. South of Bridgetown is the par-36, nine-hole course at Club Rockley which covers 2,736 yards. The 6,805-yard, par-72 Barbados Golf Club, located in Christ Church Parish, was originally designed by Col. J. Harris in 1974, then redesigned by Ron Kirby for its reopening in 2000.

Local Attractions

Founded in 1628, Bridgetown stands on the banks of the Constitution River, its wide mouth forming a harbor called the Careenage where boats moor alongside. Spanning the Careenage is the Chamberlain Bridge, its south end graced with the Independence Arch. At the north end of the bridge is **1**

(Above) Crane Bay offers fine white sand and some surf.
(Below) Atlantic swells roll ashore at Bathsheba Beach.

Trafalgar Square, in the center of which stands a statue of Horatio Nelson which predates the one in London. The neo-Gothic Public Buildings on the north side of the square were erected in 1872 and they house the island's Parliament.

Other historic buildings in the downtown core include **2 St. Michael's Cathedral** (rebuilt after it was destroyed by a hurricane in 1780), the 18th-century **3 St. Mary's Church**, and the beautifully-restored **4 Nidhe Israel Synagogue** which was originally built in 1654 and has won an

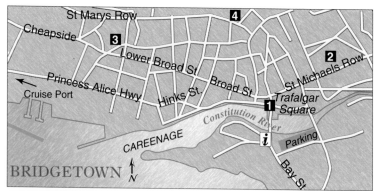

The Parliament Buildings and Trafalgar Square stand on the north side of the Careenage.

American Express Preservation Award. Streets of interest include Hinks Street, with its old sugar warehouses, and Broad Street with its elegant shops and colonial buildings. A convenient parking lot is located between the two bridges on the south bank of the river.

Island Attractions

The Barbados National Trust preserves and operates a number of island attractions that have historic importance or natural beau-

ty. These are indicated below with a star (*) and can be visited individually (a discount system is in place for those who visit more than one attraction). Ship-organized tours visit several National Trust properties (some of which are closed on Sundays and public holidays). In addition to those mentioned below, Trust properties include the Sir Frank Hutson Sugar Museum, Codrington College, Oughterson House & Barbados Zoo Park, and the elegant Francia Plantation House (near Gun Hill) which was built by a Frenchman for his bride at the turn of the century. In the historic Garrison area just south of Bridgetown are the **5 Barbados Gallery of Art and The Barbados Museum*** which contains archaeological and historical exhibits as well as African and European decorative arts.

6 The Mount Gay Rum Visitor's Center*, just north of Bridgetown, offers 45-minute tours which end with a sampling of the company's famous rum.

The authentic chattel houses at **7 Tyrol Cot Heritage Village*** are centered around an 1854 mansion, the former home of Sir Grantley and Lady Adams, and the village includes a popular market selling local arts and crafts.

In the 19th century, a series of signal stations were established by Britain's Royal Artillery along the island's high points to signal the approach of enemy ships or the safe arrival of cargo ships. The signal men communicated between stations using telescopes and flags. **8 Gun Hill Signal Station***, situated on the highland of St. George with a magnificent view of the west coast, was built in 1818 and restored by the Barbados National Trust in 1982. On the hill below the station, visible from the road when exiting the premises, is a British Military Lion that was carved by British soldiers.

At **9 Harrison's Cave*** trams take visitors on a spectacular subterranean ride past limestone stalactites and stalagmites that took millions of years to form. An underground stream of clear water runs through the cave, fed by rain that is filtered through 200 feet of coral before reaching a natural underground reservoir which is the island's supply of pure drinking water.

Administered by the Barbados National Trust, **10 Welchman Hall Gully*** is an oasis of ornamental plants and trees nestled in a deep gully rimmed with cliffs. Located near Harrison's Cave, it was once part of a series of caves, the roofs of which collapsed to cre-

ate the gully now filled with tropical plants and pathways. Its jungle setting is also a habitat for the Barbados Green Monkey which is frequently seen here in the early morning or late afternoon.

The 50-acre **11 Flower Forest** is a cross between a botanical garden and a nature trail. Located on a hillside of the Scotland District, its paths contain several seats, and walking sticks and umbrellas are provided. In addition to bar and restaurant facilities, the premises contain a Best of Barbados gift shop.

One of the oldest great houses in the Caribbean, **12 St. Nicholas Abbey*** is maintained by the National Trust. It was built by a British colonel around 1650 in the Jacobean style with Dutch gables and corner fireplaces – an unlikely feature for the tropics. Its second owner, Sir John Yeamans, colonized Carolina and became the third Governor of South Carolina. The current owner is Lieutenant Colonel Stephen Cave whose family has owned the estate since 1820. One of only three remaining great houses of its period in the Western Hemisphere, the ground floor is open for viewing and is furnished with English and Barbadian antiques. The wine cellar is now a gift shop.

A restored signal station is located at **13 Grenade Hall Forest & Signal Station*** in St. Peter. A panoramic view can be enjoyed from the signal station, and the surrounding forest contains coral pathways for viewing the various species of trees, vines and herbs.

Established in 1985 on four acres of mahogany forest, the non-profit **14 Barbados Wildlife Reserve** includes a research center that focuses on conservation of the Barbados Green Monkey. The animals wander freely here and visitors are encouraged to take their time while walking quietly along the shady paths or pausing on a bench to wait and see which creatures appear.

At **15 Farley Hill National Park***, officially opened by Queen Elizabeth in 1966, visitors can wander the ruins of what was once the most opulent plantation estate on the island. Situated in the Scotland District at the north end of the island, the park's ridge-top location provides sweeping views of the surrounding countryside and the island's Atlantic coast. The mansion, built in stages in the 19th century, was gutted by fire in the late 1950s shortly after the filming of *Island In The Sun* starring Harry Belafonte. Its stone walls remain, as do the trimmed lawns and narrow lanes shaded by a corridor of palm trees. The park is a cool and breezy place to enjoy a picnic lunch, just as royal guests Prince Albert and Prince George (later King George V) did in 1879.

16 Morgan Lewis Mill*, a Barbados National Trust Property in the rugged Scotland District, is the only complete sugar windmill surviving in the Caribbean. Built in the 18th century to grind sugarcane, hundreds of such mills used

(Left) Gun Hill Signal Station.
(Below) Farley Hill ruins.

to dot the countryside when sugar was 'white gold' and Barbados was Britain's most valuable possession in the Americas.

The six acres of individual tropical gardens at 🔢 **Andromeda Botanic Gardens*** contain rare and unique species of plants.

One of the oldest and most picturesque churches on the island, 🔢 **St. John's Parish Church** stands atop an inland bluff overlooking the east coast. Originally built of wood, its stone replacement was destroyed by several hurricanes. The present structure dates from 1836 and the churchyard contains the tomb of Ferdinand Paleologus, who was a great-grandson of Thomas, brother of the last Byzantine Emperor. Ferdinand served in the British army before sailing to Barbados, where he was church warden from 1655 to 1656.

The original 🔢 **Villa Nova** was destroyed by a hurricane in 1831. Rebuilt in 1834 and now a luxury resort, its previous owners include British Prime Minister Sir Anthony Eden and the Earl of

Avon, whose garden parties were attended by Lady Churchill and Queen Elizabeth.

🔢 **Sunbury Plantation House*** is a beautifully preserved great house built in the 1600s by the Chapmans, one of the first planter families on Barbados. The residence was officially opened to visitors as a Heritage House in 1984. The mansion is filled with mahogany antiques and the grounds contain gardens, a gift shop, and a unique collection of horse-drawn carriages.

(Right) St. Nicholas Abbey.
(Below) The view from Farley Hill National Park.

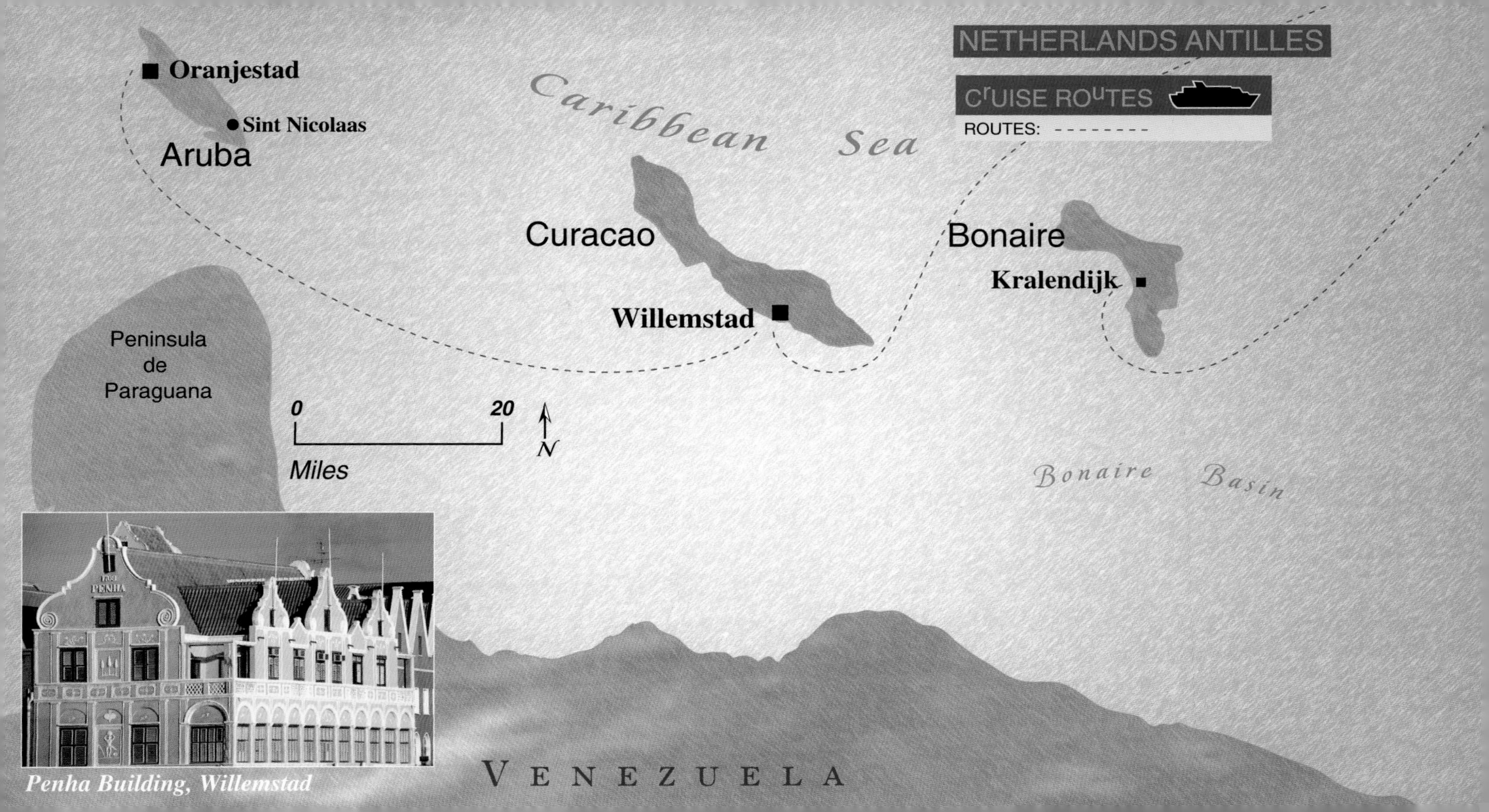

NETHERLANDS ANTILLES

CRUISE ROUTES

ROUTES: ------

Caribbean Sea

Bonaire

Kralendijk ■

Bonaire Basin

Curacao

Willemstad ■

VENEZUELA

N

20

0   Miles

Oranjestad ■

● Sint Nicolaas

Aruba

Peninsula de Paraguana

Penha Building, Willemstad

CHAPTER EIGHTEEN

ARUBA, CURACAO & BONAIRE

The Dutch islands of Aruba, Bonaire and Curacao (the ABCs) lie off the coast of Venezuela, outside of the hurricane belt. Unlike the other Lesser Antilles, they receive little rain in summer, their vegetation consisting of drought-resistant cacti and divi-divi trees bent by the steady trade winds. Their stark landscapes of wave-eroded rock formations and brilliant white beaches are in contrast to the colorful ports where Dutch gabled, pastel-painted buildings line the waterfront.

The islands' semi-arid climate, interrupted by a brief rainy spell each winter, is one reason they were deemed 'useless' by the early Spanish explorers. They were inhabited at the time by Caiquetios, a tribe of peaceful Arawak Indians who lived in villages and caves, the walls of which contain pictographs they left behind. Their food came mostly from the rich bounty of the sea, the surrounding waters filled with colorful coral gardens and an abundance of fish. Other foodstuffs were obtained from mainland tribes in exchange for salt, one of the few natural resources found on these barren islands.

Located within 40 miles of the Venezuela coast, the ABCs are actually part of the Andes chain of mountains which snakes up the western side of South America and branches into smaller ranges at the north end of the continent.

Dutch colonial architecture lines a shopping street in Oranjestad.

Underwater volcanic activity helped form the islands, which consist of batholith rock as well as younger limestone formed before uplifting slowly brought the islands to the sea's surface.

The treasure-seeking Spaniards were the first Europeans to discover the ABCs when, in 1499, a Spanish sea captain en route to South America left some of his scurvy-afflicted sailors on one of the islands to die. When he returned less than a year later, he found them all alive and well. Hence the name Curacao – based on the Portuguese word for 'the cure'. Yet, despite its promising name, Curacao did not impress the Spanish for it was a dry, prickly place with no apparent gold deposits. Even the Valencia orange trees brought from Spain produced a bitter, almost inedible fruit when planted here.

It took the resourceful Dutch to see the potential of Curacao and make it an integral part of their trading empire. They seized the island in 1634, transferring the few Spanish settlers and Arawak Indians to the mainland, and took possession of Aruba and Bonaire a year or so later. Some Arawaks lived on Aruba where they maintained the cattle and horses that roamed freely on the island.

The Dutch West India Company was initially attracted to Curacao as a source of salt and hardwood, but it soon became a base for raiding settlements on other islands and the coastal mainland. Its sheltered harbor was fortified on either side at the entrance and, under the governorship of Peter Stuyvesant from 1642 to 1647, Willemstad became an important world port. With the soil unable to support sugar cane or other cash crops, Curacao's survival depended on trade, which came in the form of slaves. Throughout the latter half of the 1600s and well into the 1700s, Curacao was an enormous slave depot for the Caribbean and South America.

Meanwhile, Aruba was maintained as a vast cattle ranch, and corn was grown on Bonaire to feed the slaves passing through Curacao, which also became a commercial meeting place for pirates, American rebels, Dutch merchants and Spaniards from the mainland. As for those bitter-tasting oranges brought from Spain, it was discovered that their sun-dried peels contained an etheric

Fort Amsterdam was the center of the fortified town of Willemstad, Curacao.

oil which became the basis for Curacao's famous liqueur. The ABCs remained for the most part Dutch, briefly besieged by the British in 1804, and occupied by British troops from 1807 to 1814.

Slavery was finally ended in 1863 and the islands had to develop new resources. Trade with Venezuela became the mainstay of Curacao's economy and was helped greatly when the Dutch government lifted all import taxes on goods from the Netherlands, which local merchants could then exchange at a profit for Venezuelan products. On Aruba and Bonaire, the aloe plant became an important crop, its gel used in numerous pharmaceuticals, and the pods of the divi-divi tree were also exported for use in leather tanning.

In 1824, alluvial deposits of gold were found on Aruba and the island's mines, which operated for nearly a century, yielded more than three million pounds of gold. When, following World War I, oil was discovered at Lake Maracaibo in Venezuela the oil companies, seeking a stable place to locate their refineries and storage facilities, chose the nearby Dutch islands. When the demand for oil slumped, the islands developed yet another untapped resource which continues today – tourism.

Blessed with natural appeal – beautiful beaches, turquoise waters, colorful coral reefs, and a climate that's sunny and dry – the islands have added duty-free shopping, waterfront casinos and championship golf courses to their growing list of attractions. Their residents, who descend from a mix

of races and cultures, are a people known for their racial and religious tolerance. They are also multilingual, learning Dutch – the official language – at school, and are often fluent in English and Spanish, as well as their native tongue of Papiamento, which is a lilting blend of Spanish, Portuguese, Dutch, English and African dialects.

All three islands are part of the Kingdom of the Netherlands but Aruba is no longer part of the Netherlands Antilles, of which Curacao is the capital and Bonaire is a member, along with the Leeward Islands of St. Maarten, Saba and St. Eustatius. Aruba, seeking more autonomy in connection with its oil revenues, became a separate entity in 1986.

Aruba

Once a cacti-studded cattle ranch, Aruba is today a holiday paradise with miles of blinding white beaches and crystal-clear turquoise waters. The island's first inhabitants, the Caquetio Indians, had established themselves at the mouth of Venezuela's Aroa River until repeated attacks by the Carib Indians prompted them to leave. Some of the tribe members moved to the shores of Lake Maracaibo and still bear the name Arubaes. Others moved to the island now called Aruba.

The island's southwest coast has beach resorts, shopping malls and casinos; its rugged northeast coast is where wave action has carved coral cliffs into dramatic sea arches. In between lies a hilly desert of caves, cacti and scrub.

A ship docks at the Oranjestad cruise terminal.

Splashes of color are provided by flamboyant trees, in bloom from June through August, and gardens of homes which often contain a variety of tropical flowers. Wells tap into the island's water table but a huge saltwater distillation plant at Spanish Lagoon, once a hideout for pirates, is the island's main source of fresh water.

Getting Around

The cruise ships dock in the heart of **Oranjestad**, within easy walking distance of the shops and other attractions. Taxis are unmetered and rates are fixed, based on a carload of up to four passengers, but be sure to establish a fare before departing. People returning from the beach in wet bathing suits are usually refused, so be sure to dry off and take a cover-up. US currency is accepted,

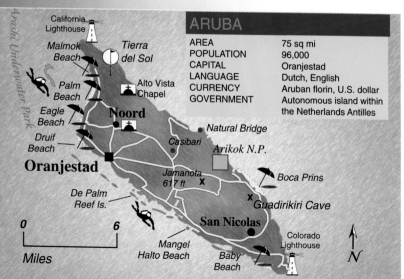

ARUBA

AREA	75 sq mi
POPULATION	96,000
CAPITAL	Oranjestad
LANGUAGE	Dutch, English
CURRENCY	Aruban florin, U.S. dollar
GOVERNMENT	Autonomous island within the Netherlands Antilles

California Lighthouse
Malmok Beach
Tierra del Sol
Palm Beach
Alto Vista Chapel
Eagle Beach
Noord
Druif Beach
Natural Bridge
Casibari
Arikok N.P.
Oranjestad
Jamanota 617 ft
Boca Prins
De Palm Reef Is.
Guadirikiri Cave
San Nicolas
Mangel Halto Beach
Baby Beach
Colorado Lighthouse
Arashi Underwater Park
0   6
Miles
N

but not large bills (i.e. $50 or $100). The minimum rate to any destination is $4, and the hired rate per hour is $30. Some sample fares (in US$) from the cruise terminal: Eagle Beach ($7); Noord ($9); Mangel Halto Beach ($14).

Most major American car rental companies operate on Aruba, in addition to several local companies. Avis has an office at the cruise ship terminal. A valid driver's license is all that's required to rent a car. The island is 19-1/2 miles long by six miles wide, the main roads are paved, and driving is on the right. It's hard to get lost, and the divi-divi trees – bent by the trade winds – all point toward the island's leeward side where Oranjestad is located.

The official currency is the Aruban Florin (AWG) but US dollars are readily accepted island wide, and major credit cards are

(Above) Aruba has several good dive sites. (Below) Palm Beach is one of the best swimming beaches in the Caribbean.

Shore Excursions

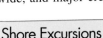

Shore excursions include countryside drives and feature such island attractions as the Butterfly Farm (near Palm Beach) and the Ostrich Farm (on the road leading to the Natural Bridge). Also offered are ATV adventures, 4WD safaris, mountain biking and horseback riding, as well as guided hikes in Arikok National Park and historic walking tours of Oranjestad. Submarine rides, semi-submersible cruises and glass-bottom boat rides are available, as are kayaking, snorkeling, helmet diving and scuba diving. Beach breaks include Palm Beach and De Palm Island. Golf is available at Tierra Del Sol.

(Above) Souvenir stand and Seaport Marketplace in Oranjestad. (Opposite) A cruise ship departs Aruba.

accepted at most establishments. The bank rate of exchange is fixed at 1.77 Afl. to $1 US (stores exchange at AWG 1.75 to $1 US).

Beaches – A string of fine beaches lie along the coast northwest of the cruise terminal, starting with Druif Beach (about 2 miles away), which is adjacent to Manchebo Beach (where hotel facilities are available) which is adjacent to Eagle Beach, where watersports equipment is available. About four miles from the terminal is Palm Beach, considered one of the best beaches in the Caribbean and extremely popular for its good swimming, sailing and hotel facilities. Hadikurari is popular

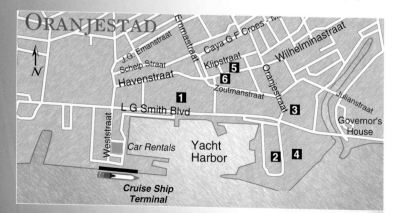

with windsurfers, where rental equipment is available. Arushi Beach, near the island's northern tip, is a wide expanse of sand dotted with beach huts and within sight of the California Light House. At the island's southeastern tip are Rodgers Beach and Baby Beach, the latter being ideal for young children with its calm, shallow waters and shady areas. Picnickers enjoy the romantic setting of Boca Prins, backed by sand dunes and pounded by the nearby surf, which makes swimming dangerous.

Dive and Snorkel Sites – The shallow waters and abundance of fish off Malmok Beach (8 miles from the terminal) make it an ideal spot for snorkelers but there are no facilities nearby. Arashi Reef and the Antilla, a German freighter destroyed during World War II, are popular dive sites, and can also be viewed by semi-submersible and submarine, both available through ship-organized shore excursions. Seaworld Explorer transports passengers by bus to the north end of the island where their semi-submersible is boarded, while Atlantis transports passengers to and from their sub site by ferry from Seaport Village Marina. Another good snorkeling beach is Manguel Halto beach, with its nearby barrier reef. De Palm Island (reached by ferry) also offers excellent snorkeling; the full-day admission charge ($89 for adults/half price for children) covers all beach facilities and waterpark slides, an open bar and an all-you-can-eat buffet (or chef-prepared lunch) as well as snorkel equipment, instructions and guided tours. Scuba and seatrek (helmet diving) are available for an additional cost.

Golf – An 18-hole course designed by Robert Trents Jones Jr is situated at Tierra del Sol near the island's northwestern tip. This par-71 course with water on two sides, has stunning sea views and is dotted with giant cacti and clusters of natural grasses.

Shopping – Shopping malls are located at the harborfront, in town and stretching northwest along the coast. **1**

Seaport Village Mall, a five-minute walk from the cruise terminal, is Aruba's largest shopping and entertainment complex with dozens of stores, boutiques and a casino. The nearby **2 Seaport Marketplace** is also popular with its shaded central walkway and sidewalk cafes. Oranjestad's main shopping street is Caya G.F. Betico Croes, with chic boutiques and shops.

International items to look for include perfumes, designer fashions, china, crystal, jewelry, watches and cameras. There are also good buys in Peruvian hand-knit sweaters, Venezuelan shoes and handbags, Colombian emeralds, and locally made aloe vera products. Clay pottery and other local artwork is sold at outdoor stands along the waterfront.

Local Sights – 3 Fort Zoutman is the oldest building in Oranjestad, erected in 1796 and named for a Dutch Rear Admiral. Added to the fort in 1868 was King Willem III Tower which served as a lighthouse and now houses a heritage museum.

4 Queen Wilhelmina Park, adjacent to the Seaport Marketplace, contains a marble statue of the former Dutch queen. Wilhelminastraat contains interesting colonial architecture including the **5 Protestant Church**, built in 1846. The **6 Archaeological Museum** on Zoutmanstraat contains artifacts and pottery of the island's first Indian inhabitants.

Island Attractions – Santa Anna Church in **Noord** was built in the 1770s, and its hand-carved oak altar won the exhibition award in Rome in 1870 (see photo, page 77). The **Chapel of Alto Vista**, built by a Spanish missionary, is a place of pilgrimage situated on the north coast overlooking the sea. The interesting rock formations at **Casibari** can be climbed via some steps to the top for a view of the island. Aruba's most famous landmark is the **Natural Bridge**, made of coral and carved by the sea on the island's windward coast. The arch is over 100 feet long and stands 23 feet above sea level.

Arikok National Park contains natural and man-made paths, a restored *cunucu* (countryside house), a traditional stone well and the Natural Pool, near Boca Keto, which is surrounded by rocks and filled with sea water. Several caves are situated along the north coast, including **Guadirikiri Cave**, its caverns containing stalactites and ancient drawings.

Natural Bridge, Aruba.

Curacao

A ship arriving in Willemstad.

Few Caribbean ports of call can surpass the arrival awaiting passengers at Curacao. Here the Queen Emma Pontoon Bridge swings open to allow ships to enter the canal-like entrance of St. Anna Bay and glide past the waterfront buildings of colonial **Willemstad**. A centuries-old capital, its channel-side streets are lined with gabled buildings which were painted a variety of colors in 1817 when the Governor com-plained that the sun's glare off the stark white buildings was giving him headaches.

Initially founded as Santa Anna by the Spanish, the port's name was changed to Willemstad when Holland took possession of the island in 1634. Settlement grew on both sides of the channel with the eastern side called Punda and the western side Otrabanda ('other side').

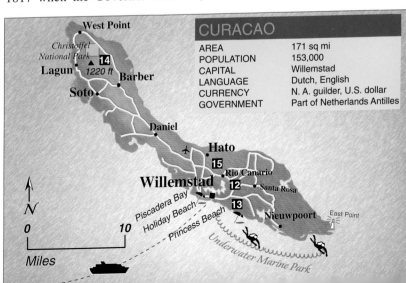

CURACAO

AREA	171 sq mi
POPULATION	153,000
CAPITAL	Willemstad
LANGUAGE	Dutch, English
CURRENCY	N. A. guilder, U.S. dollar
GOVERNMENT	Part of Netherlands Antilles

West Point

Christoffel National Park

Lagun

14 1220 ft

Barber

Soto

Daniel

Hato

15

Rio Canario

Willemstad

12

Santa Rosa

13

Nieuwpoort

East Point

Piscadera Bay

Holiday Beach

Princess Beach

Underwater Marine Park

N

0   10

Miles

Willemstad's golden Penha Building is a town landmark.

Ferry boats have long transported residents across the channel but in the late 1900s the American consul, Leonard Burlington Smith, suggested a pontoon foot bridge be built. Fixed at one end so it could open whenever a vessel had to pass, the bridge was completed in 1888. A toll charge was based on each person's ability to pay – those wearing shoes were charged 2¢ and those walking barefooted were free. It's said that the poor would borrow shoes to prove their ability to pay, while the rich would take off their shoes to save 2¢. Today there is no charge for either the bridge or the passenger ferries which run continuously throughout the day.

Getting Around

Dutch charm and duty-free shopping await the visitor to Willemstad. The official currency is the Netherlands Antilles guilder (NAfl) but U.S. dollars

are widely accepted. The cruise ships dock on the Otrabanda side of the channel and passengers can make their way to the Punda side on foot over the pontoon bridge, via the free passenger ferry which docks at Mathey Wharf, or by taxi (about $6 US) over the Queen Julianna Bridge which spans the harbor at a height of 185 feet. Taxis are unmetered and the fee should be agreed upon before departing. Sample fares, per taxi, from the cruise pier: Holiday Beach – $6; Piscadera Bay – $7; Princess Beach – $12; island sightseeing – $30 per hour.

There are several tourist information booths along the

Dutch gabled buildings line Willemstad's waterfront.

Otrabanda waterfront, and the main office is located on the Punda side at the east end of Wilhelminaplein. A post office is directly east of the Central Market.

Beaches – Curacao's southern coast is indented with beach-lined bays and coves. Private beaches charge a small entrance fee, as do some of the hotel beaches. A popular hotel beach close to the cruise port is Holiday Beach. Farther west is the private beach at Blaauwbaai (Blue Bay) – considered one of Curacao's best with its white sand, shaded areas and change facilities. More hotel beaches are located at Piscadera Bay, including the Sonesta Hotel, Las Palmas and Curacao Caribbean. Fine beaches east of Willemstad include Princess Beach, where a hotel is located, and Seaquarium Beach and Santa Barbara Beach, both private beaches with change facilities and snack bars.

Dive & Snorkel Sites – Excellent snorkeling and diving

are available all around the island with visibility of 60 to 80 feet, and sometimes up to 150 feet. The Curacao Underwater Park, ideal for both diving and snorkeling, protects 12-1/2 miles of unspoiled coral reef along which is an underwater nature trail and spectacular dive sites which include coral beds, sheer walls and shipwrecks. Klein Curacao, lying off East Point, is an uninhabited islet with beautiful beaches and good snorkeling and diving.

Golf – A nine-hole course with sand greens is open mornings at the Curacao Golf & Squash Club just north of the Willemstad Harbor.

Shopping – Duty-free bargains in Willemstad include brand-name jewelry, watches, European fashions, perfumes, crystal, china, electronics and cameras. Fine stores are located

The Queen Emma Pontoon Bridge connects the two sides of Willemstad and can be accessed from the cruise docks.

on Handelskade, Heerenstraat and Breedestraat, with more shops and boutiques located in the restored **3** Waterfort Arches. Local crafts are sold at the Central Market, located in a large circular building east of the **6** Floating Market, and at various shops in Punda such as Tropical Visions in the **5** Penha Building. Along the Otrobanda waterfront, facing the cruise pier, are a number of shops selling duty-free liquor and local handicrafts, including pottery at the Arawak Craft Factory opposite West Wharf.

Local Attractions

Located at the harbor entrance within the battlements of **1** **Waterfort** (built in 1634), and within hailing distance of ships entering the harbor, is the Van der Valk Plaza Hotel – one of only two hotels in the world that is covered by marine collision insurance. Still attached to the sea wall are iron rings once used to secure a chain that was stretched across the channel to prevent enemy ships from entering the harbor. During World War II, a steel net was stretched across the channel between Waterfort and **2** **Riffort** – built on the other side in 1838. Stretching east of Waterfort along the sea front are more old battlements, including the **3** **Waterfort Arches**, housing shops and restaurants.

4 **Fort Amsterdam** with its mustard-colored walls, was the center of the fortified town from 1648 to 1861. Today it's the seat of the Netherlands Antilles government. Its inner courtyard, entered through an arched walkway, is formed by the Governor's Palace (facing the water), the Fort Church Museum (opposite), and government offices on each side. In case of siege, the church was built with a cellar for provisions and an adjacent water cistern. A cannon ball fired in 1804 by English troops, led by Captain Bligh of Bounty fame, remains embedded in its front wall.

The much-photographed **5 Penha Building**, golden yellow with white trim, stands at the corner near the east end of the pontoon bridge. One of Curacao's oldest examples of Dutch colonial architecture, the building was formerly a social club with a gallery overlooking the harbor. Other waterfront buildings along this block resemble the canal houses of Amsterdam, one of which houses Gallery '86 – a showcase for the works of well-known artists of the Caribbean and Netherlands.

At the other end of the block is the **6 Floating Market** where Venezuelan boats loaded with fruit, vegetables and fish sell their wares. At the east end of the market is the **7 Queen Wilhelmina** Bridge which spans the Waaigat and leads to the former residential district of **8 Scharloo** where wealthy merchants built opulent homes, their architectural styles ranging from 18th-century colonial to Victorian.

In 1651, a dozen Jewish families from Amsterdam arrived in Willemstad and by the early 1700s the local Jewish community numbered 2,000. The **9**

Mikve Emanuel Synagogue, built in 1732 and similar in style to the old Portuguese one in Amsterdam, is today the oldest active synagogue in the Western Hemisphere. The Jewish Cultural Museum is entered off the synagogue's courtyard. Other museums in Punda include the **10 Postal Museu**m, housed in a 1693 building at the corner of Keukenstraat and Kuiperstraat, and the Numismatic Museum on Breedestraat.

The town's central park, **11 Wilhelminaplein**, contains a statue of Queen Wilhelmina, as well as shaded benches and a playground. Opposite the park's east side is the former Jewish Reformed Synagogue Temple Emmanuel (the Temple Building) and City Gate, which marks the boundary of Willemstad when it was a fortified settlement.

The passenger ferry is one way to cross the channel running through the center of Willemstad.

Island Attractions – Outside of Willemstad the attractions include beautiful beaches, secluded coves, village churches and restored land houses which are former country estates situated on hilltops so the owner could watch his slaves and signal his neighbors if trouble developed. Popular attractions include the **12 Curacao Liqueur Distillery**, located in the former colonial mansion of Chobolobo on the east side of Willemstad's harbor, and the **13 Curacao Seaquarium** where visitors can view 400 species of sea life native to local waters, including various sharks and stingrays. Beside the aquarium is a full-facility beach of white sand.

At the north end of Curacao is **14 Christoffel National Park**, a 4,500-acre nature reserve containing the island's highest point of Mount Christoffel (1,239 feet), Indian caves and trails.

The prehistoric caves at **15 Hato** were recently opened to the public, their limestone terraces containing fossilized coral that formed before tectonic uplifting brought the submerged island to the sea's surface.

Bonaire

Boomerang-shaped Bonaire is one of the best islands in the Caribbean for diving and snorkeling. The island's shoreline is a protected marine park, where coral reefs are home to more than a thousand different species of aquatic creatures, including sea horses and turtles. There are 86 charted dive sites on the island, many of these located on the sheltered western side of the island, clustered north of Kralendijk and around the offshore islet of Klein Bonaire. Reefs and wrecks, beach dives and drop-offs – the variety of dive sites and the clarity of the water is spectacular. Conditions are also ideal for snorkelers, with little current and plenty of shallow water snorkeling sites.

The island capital of **Kralendijk**, meaning 'coral dike', is a quiet place where about 3,000 of the island's 15,000 residents live. Shops carrying duty-

Bonaire's famous and protected underwater sites include three vertical wall dives.

free and local items are found at the Harborside Shopping Mall and along the main street which runs parallel with the waterfront. Historic sights include Fort Oranje, two churches and a museum. Wild donkeys and goats roam free on this unspoiled island where the centuries-old industry of salt mining has been joined by oil bunkering and tourism.

Bonaire's land-based attractions are as fascinating as its underwater world, for the island is home to one of the largest **flamingo colonies** in the Western Hemisphere. More than 15,000

Pink Beach is ideal for swimming, snorkeling and scuba diving.

flamingos nest in the island's salt pans and, in addition to two flamingo sanctuaries, a 13,500-acre game preserve (Washington-Slagbaai National Park) has been established at Bonaire's north end. Here iguanas and green-tailed lizards can be viewed in addition to flamingos and other birds such as yellow-winged parrots, often seen perched on the giant cacti that grow as high as 30 feet.

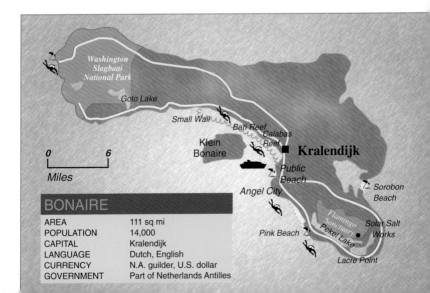

Washington Slagbaai National Park

Goto Lake

Small Wall

Bari Reef

Klein Bonaire

Calabas Reef

Kralendijk

Public Beach

Angel City

Sorobon Beach

Flamingo Sanctuary

Pekel Lake

Solar Salt Works

Pink Beach

Lacre Point

0   6

Miles

BONAIRE

AREA	111 sq mi
POPULATION	14,000
CAPITAL	Kralendijk
LANGUAGE	Dutch, English
CURRENCY	N.A. guilder, U.S. dollar
GOVERNMENT	Part of Netherlands Antilles

TRINIDAD & TOBAGO

AREA	1,981 sq mi
POPULATION	1.3 million
CAPITAL	Port-of-Spain
LANGUAGE	English, Hindi, French
CURRENCY	Trinidad dollar
GOVERNMENT	Parliamentary democracy

0   100
Miles

N

Caribbean Sea

Isla de Margarita

La Asuncion

Porlamar

Cumana

Puerto La Cruz

La Guaira

CARACAS

Atlantic Ocean

Tobago

Scarborough

Buccoo Reef
Pigeon Pt.

Asa Wright Nature Center

Maracas

Northern Range (3084 ft)

Arima

Sangre Grande

Port of Spain

Trinidad

Santa Cruz

San Fernando

Brighton

San Francique

Gulf of Paria

ORINOCO RIVER

Ciudad Bolivar

Canaima Nat

La Guaira, Venezuela

CHAPTER NINETEEN

VENEZUELA, TRINIDAD & TOBAGO

The sight of native villages set on stilts above the water prompted an early Spanish explorer, when exploring the northern coast of South America in 1499, to name the area Venezuela – 'little Venice.' Venezuela is, however, anything but little. Its 350,000 square miles of scenic wonders encompass one of South America's longest rivers, the Orinoco, which rises in the Guiana Highlands of South Venezuela and carves its serpentine course through tropical rainforests and savannahs for some 1,600 miles before terminating in a vast marshy delta where its many arms drain into the Atlantic Ocean. Canaima National Park, situated deep in the Tepui mountains, which rise 7,000 feet above a valley floor and from which mul-

tiple waterfalls cascade, is home to spectacular Angel Falls – which plunges 3,200 feet and is the highest uninterrupted waterfall in the world. The country's Caribbean coastline is nearly 1,800 miles long and its numerous offshore islands include Margarita, famous for pearl fishing.

Venezuela is also a country of great oil wealth, although many Venezuelans live in poverty, their shacks covering the hillsides around Caracas – the nation's capital and birthplace of the great liberator and military leader Simon Bolivar, born to a wealthy Creole family, who liberated

Playa Puerto Cruz on Margarita Island, with the Dunes Hotel & Beach Resort in the foreground.

Venezuela from Spanish rule in the early 1800s. Hugo Chavez, Venezuela's current president, is a former paratroop commander who considers himself an heir to the mantle of Simon Bolivar. Chavez survived a military coup in 2002 and easily won re-election in 2007, vowing to redistribute his country's wealth, but his opponents regard him as a socialist dictator abusing his power.

Caracas, accessed from the port of La Guaira, enjoys a magnificent setting atop a mountain plateau. Shore excursions include a cable car ride up Mount Avila from the Humboldt Hotel for a spectacular view of the city. Other tours include a visit to Bolivar Plaza with its complex of fountains, sculptures and colossal statues, and to the Museum of Modern Art. Hiking is available in Avila National Park to an elevation of 1,200 feet.

Margarita Island

Only 25 miles from the mainland, Isla de Margarita has long been a vacation hot spot for Venezuelans drawn to the island's pristine beaches and duty-free shopping. Margarita was sighted by Columbus in 1498 and was used briefly as a rebel base by the brutal conquistador Lope de Aguirre in 1561. In the 1800s, Margarita Island's inhabitants supported South America's revolutionary leader Simon Bolivar and, following independence from Spain, the island – along with smaller neighboring islands – was made a state of Venezuela. La Asuncion is the state capital and Porlamar is the economic center. Pearl fishing remains an important industry, along with fish canning and boat building. Construction of a freshwater pipe from the mainland has allowed the island to prosper.

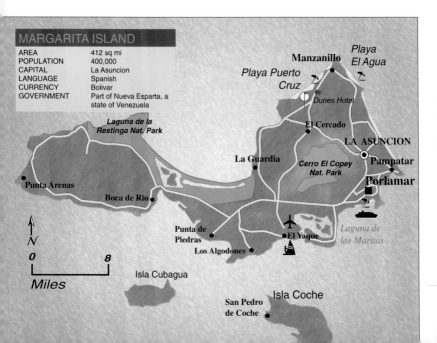

MARGARITA ISLAND

AREA	412 sq mi
POPULATION	400,000
CAPITAL	La Asuncion
LANGUAGE	Spanish
CURRENCY	Bolivar
GOVERNMENT	Part of Nueva Esparta, a state of Venezuela

Playa El Agua

Manzanillo

Playa Puerto Cruz

Dunes Hotel

Laguna de la Restinga Nat. Park

El Cercado

LA ASUNCION

La Guardia

Cerro El Copey Nat. Park

Pampatar

Porlamar

Punta Arenas

Boca de Rio

Punta de Piedras

El Yaque

Laguna de las Maritas

Los Algodones

N

0   8

Miles

Isla Cubagua

Isla Coche

San Pedro de Coche

Getting Around 🚕

The cruise ship pier is located at **Porlamar**, where a waterfront promenade called La Punta Commercial Boulevard is lined with local artisans selling their handcrafted wares. Good buys can be made in leather goods, pottery, ceramics, woven baskets, hammocks and locally harvested pearls (a good-quality strand costs about US$15-20). (Porlamar is a duty free area, with designer clothing and electronic goods available at the large shopping malls on the city's outskirts). The official currency is the bolivar, but bring U.S. cash and do not plan on using a credit card or ATM card. Spanish is the official language but English is widely spoken.

Beaches – At the far end of the shopping boulevard lies a nice swimming beach. Other excellent beaches

ring the island and Playa El Agua is one of the best, with over two miles of fine white sand and plenty of palm-shaded restaurants; lounge chairs and umbrellas are available for rent. A taxi from the cruise port to Playa El Agua costs about $16.

Numerous fortifications were built on Isla de Margarita during the Spanish colonial period to protect it from pirate attacks, and these include Castillo de San Carlos at Pampatar, a picturesque port located six miles north of Porlamor. The historic buildings of La Asuncion, founded in 1565, include a 16th-century cathedral said to be the oldest in Venezuela. Also of historic interest is the Virgin of the Valley Sanctuary, which is located in a village near Porlamar.

Trinidad & Tobago

Trinidad and Tobago, lying off the coast of Venezuela, were once part of the South American subcontinent, with Trinidad becom-

Margarita Island

Ship-organized **shore excursions** include a beach getaways to Playa El Agua and to the Dunes Resort at Playa Puerto Cruz, as well as a catamaran sail to Coche Island where the beaches are pristine and the pearl beds were a major source of wealth during the colonial era. Other natural attractions include La Restinga National Park, where boat rides can be taken through mangroves. Some cruise lines offer a flightseeing tour of Canaima National Park and Angel Falls on the Venezuelan mainland. Kayaking, snorkeling and horseback riding are offered, as are sightseeing tours of the island.

Pigeon Point, Tobago

ing an island as recently as 10,000 years ago when the last Ice Age ended and sea levels rose. The variety of flora and fauna is matched by the diversity of cultures found in this two-island nation. Trinidad (named by Columbus for its three southeastern peaks) and Tobago (named

for pipe tobacco by British settlers) were fought over and farmed by various nationalities, including the Portuguese, Dutch, Spanish, French and British.

Trinidad's capital, **Port of Spain**, is an amalgam of European, African and Indian heritage with churches, mosques, markets and museums built in a diversity of styles – Moorish, neo-Gothic, Italian Renaissance, Victorian and West Indian gingerbread to name a few. There's even a German castle resembling the medieval castles of the Rhine which, along with the official residences of the prime minister and governor general, overlooks Queen's Park Savannah – the site of glittering revelry during Trinidad's famous Carnival when the Parade of Bands proceeds up Frederick Street on the final day of street parties and calypso competitions.

(Left) Trinidad's famous Carnival. (Below) Port of Spain's Red House houses parliament.

In contrast to the pulsating beat of Trinidad is the unspoiled holiday island of **Tobago**, 21 miles away but a world apart. Scarborough is the island's main port and nearby is Pigeon Point with its glorious beaches and famous Buccoo Reef, where colorful coral gardens, popular with divers and snorkelers, can be viewed by glass-bottom boat.

The two islands, both of which prospered as producers of sugarcane during colonialism, were joined together under one government at the end of the 19th century and gained independence from Britain in 1962. Trinidad is the larger and more heavily populated of the two islands, with only 45,000 of a total 1.3 million inhabitants living on Tobago. Both islands boast lush rainforests, rare birds and brilliant butterflies, their colorful wings copied in the elaborate costumes of Trinidad's world-famous Carnival.

Trinidad's most beautiful beach is at **Maracas Bay**, about a 45-minute drive from the cruise terminal, where port-approved taxis are available. A ship-organized shore excursion is usually offered for Maracas Beach.

Other shore excursions in Trinidad include a half-day scenic drive and city tour of Port of Spain. Trinidad's bird life can be appreciated on a nature walk at the Asa Wright Nature Center or a boat ride through the mangroves of Caroni Bird Sanctuary. A guided hike to Maracas Waterfall includes swimming in a freshwater pool.

Golf is available at St. Andrews, an 18-hole course that sprawls along the Santa Cruz Valley and is flanked by steep mountains.

One of Trinidad's most beautiful beaches is at Maracas Bay.

Carnival Liberty (2005)
2,974 passengers, 110,000 tons

Carnival Spirit (2001)
2,124 passengers, 85,920 tons

Summit (2001)
1,950 passengers, 91,000 tons

CARNIVAL CRUISE LINES: This mainstream cruise line, which started in the early 1970s, has mushroomed into the largest cruise corporation in the world, with Carnival Corporation owning numerous lines, including Cunard, Princess and Holland America. Carnival can take credit for changing the public's perception of cruising, from its being stuffy and formal to its being casual and fun. The ships' interiors reflect this outlook, with an enthusiastic use of color and contemporary themes. Carnival attracts a high number of first-time cruisers and, with extensive facilities for children and teens, families. With a fleet of 18 'Fun Ships' in the Caribbean, many of these remaining there year-round, Carnival has a wide range of itineraries, offering everything from 2- and 3-day cruises to the Bahamas to 7- and 8-day cruises into the southern Caribbean. Base ports are Miami, Tampa, Port Canaveral and Jacksonville, as well as Galveston, New Orleans, Mobile, New York and San Juan, Puerto Rico. Officers are Italian. *(www.carnival.com)*

CELEBRITY CRUISES: Founded in 1990 as an offshoot of the Greek line Chandris Inc., Celebrity Cruises is now owned by Royal Caribbean International. A premium cruise line, Celebrity ships are modern in decor and highly rated by the readers of Conde Naste magazine. The service is attentive and the cuisine is very good, as are the children's facilities and programs. Celebrity has five ships in the Caribbean, departing from the base ports of Miami, Fort Lauderdale, Tampa, New York and San Juan, Puerto Rico. Celebrity's private-island stops are Casa de Campo / Catalina Island in Dominican Republic, and Coco Cay in the Bahamas. Ship officers are Greek and service staff is international. *(www.celebritycruises.com)*

COSTA CRUISES: The Costa shipping family of Genoa, Italy, introduced their first passenger ship in 1948, and today the Costa fleet is Europe's most popular cruise line, appealing to anyone who loves Italian food, music and dancing. Costa positions two ships in the Caribbean, sailing 5- to 8-day cruises out of Fort Lauderdale to the Western and Eastern Caribbean. Costa's 'Italian style' of cruising is upbeat, with an international ambiance and authentic Italian cuisine. Officers and crew are international. *(www.costacruise.com)*

Costa Mediterranea (2003)
2,114 passengers, 86,000 tons

CRYSTAL CRUISES: Owned by NYK of Japan, this luxury line offers a handful of Caribbean itineraries – 14-day roundtrip from Miami, or 11-day cruises between Caldera, Costa Rica, and Miami. Crystal features tailor-made shore excursions to suit individual preferences and the line's ships, which carry 960 passengers each, are finely appointed with spacious interiors and almost all outside cabins. *(www.crystalcruises.com)*

Crystal Serenity (2003)
1,080 passengers, 68,000 tons

CUNARD: This prestigious British line (now owned by Carnival Corporation) began operations in 1840 when Sir Samuel Cunard's fleet of four ships began carrying mail between Liverpool, Halifax and Boston. Cunard's classic ocean liners – *Queen Mary 2* and *Queen Victoria* – are modern ships offering traditional elegance and British ambiance. Roundtrip, 10-day Caribbean cruises are available on *Queen Mary 2* from New York and Fort Lauderdale. Officers are British; service staff is international. *(www.cunard.com)*

Queen Mary 2 (2004)
2,620 passengers, 150,000 tons

DISNEY CRUISE LINE: Appealing to the family market, Disney Cruise Line offers roundtrip cruises from Port

Canaveral – 4-day itineraries to the Bahamas and 7-day itineraries to the Eastern and Western Caribbean. The company's private island is Castaway Cay in the Bahamas. Officers are European. (*www.disneycruise.com*)

Westerdam (2006)
1,848 passengers, 85,000 tons

HOLLAND AMERICA LINE: This company's connection with North America began in 1873 with regular service between New York and Rotterdam. Now based in Seattle, HAL has established a loyal following for its worldwide itineraries. A premium cruise line, HAL positions eight ships in the Caribbean. HAL ships cut a fine profile with their distinctive sheer and blue hull, and such classic features as a wraparound teak deck. The ships' spacious interiors contain extensive artwork to complement each ship's thematic decor. Holland America's Dutch officers and service staff of Indonesians and Filipinos have built a solid reputation of well-run, immaculate ships with a high level of service. HAL offers a good range of 7- to 16-day cruises to most Caribbean ports from base ports Fort Lauderdale, Tampa and New York. In 1997 HAL debuted its private island – Half Moon Cay – after purchasing the uninhabited Bahamian island of Little San Salvador and developing shoreside facilities for its passengers. (*www.hollandamerica.com*)

MSC Musica (2006)
2,550 passengers, 89,000 tons

MSC ITALIAN CRUISES: This Italian line is owned by Mediterranean Shipping Company, one of the world's largest freight container companies. MSC appeals mainly to European cruisers. MSC offers 8- and 11-day roundtrip cruises from Fort Lauderdale. Ports of call include Samana (Dominican Republic) for the line's private retreat, Cayo Levantado. Officers and service staff are Italian. (*www.msccruises.com*)

NORWEGIAN CRUISE LINE: This company first introduced trips from Miami to the Bahamas in the mid-1960s. NCL also pioneered the concept of a private-island port of call when it purchased Great Stirrup Cay from the Bahamian government in 1977. The line appeals to young couples and families, with its fleet of modern ships offering a casual onboard atmosphere, unstructured dining and good facilities for children. NCL's Caribbean itineraries include 7- and 9-day cruises from Miami, 7-day Western itineraries from Houston and New Orleans, and 10- and 11-day cruises from New York. Officers are Norwegian, service staff is international. *(www.ncl.com)*

Norwegian Jewel (2005)
2,400 passengers, 92,000 tons

OCEANIA CRUISES, INC: This luxury line's mid-sized ships offer gourmet cuisine and attentive service in a country-club casual atmosphere. Oceania offers a variety of 10- to 14-day roundtrip itineraries from Miami. The line's private beach stop is a pristine peninsula at Samana, Dominican Republic. Officers and service staff are international. *(www.oceaniacruises.com)*

Regatta (1998)
684 passengers, 30,000 tons

PRINCESS CRUISES: Well known for its role in *The Love Boat* television show in the 1970s, this line has always been an innovator with its ships and itineraries. Like other cruise industry leaders, Princess has experienced phenomenal growth in the last decade and has launched over half a dozen new ships since 1996. These new megaships have all the modern facilities cruise passengers have come to expect, including health spas and internet cafes, as well as traditional features such as wraparound teak promenade decks and intimate wood-panelled pubs. A high percentage of staterooms on these new ships have a verandah, while the public areas are

Grand Princess (1998)
2,600 passengers, 109,000 tons

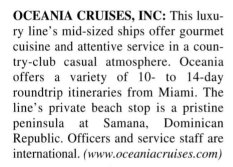

Diamond Princess (2003)
2,674 passengers, 113,000 tons

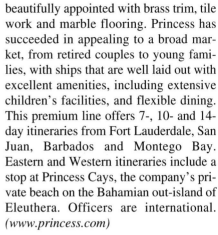

Seven Seas Navigator (1999)
490 passengers, 30,000 tons

Brilliance of the Seas (2002)
2,112 passengers, 90,000 tons

beautifully appointed with brass trim, tile work and marble flooring. Princess has succeeded in appealing to a broad market, from retired couples to young families, with ships that are well laid out with excellent amenities, including extensive children's facilities, and flexible dining. This premium line offers 7-, 10- and 14-day itineraries from Fort Lauderdale, San Juan, Barbados and Montego Bay. Eastern and Western itineraries include a stop at Princess Cays, the company's private beach on the Bahamian out-island of Eleuthera. Officers are international. *(www.princess.com)*

REGENT SEVEN SEAS: This luxury line (formerly called Radisson Seven Seas) offers small-ship intimacy, spaciousness and fine cuisine. Caribbean itineraries range from 3 to 14 days, roundtrip from Fort Lauderdale to a mix of ports, often including one or two smaller, less-visited islands. Officers are European. *(www.rssc.com)*

ROYAL CARIBBEAN INTERNATIONAL: One of the original cruise lines to set up shop in the Caribbean in the late 1960s, Royal Caribbean maintains a strong presence with a cruise product appealing to young couples and families. This line is not afraid of innovation and was the first to introduce an 18-hole miniature golf course and, most recently, an onboard rock-climbing wall – the company's trademark. RCI's modern megaships offer spacious and impressive public areas, including a multi-deck atrium with glass elevators and a glass-wrapped observation lounge on the highest deck. Family suites, a spacious playroom and a teen center make these ships ideal for passengers with children. RCI offers cruises from the Florida ports of Miami, Fort Lauderdale,

Port Canaveral and Tampa as well as San Juan, New Orleans, Galveston, Norfolk, Baltimore and New York Harbor. The company's Caribbean fleet includes some of the largest ships in the world, and itineraries range from 3-night cruises to the Bahamas to 11-day Southern Caribbean cruises out of San Juan. The company has two private beach stops – Labadee on the north coast of Haiti and CocoCay, a Bahamian island that RCI acquired in 1988 (then called Little Stirrup Cay). *(www.royalcaribbean.com)*

Legend of the Seas (1995)
1,804 passengers, 69,000 tons

STAR CLIPPERS: This line offers a unique product for those seeking sailing adventure with plenty of onboard comforts. The ships (carrying 170 to 228 passengers) offer an authentic tall-ship experience (*Royal Clipper* flies 42 sails from her five masts) but with modern amenities such as marina platforms on the stern. Itineraries are seven days using Barbados as a base port for sailing to many of the smaller, less-visited islands. *(www. starclippers.com)*

Royal Clipper (2000)
228 passengers, 5,000 tons

SEABOURN CRUISE LINE: Widely considered the ultimate in luxury cruising, Seabourn operates a small fleet of mega-yachts, each carrying 208 passengers in outside suites, many of these with balconies. In addition to providing gourmet cuisine, white glove service, and spacious accommodations, Seabourn combines interesting itineraries with unique shore excursions. The line currently offers 7- and 14-day cruises out of Barbados, St. Thomas and Fort Lauderdale. Officers are Norwegian. *(www. seabourn.com)*

Seabourn Spirit (1989)
208 passengers, 10,000 tons

SEA DREAM YACHT CLUB: Founded in 2001 by Norwegian industrialist Atle Brynestad (founder of Seabourn) this innovative company's

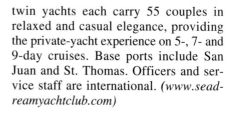

SeaDream II (1985)
110 passengers, 4,250 tons

twin yachts each carry 55 couples in relaxed and casual elegance, providing the private-yacht experience on 5-, 7- and 9-day cruises. Base ports include San Juan and St. Thomas. Officers and service staff are international. *(www.seadreamyachtclub.com)*

Silver Whisper (2001)
382 passengers, 28,250 tons

SILVERSEA: Consistently rated the Number One Small Ship Cruise Line by the readers of Conde Nast Traveler, this luxury line consists of four ships and offers 7- to 15-day Caribbean cruises from Fort Lauderdale, San Juan and Barbados. *(www.silversea.com)*

WINDJAMMER CRUISES: This fleet of small sailing vessels is one of the Caribbean's cruise pioneers, with over four decades of experience. Started by Mike Burke in the early 1960s with one small sailing ship, the line now has a fleet of ships offering 7-day cruises from St. Maarten, Tortola, Grenada and Aruba. Officers and crew are international. *(www.windjammer.com)*

Wind Spirit (1988)
140 passengers, 6,000 tons

WINDSTAR CRUISES: This is a premium line of high-tech sailing ships, each accommodating about 150 passengers (except *Wind Surf* which carries 312 passengers). Noted for their fine cuisine and good service, Windstar ships appeal to cruisers seeking luxury in a casual setting as well as a bit of sailing adventure. The line offers 7-day cruises from Barbados and St. Thomas to an array of islands. *(www.windstarcruises.com)*

PHOTOGRAPHY

Michael DeFreitas photos: 5, 9, 37 (top), 47, 57, 67, 74 (top & middle), 75 (inset, middle, bottom), 78, 86 (bottom), 87 (bottom), 90, 91, 93 (top), 94 (bottom left), 95 (all), 96, 97, 98, 99, 100, 158, 161, 165, 168, 171, 177 (bottom), 180, 200, 201 (bottom left), 202, 204 (top), 205 (top), 208, 209 (all), 235, 213, 220 (bottom), 237, 238, 240, 248, 257, 271,278 (top), 287, 302 (bottom), 305, 306 (middle), 307 (top), 325 (all), 330, 331, 334, 335, 339, 340 (all), 341
Additional Photography:
Gordon Persson, 3, 166, 181
Windstar Cruises:
Gerald Brimacombe, 5; 245; Harvey Lloyd, 14; 278 (bottom), 306 (bottom), 307 (bottom);
Bernard Gvilly, 306 (top).
Royal Caribbean International, 13 (top), 28, 29,
Celebrity Cruises, 16 (top), 17 (top), 86 (top), 94 (bottom right), 145, 147 (top), 148, 149,
Holland America Line, 30, 162, 167,
Sanford/Agliolo/Corbis, 40
Library of Congress, 42
NOAA, 45, 46
Mary Evans Picture Library, 51, 59, 64
St. Croix Landmarks Society, 55, 58, 60, 61, 68, 69
George Brizan, 56
Puerto Rico Tourism Company, 62
Fred Jensen, 12 (inset),
72, 77, 267 (top), 328,
Ueli Frey, 80
Corbis, 87 (top), 112
Tom Brakefield/Corbis, 101,
George Rhodes, 102
Ports America Inc., 104 (top)
Cunard, 104 (bottom)
Norwegian Cruise Line, 105
Cunard, 106
Port of Norfolk, 107
Port of Miami, 109
Port Everglades, 123
Port Canaveral, 127
Florida Division of Tourism,130
Donn Young, Port of New Orleans, 136
Michael Terranova, 137 (top)
Mariano Advertising, 137 (bottom).
Port of Galveston, 140, 141.
Judi Lees, 159
Raymond Norris-Jones,174.
Johnnie Black, 175.
Princess Cruises, 182, 198,
Martin Gerretson, 195, 291, 304,
Bob Krist, 205 (middle).

All other photography by Anne Vipond.